Regional Economic Cooperation and Integration

COMESA EU SAARC

About the book

Prompted by the uncertain outcome of the GATT/Uruguay Round negotiations, regional agreements mushroomed in different parts of the world. The collapse of the Soviet Union gave a renewed impulse to economic interactions at the expense of political and strategic preoccupations. Inter-regional co-operation reduces economic and social fragmentation created by national frontiers and hence facilitates integrated development of participating states. In Africa, as in other parts of the world, regional co-operation is a major factor in internal and international politics.

This book focuses on the regional co-operation efforts in the three continents of the world, viz. Africa, Asia and Europe and their role in promoting and strengthening *African Capacities*. It examines various dimensions of regional co-operation with focus on bilateral relations between a community of highly developed states (European Union) and a group of developing countries, viz. COMESA (Common Market for Eastern and Southern Africa). The latter part of the book focuses on inter-regional co-operation between South Asian countries, particularly India, and COMESA. These two regions of the world share a common colonial legacy and are striving to improve the socio-economic conditions of their people. Inter-regional cooperation and integration is a vital necessity in a world witnessing trade liberalisation, foreign investments and reduced role of governments in economic affairs.

Author's Profile

Sonu Trivedi is a Research Associate at the Centre for Policy Research (CPR), Chanakyapuri, New Delhi. She specialises in regional economic cooperation in Africa and Southeast Asia. She has to her credit a number of articles published in reputed journals. Her recent works include *A Handbook of International Organisations*. Currently, she is working on a project titled Challenges of Multilateralism in the World Economy.

Regional Economic Cooperation and Integration

COMESA EU SAARC

Sonu Trivedi

New Century Publications
New Delhi, India

NEW CENTURY PUBLICATIONS
4800/24, Bharat Ram Road,
Ansari Road, Daryaganj,
New Delhi-110 002
Tel.: 23247798, 55396605
E-mail: indiatax@vsnl.com
www.newcenturypublications.com

Editorial office:
34, Gujranwala Town, Part-2,
Delhi - 110 009
Tel.: 27247805, 27464774

First Published 2005

ISBN: 81-7708-098-9

Published by New Century Publications and printed at Singhal Print Media, Delhi -110 007

PRINTED IN INDIA

Preface

The years since 1990 have witnessed a renewed and stronger trend for regional and bilateral economic groupings world-wide, led by developed countries and followed by developing countries. There has been a widespread recognition among several nations that, under the present conditions, joining regional cooperative groupings is an appropriate strategic response to the intensification of the ongoing process of globalisation. The future of regional co-operation in Africa and the rest of the developing world is closely linked with the future of international co-operation and the world economy.

In Africa, as in other parts of the world, regional co-operation is a major factor in internal and international politics. Many countries have become members of two or more regional economic organisations with overlapping privileges and obligations. No African state is large enough to conduct a modern economy alone.

Regional agreements mushroomed, prompted by the uncertain outcome of the GATT/Uruguay Round negotiations, and apprehensions about a possible transformation of the EU into *fortress Europe*. The collapse of the Soviet Union further hastened the tendency to emphasise economic interactions at the expense of political and strategic preoccupations.

Recognising the need for and the proven utility of cooperative linkages between (and among) regional economic groupings, leading organisations of the world have already entered into agreements with other similar organisations in specified areas of inter-regional cooperation. The working of such inter-organisational cooperative agreements provides valuable lessons for any regional economic grouping desirous of networking with other similar groupings.

This book focuses on the regional co-operation efforts in the three continents of the world, viz. Africa, Asia and Europe and their role in promoting and strengthening *African Capacities*.

In this context, the book examines regional co-operation with focus on bilateral relations between a community of highly developed states (European Union) and a group of developing countries (COMESA). The latter part of the book focuses on inter-regional co-operation between South Asian countries, particularly India, and COMESA. These two regions of the world share a common colonial legacy and are striving to improve the socio-economic conditions of their people. Inter-regional cooperation and integration is a vital necessity in a world witnessing trade liberalisation, foreign investments and reduced role of governments in economic affairs.

The book contains 11 chapters.

Chapter 1 explains the concept of regionalism, its evolution and spread in the global trading system.

Chapter 2 deals with the regional co-operation and integration process in Africa.

Chapter 3 provides an overview of Common Market for Eastern and Southern Africa (COMESA).

Chapter 4 looks into the origin, evolution and growth of European Union (EU) and traces its achievements over the years.

Chapter 5 gives an overview of Economic Partnership Agreements (EPAs), particularly between EU and African Caribbean and African (ACP) countries and explains the Lome Conventions and Cotonou Agreement.

Chapter 6 focuses on economic partnership between EU and Africa and explains how EU-Africa relations can be further strengthened.

Chapter 7 is devoted to EU's relations with COMESA member states. It provides a country-wise analysis of EU's efforts in promoting economic development in the African continent.

Chapter 8 deals with regional co-operation and integration in South Asia with focus on South Asian Association for Regional Co-operation (SAARC). It also highlights the common problems of the two regions (COMESA and SAARC).

Chapter 9 traces the historical relations between India and Africa. It focuses on the major challenges faced by India and

Africa and highlights potential areas of co-operation between the two regions.

Chapter 10 examines the role of India and COMESA in exploring South-South Co-operation. It also explains bilateral trade between India and COMESA.

Chapter 11 analyses the role of EU and India in strengthening *African Capacities* and explores the various possibilities of close co-operation between EU, India and Africa.

I take this opportunity to express my gratitude to Professor K. Mathews, former Head, Department of African Studies, University of Delhi and presently Professor of International Relations, Addis Ababa University, Ethiopia, for his guidance and encouragement to complete this work. Thanks are also due to Mr. Sandeep Sury, Chief Executive, New Century Publications, New Delhi for keeping patience when the manuscript was being updated and revised and bringing out this book in the shortest possible time after the submission of the final manuscript.

Delhi
May 20, 2005

Ms. Sonu Trivedi

List of Acronyms

AACB	—	Association of African Central Banks
AAPC	—	All-African Peoples Conference
AAPSO	—	Afro-Asian Peoples Solidarity Organization
ACMS	—	African Centre for Monetary Studies
ADB	—	African Development Bank
ADF	—	African Development Fund
AEF	—	Institution d' Emisson de I' Afrique Equatoriale Francaise (Bank of French West Africa and Cameroon)
AOF	—	La Banque de I' Afrique de I' Ouest Francaise et de Togo (Bank of French West Africa and Togo)
BAO	—	Banque de I' Afrique de I' Ouest (Bank of West Africa)
BCEAO	—	Banque Centrale des Etats de I' Afrique de I' Ouest (Central Bank of West African States)
BDEGL	—	Banque de Development des Etats des Grand Lacs (Development Bank of the Countries of the Grand Lakes)
BEAC	—	Banque des Etats de I' Afrique Centrale (Bank of Central African States)
BOAD	—	Banque Ouest Africaine de Development (West African Development Bank)
CACH	—	Central African Clearing House
CAR	—	Central African Republic
CEAO	—	Communite Economique de I' Afrique de I' Ouest (Economic Community of West Africa)
CEDEAO	—	Communite Economique des Etats de I' Afrique de I' Ouest (ECOWAS)
CEEAC	—	Communite Economique des Etats de I' Afrique Central (ECCAS)

CEPGL —	Communite Economique des Pays des Grand Lacs (Economic Community of the Countries of the Grand Lakes)
CET —	Common External Tariff
CFA —	Communite Financiere Africaine (African Financial Community)
CIAS —	Conference of Independent African States
CODESRIA—	Council for the Development of Social Science Research in Africa
CPCM —	Conseil Permanent Consultatif Maghrebin (Maghreb Permanent Consultative Committee)
EACB —	East African Currency Board
EACM —	East African Common Market
EADB —	East African Development Bank
EAEC —	East African Economic Community
ECA —	Economic Community for Central Africa
ECCAS —	Economic Community of Central African States
ECCM —	East Caribbean Common Market
ECOWAS —	Economic Community of West African States
ECUCA —	Economic and Customs Union of Central Africa
IBRD —	International Bank of Reconstruction and Development
ICMCWA —	Interim Council of Ministers of the Countries of West Africa
IGO —	Intergovernmental Organizations
IMF —	International Monetary Fund
LPA —	Lagos Plan of Action
LLPI —	Leather and Leather Product Institute
MAU —	Maghreb Arab Union
MCCA —	Mercado Comun Centroamericano (Central American Common Market)
MFN —	Most Favored Nation

MRU	—	Mano River Union
OAU	—	Organization of African Unity
OERS	—	Organization des Etats Des Rivieres Senegaleses (Organisation of Senegal River Stages)
OMVS	—	Organization for the Development of the Senegal River
PAEC	—	Pan-African Economic Community
PAFMECSA	—	Pan-African Freedom Movement of East Central & Southern Africa
PTA	—	Preferential Trade Area for Eastern and Southern African States
RSA	—	Republic of South Africa
SACCAR	—	Southern African Centre for Cooperation in Agricultural Research
SACU	—	Southern African Customs Union
SADC	—	Southern African Development Community
SADCC	—	Southern African Development and Coordination Conference
SAP	—	Structural Adjustment Program
UDAO	—	Union Douaniere de I' Afrique de I' Ouest (West African Customs Union)
UDEAC	—	Union Douaniere des Etats de I' Afrique Centrale (Customs Union of Central States)
UDEAO	—	Union Douaniere et Economique de I' Afreque de I' Ouest (West African Customs and Economic Union)
UEAC	—	Union des Etats de I' Afrique Centrale (Union of Central African States)
UNCTAD	—	United Nations Conference on Trade and Development
UNDP	—	United Nations Development Programme
WACH	—	West African Clearing House
WAFTA	—	West African Free Trade Area
WAMU	—	West African Monetary Union

Contents

1

Regionalism in the World Economy

Regional cooperation as an antithesis of autarky and global cooperation has become an inevitable intermediate link in the system of international cooperation and interdependence. The epoch of global One-worldism appears to be premature, given the as yet utopian nature of attempts to consolidate the world's highly unequal sovereign nation-states into a single world system. At the present time, the balanced progress towards greater regional focus motivated by considerations of economic and social benefits and requirements, offers the best alternative.

The basis for regional cooperation lies in common national interests deriving from propinquity, similarity of socio-political systems, comparable levels of development and complementarity of economies and affinities of language, culture, historical tradition and religion. The smallness of most of the Third World countries' individual markets compels them to join forces to develop their industries and reap the benefits of economies of scale, attract foreign investors by organising a frontier-less market with a critical mass of potential consumers and create the jobs that their constantly expanding populations demand.

However, on the whole, the majority of the attempts made in the developing world have been plagued by serious difficulties. Some of these have stemmed from the unequal level of development of the member states, others from inequalities in resources and labor forces and the economic and political ideals, and still others from the insufficiently developed linkages between the nascent regional units and the rest of the world economy. Unequal distribution of the costs and benefits of regional cooperation has often led to resentment and resistance, which sacrificed long-term benefits to be achieved through more equitable cooperation to the short-term advantages of a return to bilateral economic relationships. Success among the attempts at regional cooperation have been achieved mainly in regions with a relatively developed economic, educational, technological, and scientific infrastructure, and with the capability and the will to provide a significant and dependable level of investment in programmes of economic cooperation.

Regional economic integration involves various steps. The first step is a free trade area in which tariffs are eliminated among the member states. The second step is a customs union, which establishes a common policy of protection for the members with other countries. The customs union, which is also a free trade area, is difficult to form because each nation has its own industries that face international competition. A further step in regional integration is a common market, which is a customs union without restriction on the movement of labor and capital across member states. A final stage of regional economic integration will be an economic union, with member states sharing a common currency.

The benefits of regional integration include an improvement of efficiency and an increase in economic welfare. However, national sovereignty and governance by the domestic political elite will be eroded by economic integration. Political leaders benefit from the process of integration that increases national welfare, which helps them get selected in office. In the long-run, however, the outcome of integration will lead to the diminution of power that future domestic political elite can wield when their time comes. Given all the economic benefits and political rationale of regional integration, there are successful cases as well as negative ones involving regional integration.

Regional economic arrangements of the variety, more generally recognised now, emerged and were continually refined under colonial rule between 1870 – 1950 in various parts of developing world such as in South Asia, East Asia and the Middle East as well as in various sub-regions of Africa and the Caribbean. The most successful form of regional cooperation, that evolved and culminated in full economic and political union on a more or less voluntary and democratically determined basis, was the progressive expansion and the formation of the USA during

1820-1920. This unique, experience, however is not usually seen as an example of Regional cooperation among nations as such but as exemplifying the evolution and expansion of a federation welding together functions of semi – sovereign, constituent states. First cogent and articulate version of regionalism was laid down in the United Nations Charter. The chapter VIII of the UN charter deals exclusively with the Regional Arrangement. The charter confirms that its universal principles of maintenance of international peace can collaterally exist with regional arrangements based on their regional interests – political or economic. It implies that as per the charter of the UN, Universalism and regionalism are not contradictory but confirmatory to each other in that any regional arrangements which confirm to the principles of the UN may be helpful in sustenance of international peace and security.

1.1 Evolution of Regionalism

The urge for cooperative relations between states is as old as the beginning of civilized life, but the experimentation of this concept gained currency after the Second World War. A treaty of 1278 BC between the Pharos and the Hitties incorporate almost every stipulation that a treaty of regional cooperation might contain today. The Greek history reveals that their existed a number of regional organizations, viz. Amphictyomic League from the pre-historic period, Lacedaemonian League in the sixth century, the Peloponesian League and the Athenian League. Before the period of Waterloo, many alliances took place. In 1800, Baltic powers entered into an alliance among themselves to maintain the freedom of the seas against the monopoly of England. Following the Napoleanic wars, the European monarchs entered into the Holy Alliance and the Quadruple Alliances against France. Numerous regional arrangements came into existence in the inter-war period (1918-39) of which the Draft Treaty of Mutual Trust and Locarno Pact are significant. League Covenant also provided for regional understanding for securing peace.

The emergence of bipolarity after the Second World War led to the formation of a number of treaties, pacts and regional integration schemes in both the developed and the developing world. The nations of the Americas are working more closely together than ever before – strengthening democracy, advancing human rights, promoting peace and security, expanding trade and tackling complex problems caused by poverty, drugs and corruption. The Organization of American States (OAS) is playing a central role in working toward many of the goals that are shared by the countries of North, Central and South America and the Caribbean.

The first specific and important manifestations of the Latin American economic integration process were the Central American Common Market (CACM, 1960) and the Latin American Free Trade Association (LAFTA, 1960). The former linked the five Central American countries and other economic areas in trade, in order to establish a unified market, and diverse institutions were created to promote its operations. The latter - comprising ten South American countries and Mexico - was a more flexible and less ambitious mechanism for drawing closer to a Free Trade Zone by the negotiation of trade preferences on the basis of product lists.

Subsequently, the signing of the Cartagena Agreement (1969) and the creation of the Andean Development Fund (CAF, 1969) led to the establishment of the Andean Group, a sub regional scheme incorporating a number of intermediate and lesser developed countries among the LAFTA member countries, and that included accelerated and strict integration mechanisms, along with a common treatment for foreign investments and a Joint Industrial Development Program. Concomitantly, in 1968, five Caribbean English-speaking countries established the Caribbean Free Trade Area (CARIFTA) which in just a short time was transformed into the Caribbean Community (CARICOM). The establishment of the Caribbean Community and Common Market (CARICOM) was the result of a 15-year effort to fulfill the hope of regional integration which was born with the establishment of the British West Indies Federation in 1958. The West Indies Federation came to an end in 1962 but its end, in many ways must be regarded as the real beginning of what is now the Caribbean Community. The Community has concentrated on the promotion of functional cooperation, especially in relation to human and social development, and in integrating the economies of Member States.

The idea of European integration was first proposed by the French Foreign Minister Robert Schuman in a speech on 9 May 1950. The European Union (EU) is the result of a process of deep regional cooperation and integration that began in 1951 among Benelux Countries (Belgium, Netherlands & Luxembourg) and grew to include Germany, France and Italy. In 1952, Treaty of Paris was signed establishing the European Coal and Steel Community (ECSC). The logic behind this was that, if the two basic industries which had provide the where-withal to make war were placed under joint, rather than national, control, the inclination to resort to force to settle disputes would be thwarted. The power to take decisions about coal and steel industries, in those countries was placed in the hands of an independent, supranational body called the "High Authority". The ECSC was such a success that, within a few years, their same countries decided to go further and integrate other sectors of their economies. In 1957, these same countries signed the Treaty of Rome which established the European Atomic Energy Community (EURATOM) and the European Economic Community (ECC). A preamble to this treaty defined the ultimate purpose of the great European enterprise as 'ever closer union among the peoples by Europe'. The member states set about removing trade barriers between them and forming a "common market".

In 1967, the institutions of the three European communities were merged. From this point on, there was a single Commission and a single Council of Ministers as well as the European Parliament. All the above three bodies collectively came to be known as European Community. Amendments were carried out to the earlier treaties by the Single European Act of Luxembourg in 1985. The collapse of the Soviet Union and the reunification of Germany in 1989 presented European leaders with provable challenges. They realised that the opportunities offered by the end of the cold war reinforced the need for further integration in the Western half of the continent. As a result of these developments, Maastricht Treaty was signed in 1992. It introduced new forms of cooperation between the member state governments and led to the creation of European Union.

In Africa, demands for the Pan-African unity were especially noticeable in the early 1960s after most of the African States achieved independence. This was realized in the establishment of the Organization of African Unity (OAU) in 1963. A number of regional economic organizations were established within the different sub-regions in Africa, such as, the ECOWAS in West Africa, SADC in Southern Africa, Maghreb in North Africa, the COMESA for Eastern and Southern Africa, and CEEAC/ECCAS for Central African States. The end of the Cold War and emergence of a United Europe after the establishment of European Union (EU) confronted Africa and the rest of the developing world with enormous challenges. Consequently the OAU in June 1991, at its 27th annual summit in Abuja, Nigeria, adopted the Abuja Treaty to establish the African Economic Community (AEC) by the year 2025. This Treaty came into force in May 1994. Since then the idea of African unity and cooperation has assumed new dynamics and direction. The Abuja Treaty also recommended the establishment of an African Union (AU) and a Pan-African Parliament (PAP). The OAU endorsed the Abuja Treaty proposal for an African Union in 1999. The OAU summit in Lome in July 2000 declared the establishment of African Union by a unanimous decision. It came into existence on 26 May 2001. It was formally launched in Durban, South Africa on July, 9, 2002. The African Union which has replaced the OAU aims at "achieving greater unity and solidarity between the African countries and the peoples of Africa" and "accelerate the political and socio-economic integration of the continent".

The establishment of regionalism in Middle East was not a product of the moment but an institutional embodiment of a historical, social and cultural reality. Deep religious and cultural ties link these states, and strong kin relations prevail among their citizens. All these factors, enhanced by one geographical entity extending from sea to desert, have facilitated contacts and interaction among them, and created homogeneous values and characteristics. League of Arab States was formed in 1945 for strengthening ties among the member states, coordinate their policies, and promote their common interests. The Organization of the Islamic Conference (OIC), set up by the Kings and Heads of State and Government of Islamic States, in 1969, was the concrete expression of a great awareness, on the part of the Ummah, of the necessity to establish an Organization embodying its aspirations and capable of carrying out its just struggle against the various dangers which threatened it and still persist. Gulf Cooperation Council (GCC) established in 1981 is a continuation, evolution and institutionalisation of old prevailing realities; it is, on the other, a practical answer to the challenges of security and economic development in the area. It is also a fulfilment of the aspirations of its citizens towards some sort of Arab regional unity.

The first ever attempt at regionalism in Asia was made at the Asian Relations Conference in March 1947, but it largely focused on the de-colonization movements taking place in Asia. The region witnessed a few efforts by mid 1950s. However, these efforts were either promoted by anti-colonial ethos or by the prodding of ex-colonial masters. Their scope and membership even included extra regional powers and invariably remained too diffused to have any lasting and visible impact. During the Cold War period, regional politics in South Asia emerged primarily to support and sustain military alliances and to rebuild, coordinate and integrate markets and economies of allies. The South Asian nations could not do more than preoccupy themselves with quarrels and conflicts. In fact, the divisions and conflicts in South

Asia were seen to serve the greater and better purpose in Cold War politics.

The first regional grouping in Asia emerged in East Asian region. It was the SEATO (South East Asian Treaty Organization), a military alliance supported by the United States. From South Asia, Pakistan became a member of SEATO, as well as CENTO (Central Treaty Organization), a military and economic alliance of Britain, Iran, Pakistan and Turkey. After the Bandung Conference of 1955, Non-Alignment as an international group emerged at the Belgrade Conference of 1961. Except Pakistan, all other South Asian countries became its member. A sense of external threats to the Southeast Asia region from China and the Vietnam War combined to allow the creation of the Association of Southeast Asian Nations (ASEAN) in August 1967 through the Bangkok Declaration India, due to its dominant position was a leading player in the region. In the mid 1980s, regionalism eventually came into being in South Asia with the formation of SAARC. The urgency of greater and closer trade and economic cooperation in South East Asia has led to the formation of more and more regional and sub-regional groupings such as BIMST-EC (Bangladesh, India, Myanmar, Sri Lanka and Thailand Economic Cooperation) and IOR-ARC (Indian Ocean Rim Association for Regional Cooperation).

In a number of cases, the revival of regionalism meant reforming the so-called 'first-generation' regional organizations, which were established in the 1960s to promote integration through import-substitution strategies and 'delinking' from the global market. More frequently, regionalisation involved the creation of new groupings, such as the North American Free Trade Area (NAFTA) and MERCOSUR in the Americas; the Asia-Pacific Economic Conference (APEC) and the Free Trade Agreement of the ASEAN in Asia. In Europe, the expansion and deepening of European integration prompted the formation of the European Union (EU). The most successful case of economic regionalism is the European Union, which replaced European Community after the Maastricht Treaty of 1994. It has established a very novel system of a common market, common currency, common minimum economic policy and completely free flow of goods and services to the extent of even partially demolishing the traditional wall of sovereign nation state system. The most recent example of political and economic integration is the launching of the African Union in Durban, July 2002. The new 53 member AU is a political, economic and social project molded along the lines of the EU. It seeks a higher form of collaborative union for the continent–a single organisation with two dimensions–political and economic.

The most surprising aspect of this new face of economic regionalism or neo – regionalism in the 1990s is that none of the economic arrangements has banned member countries from any universal economic formation like the WTO or even participation in multilateral arrangements.

Far from implying the formation of mutually exclusive regional integration groupings, this process was strongly outward-oriented; regional cooperation & integration also meant the opening of discussions towards the enlargement of existing institutions and the conclusion of inter-regional agreements. This kaleidoscopic interplay between institutions, identities and socio-political factors accounts for the polymorphous nature of the so-called new regionalisation process. Closely tied to the advancement of globalisation, the regionalisation process often endorsed already existing international economic links between neighbouring states. Regionalisation, as in Europe or North America, represented an opportunity to establish a more appropriate framework for absorbing the pressures of multilateralism and globalisation. Elsewhere, as in Asia or Africa, regionalisation was associated with the trade and investment strategies of private agents who operated in the absence of – or, as in Africa, in opposition to – institutionalised regional structures.

1.2 Old and New Regionalism

The recent integration initiatives are often referred to as 'new regionalism' to distinguish them from the 'old regionalism' practised in the 1960s and 1970s. The first wave may have faltered, but it seems that the second wave is here to stay. A distinction is drawn between "old" and "new" regionalism on the basis of three features: the multipolar context of the latter (as opposed to the bipolar context of old regionalism); the dominant role of hegemonic actors (regionalism from "outside" and "above") in the creation of old regionalism as opposed to the "autonomous" nature of new regionalism(from "within" and "below"); and the comprehensiveness and multidimensional nature of new regionalism as opposed to the narrow and specific focus of the old. Of these, the last aspect deserves particular notice. Regionalism could no longer be associated with a set of relatively narrow security (whether as a dispute-settlement mechanism, or as a framework for defence against a common threat in the inter-state system) and economic (such as a framework of capitalist trade liberalisation) goals. For example, by the late 1970s, regionalism among the developing countries was geared to a wider menu of issues, from the protection of the environment, management of refugee flows, and protection of human rights. Many of these issue areas required a shift from sovereignty-bound thinking and approach on the part of regional organisations.

The lack of success, 'first round' can be attributed mainly to three shortcomings: a misplaced focus on inward-looking economic policies, the absence of basic preconditions, and weaknesses in institutional design.

During the 1960s and 1970s, the key development strategy was import substituting industrialisation using high protective barriers. The main theoretical justification for tariff protection was the 'infant industry' argument. The view was that, in order to gain a manufacturing foothold, local companies should have protection from established foreign competitors. At the same time, people were over-optimistic about the capacity of governments to plan economic development. High tariffs were needed to support import substitution, but they also became a useful source of funds for the rapidly expanding public sector. This inward-looking trade policy was reinforced by restrictive foreign exchange policies which led to overvalued currencies. Because most developing countries had small economies, it was felt that import substitution would have a better chance if pursued at a regional level and this led to various integration schemes. One element underpinning this approach was regional industrial planning. The idea was that industries would be shared out among participating countries, on the basis that they would then go on to supply the whole regional market.

This strategy led to massive underutilization of production capacity and a lack of competitiveness. It did not encourage technical innovation and acted as a strong disincentive for export activities. This, however, only partly explains the failure of the first wave of integration. Even if inefficient, one might reasonably expect such a strategy to increase intra-regional trade, but there is little evidence that this actually occurred. There were clearly other problems as well.

Regional integration can only succeed if certain economic and non-economic preconditions are fulfilled. Important aspects here include structural stability (peace and security), the rule of law, good governance, and macroeconomic and monetary stability. In many of the countries that participated in the 'first wave' of regionalism, one or more of these preconditions were lacking. Two examples suffice to illustrate the problem. The absence of good governance can lead to a battery of irregular non-tariff barriers which restrict the flow of goods across national borders within a region. And if there is conflict or civil strife in one of the member states, it is hardly realistic to expect any meaningful progress towards economic integration.

Inadequate institutional design also contributed to the difficulties. Most literature on economic integration glosses over such matters. If countries say they want to form a customs union or free trade area, it is simply taken for granted that they can do it, provided only that they devise a workable scheme on paper. However, fixing the core part of the menu, and is similar to variable geometry, but with a thematic rather than a geographic orientation. However, the actual implementation is a delicate process covering the setting of realistic targets, negotiation, implementation, control and resolution of disputes. It is conditioned by the nature of the decision making process which can be intergovernmental, supranational or mixed. Since its origin, the EU has been following a supranational approach on economic integration, recently complemented by an intergovernmental approach for the two new 'pillars' introduced by the Maastricht Treaty: foreign and security policy, and justice and home affairs.

For various reasons, developing countries were not keen on supra-nationalism, which would have implied the sharing of sovereignty only recently acquired. The result, in almost all cases, was the creation of regional institutions with weak secretariats and little or no authority. These bodies were invariably hampered by lack of resources, and political interference in personnel management. They were not able to ensure adequate preparation, implementation and control of agreed integration policies. And in some cases they became over-dependent on donor funding, even for their day-to-day functioning. This is clearly not a sound basis for progress.

An important aspect of institutional design is to achieve an efficient distribution of labour between different regional organisations. In some cases there were overlaps in membership and contradictory objectives. Rivalry between regional organisations sometimes contributed to failures in the implementation of agreed policies. A number of approaches have now been developed to facilitate the coherence of regional organisations as well as to deal with the accession of new member states and the introduction of new policy areas. These include: variable speed, variable geometry, integration 'à la carte' and flexible integration.

Under the variable speed approach, common objectives are agreed, but some member states can move more rapidly towards implementation. Rather than let progress be determined by the slowest member, those who are ready to proceed can do so.

Variable geometry accommodates a situation where a sub-group of member states moves towards deeper integration than the others. With 'à la carte' integration, each member can make its own selections from a menu of integration policies. Clearly, this is not very manageable in practice. Flexible integration involves defined core themes to which all state parties must subscribe and other areas where participation is voluntary. This last approach gives structure to 'à la carte' integration, by fixing the core part of the menu and is similar to variable geometry, but with a thematic rather than a geographic orientation.

Two other reasons are frequently cited to explain the relative failure of regional integration initiatives among developing countries. These are disparities between member states and lack of infrastructure. There are many types of disparity relating to income levels, development, economic size and the degree of industrialisation, as well as differences in political systems, culture, history and language. Such divergences clearly make the management of integration more complex and costly.

On the other hand, the effect of divergent income levels on the distribution of the gains of integration is often exaggerated. In the long run, economic integration will tend to reduce disparities, though in the short-term (during the transition phase), the benefits may not be evenly spread. Divergences will decrease most rapidly if integration goes well beyond trade liberalisation to include free movement of capital and workers, the right of establishment, and common competition and fiscal policies.

Lack of adequate transport and communications infrastructure is a formidable constraint that makes trade between many developing countries difficult and costly. This applies particularly to landlocked nations. Improving transport facilities has long been a priority for EU regional development cooperation. But this is not really a reason for lack of progress in economic integration. The latter usually leads to better infrastructures rather than vice versa since successful integration will result in an increased rate of return from cross-border transport and communications investments.

Why should the new integration initiatives have any better chance of succeeding than those attempted in the past? The main reason is that the current initiatives are taking place in a very different political and economic context. The key political difference is that the Cold War is over. Certain rivalries that used to hamper conflict resolution no longer exist.

In addition, many developing countries have evolved from authoritarian to democratic regimes and the influence of civil society on economic decision-making has significantly increased. On the economic front, there has been a policy shift towards more openness and reliance on market forces. Macroeconomic policies have become much more stable. Most developing countries have implemented structural adjustment programmes (SAPs) in collaboration with the Bretton Woods Institutions and other cooperation agencies. And by and large, the economic shocks that so badly affected developing countries during the 1970s and 1980s (commodity price, interest rate and exchange rate movements) have diminished.

Recent integration initiatives no longer emphasize high protective barriers or regional import substitution, and they are more outward-oriented. Additionally, the concept of regionalism has been broadened to cover a variety of issues 'beyond the borders' such as: common technical standards, competition policy, investment regulations, the provision of services and government procurement. Technological innovations especially in the areas of information management and communication, combined with increased capital mobility, have exposed the limitations of national economic policies, even in large industrial nations. A discussion on regionalism cannot ignore this globalisation process, which implies both opportunities and challenges. There is a legitimate fear in many developing countries that they will lose out unless they prepare themselves.

1.3 Regionalism as a Tool for Integration of World Economy

There is an underlying assumption that integration into the world economy will be good for economic development and social welfare. This assumption is much debated (and criticised) since a lot depends on the way in which the integration is actually achieved. An immediate question is whether developing countries should pursue this goal separately, or in a coordinated and structured way through regionalism.

Small economies and specialisation mean that most developing countries are extremely vulnerable to economic shocks. The opening up of such economies has often led to greatly increased interdependence. Countries have become 'stakeholders' in the economic policies of their neighbours. In such circumstances, some form of regional policy coordination becomes imperative. So in reality, the question for developing countries is no longer whether they should take part in regionalism, but what kind of regionalism best suits them.

Recalling the preconditions mentioned above, successful regionalism should be based on general political principles including the rule of law, respect for human rights, and government accountability and transparency. In the economic sphere, the starting point should be the basic principles of orderly monetary and economic management. These principles underpin the multilateral system and are essential for membership of the IMF and WTO. But the global arrangements are not all-encompassing, and many economic policy options remain to be determined at national or regional level.

There has always been controversy over the extent to which the multilateral system actually benefits developing countries. The latter often sought to justify import substitution strategies on the grounds that the international system was 'unfair' to them. At the same time, they neglected the possibility of exerting influence on the direction of multilateral developments. The rapidly rising developing state membership of the WTO, and the fact that more and more of these countries are fulfilling the IMF requirements on current account convertibility, suggest an important shift in attitude. This is highly significant, because it means that developing countries should become much more influential in the global system.

The WTO has a system of rules that establish rights and obligations for member states. Developing countries enjoy 'special and differential treatment', mainly in the form of longer transition periods before obligations enter into force and sometimes involving less stringent treatment. They can receive technical help to meet their obligations or deal with disputes. The WTO has also responded to the specific concerns of the least developed countries who are likely to suffer more than most from certain effects of the Uruguay Round (for example the increase in world cereal prices).

But there are limits to what the multilateral system can do. One basic limitation is that most developing countries lack the capacity to participate effectively in the structure. Another is that in many areas, the international rules offer only the legal framework an outline which must be filled in by governments. If national resources are not up to the task, a solution may be found in adopting a regional approach, as a complement to multilateralism. Thus, regional organisations can ensure that the interests of their members are taken into account in the multilateral system, as well as dealing with issues not yet covered by the latter.

Unilateral liberalisation has often been recommended, especially by the Bretton Woods Institutions, as a key strategy for developing countries. If many countries open up their economies at the same time the result is a move towards overall free trade. Unilateral reform (whether or not in the context of a formal adjustment programme) may help to achieve macroeconomic and monetary stability, and to eliminate distortions, but it does not automatically improve market access. Inefficient industries producing import substitutes may disappear before new export-oriented industries can be established. Where this happens, the result can, in fact, be renewed macroeconomic instability, not to mention an increase in social problems.

So, rapid unilateral liberalisation can pose some big risks, especially for the least-developed countries. A diversified economy may be able to respond quickly to new market opportunities' but the same is not necessarily true of a country that depends on just a few commodities for its export earnings. There are significant adjustment costs that are difficult to handle in a vulnerable economy. Balance of payments support under a structural adjustment programme can contribute to the government budget and help maintain imports, but it does not directly increase the competitiveness of the private sector. It may, therefore, not lead to new investments and the desired supply response.

Another point that most developing countries must bear in mind is that unilateral liberalisation will require major fiscal adjustments, given governments' continuing heavy reliance on trade-related taxes. Regional liberalisation should help to ease this.

Similarly, speedier and more coordinated liberalisation at the level of the regional market (vis-à-vis the world market) will mitigate the adjustment costs for the private sector. Unlike the unilateral approach, it will improve access to the markets of regional partners. Thus, regional integration taken in conjunction with an orderly and gradual opening up of markets to the rest of the world will be superior to quick unilateral liberalisation (which may be reversed if adjustment costs become too high). One final point is that regionalism reduces the influence of pressure groups who would like to see protection restored and hence, may be more credible than unilateral liberalisation.

1.4 Support for Regional Economic Integration

The EU is keen to support realistic integration initiatives among developing countries that are consistent with national Structural Adjustment Programmes (SAPs) and with the multilateral system. Recent experience has led to a strategy comprising three interrelated areas:

- capacity building (including technical assistance, training and research) on the subject of regional economic integration at the level of regional institutions and national governments;

- assistance to the private sector to facilitate restructuring in the wider regional and world markets, including improvements in the financial sector;
- support to governments that are committed to implementing regional integration, to help them cope with the transitional effect on budgetary resources (balance of payments or budgetary support).

In more concrete terms, certain orientations might be envisaged. Under the heading of 'capacity building', adequate attention must be given to the institutional design and legal framework of regional integration. There is also a need to develop analytical capacities - for example in predicting the economic effects of trade liberalisation and regional integration. The approach could cover the training of personnel responsible for policy design and for handling WTO and regional obligations. An effort is needed to upgrade customs services to deal with issues such as verification of origin, and phytosanitary and sanitary regulations. There is also a need to simplify and harmonise rules of origin. The private sector should be involved in capacity building, for example, in areas such as standardisation, quality control and international payments procedures. Regional organisations should be strengthened so that they are able to provide real services to their member states in these areas. Customs unions (and other 'deeper' integration structures) should be mandated to represent their member states in the WTO thus both saving resources and ensuring a higher profile. Multilateral surveillance of monetary and trade policies could be more closely linked to economic policy surveillance at regional level. And if all of this is to work, capacity building is essential.

The benefits of unilateral liberalisation and regional integration will materialise through decisions by the private sector. Subsidies to enterprises that are no longer viable in the regional or global markets should be resisted. This will be easier at regional level because of the reduced influence of pressure groups. At the same time, it should be recognised that adjustment and restructuring costs are real. There needs to be a new industrial policy that facilitates adoption of and transition to improved technologies. Development cooperation can play a useful role here. Special attention should also be given to integrating developing countries more effectively into the global financial markets.

Trade liberalisation may diminish government revenue. The sharpest effects will be felt in the short term as it will take time for new private sector activities to generate higher revenue for governments. Particular care will therefore be needed in undertaking fiscal adjustments. However, it should be kept in mind that reforms to increase the efficiency of customs services will tend to diminish the decline in government revenue resulting from lower tariff rates. Furthermore, trade expansion will gradually increase tariff revenue.

The EU has recently been involved in some initiatives to support economic integration among developing countries along the lines of the above-mentioned principles. Together with the African Development Bank the IMF and the World Bank, the EU is helping to facilitate regional trade in goods and services and investments and payments in Eastern and Southern Africa and the Indian Ocean (the Cross-Border Initiative). In collaboration with France, the IMF and the World Bank, it is also supporting the construction of the West African Economic and Monetary Union. Despite the widespread view that the 'second wave' of regional integration is here to stay, it is too early to declare it a success. What is clear is that the circumstances are now very different from those that pertained during the 'first wave' and important lessons have been learnt in the meantime. In view of this, regionalism may well prove to be a gangplank for developing countries striving to get aboard the global economic vessel.

1.5 Lessons Learned

From the standpoint of the Integration Process the lessons learned are the following:

- First, sustained macroeconomic stability in member countries is essential for advancing regional integration.

- Second, regional integration and cooperation needs political commitment at the highest level and sustained benevolent leadership from the major market partner(s).
- Third, regarding sub-regional or extra regional-integration agreements, consolidating quickly and preserving secure preferential market access for trade is essential "glue" for deepening integration, or even pursuing parallel cooperation programs.
- A fourth major lesson for regional integration is the importance of maintaining forward momentum in the development of transparent and equitable rules-based systems (with formal contingent mechanisms) as well as functional regional institutions and national counterparts with a capacity to formulate, coordinate, and implement regional policy. Likewise, agenda setting must be accompanied by realistic roadmaps and calendars with fallback positions that can help preserve forward momentum.
- Fifth, the effects of regional integration are highly conditioned by factors in the home market. Effective domestic policies and rules-based democratic institutions are necessary to ensure equitable public access to the benefits of regional integration and to provide social protection and conditions for socially efficient adjustment in the face of increased competition and economic transformations which create losers as well as winners. Particular attention should be given to the poor so that they benefit from the integration process.
- Finally, for regional integration to be effective, both collectively and for the individual partner, there is a need for efficient national counterparts of regional policy.

There are clear positive synergies among various regional agreements and between them and gradual unilateral opening and development of the multilateral system. Hence policies on these fronts must work in tandem.

Good and sustainable trade and integration agreements demand: good negotiations (including channels of communication with civil society and its representatives in the legislative branch);

effective implementation; and socially efficient adjustments. There are severe asymmetric capabilities on all three of these fronts in the emerging initiatives with North America, the EU, Asia and the WTO. Without capacity building these initiatives could be in jeopardy.

Broad-based functional cooperation initiatives –while not necessarily bearing the same level of political commitment as formal integration-nevertheless needs political backing from the participating countries at the highest national level and sectorally, a prioritization of agendas, forward looking calendars with precise collective work programs, benchmark reviews, monitoring and follow-up. They also need adequate collective technical, financial and logistical support.

Despite its limitations and dangers, regionalism remains an important tool for promoting a range of positive values and practical approaches in responding to the economic and strategic challenges of the 21st Century. In Europe, it has become the chief promoter of human rights and democracy. The Third World countries, unable and unwilling to follow European models and practices of regionalism, nonetheless recognise its potential to foster a greater decentralisation and democratisation of global institutions and regimes. Regionalism is no longer associated with a set of relatively narrow security (whether as a legalistic dispute-settlement mechanism, or as a framework for defence against a common threat) and welfare (such as trade liberalisation) goals. The end of the Cold War and the effects of globalisation have introduced a wider range of issues and actors into the discourses and practices of regional cooperation. New regionalism promises to foster greater respect for democracy and human rights in the international system. Regional cooperation and integration has become a crucial element of the development process. The benefits of regionalism undergoing such transformations may well outweigh its dangers and shortcomings.

In order to give the dream of an Economic Union and common currency goal a touch of reality, it is necessary to transform the entire approach and policies of Member States towards these organizations. The biggest challenge is to make the mainstream process a dynamic exercise with a multiplicity of stakeholders and institutions. Our search for pragmatism, maturity and wisdom will have to involve both Government and civil society.

References

Acharya Amitav," Regionalism and the Emerging World Order: Sovereignty, Autonomy, Identity", paper presented in the 3rd Annual Conference of the *Centre for the Study on Globalization and Regionalization*, University of Warwick, 16-18 September, 1999.

A.D.V. de S. (ed), *Globalization and South Asia: Retrospect and Prospect*, Sri Lanka Association for the Advancement of Science, 1999, Colombo.

Adisheshiah Malcom, *Regional Economic Arrangements,* New Delhi, India International Centre, 1989.

Almond Gabriel A. and James S. Coleman (eds.), *The Politics of Developing Areas,* Princeton University Press, 1960.

Bach Daniel (ed.) *Regionalisation in Africa: Integration and Disintegration,* Indiana University Press, 1999.

Baldwin, R., "The Causes of Regionalism", *World Economy*, 20(7), 1997.

Baru, S., "Regional Economic Cooperation: Threat or Opportunity?" in Gunewardena, V. (ed), *Regional Cooperation and integration: Perspective from Europe and South Asia,* European Commission to Sri Lanka, 1998, Colombo.

Brage C., *The New Regionalism and its Consequence, Washington* DC, World Bank, 1994.

Demelo And Panagariya (eds), *New Dimensions in Regional Cooperation*, Cambridge University Press 1994.

Dubey, M., *New Regionalism and the Countries of the South,* South Centre, Geneva. 1997.

Haas, Ernest B., "The Study of Regional Integration: Reflections on the Joy and Anguish of Pre-Theorizing", *International Organization* (Cambridge), Vol.24, Autumn 1970.

Feng Yi And Gaspare M. Genna, "Regional Integration and Domestic Institutional Compatibility: A Comparative Analysis of Regional Integration in Central Africa, the Americas, Pacific Asia and Western Europe", paper presented in the 3rd Annual Conference of the *Centre for the Study on Globalization and Regionalization,* University of Warwick, 16-18 September,1999.

Kennes, Walter, "Developing Countries and Regional Integration", *The Courier ACP-EU,* No.165, September-October 1997.

Krugman, P., "Regionalism Vs – Multilateralism ; An Analytical Notes", in DeMelo and Panagariya (eds), *New Dimensions in Regional Cooperation,* Cambridge University Press 1994.

Landau, A., "Multilateralism and Regionalism International Economic Relations" in Daniel C. Bach (ed.) *Regionalisation in Africa: Integration and Disintegration,* Indiana University Press, 1999.

Lawrence, Robert Z., *Regionalism, Multilateralism and Deeper Integration,* The Brookings Institution, Washington DC, 1996.

Milner Helen And Edward Mansfield (ed), *The Political Economy of Regionalism,* Columbia University Press, 1997.

Mistry, P.S., "Regional Integration and Development: Panacea or Pitfalls?", RIS Occasional Paper, No. 47, New Delhi, 1995.

Rana A. P., "Regionalism as an Approach to International Order: A Conceptual Overview", *International Studies* (New Delhi), Vol. 13, 1979.

Schiff Maurice And L. Alan Winters, Regional Cooperation and the role of International Organization and Regional Integration, *World Bank Policy Research Working Paper,* 2872, July 2002.

Sideri S., "Globalisation and Regional Integration", *European Journal of Development Research,* 9(1), 1997.

Tharp Paul A. (ed.), *Regional International Organizations: Structures and Functions* St. Martin's Press, New York, 1971.

2

Growth of Regional Cooperation and Integration in Africa

Following independence, there was universal agreement on pan-Africanism as an effective means of attaining the twin objectives of complete decolonization and rapid economic growth of the continent. However, no similar consensus was reached among African leaders, policymakers, and thinkers on how to *approach* pan-Africanism. Two points of view, diametrically opposed to each other, dominated the debate: continental-ism and functionalism. The continentalists, or the radicals, called for immediate political unification of the continent (i.e. the formation of a United States of Africa) on the grounds that what Africa needed was an integration of common economic functions. The functionalists, or the conservatives, by contrast, were in favour of creating sub-regional groupings as a realistic basis for political unity. The lack of an agreed-upon strategy resulted, in the euphoria of independence, in a disorderly cooperation drive at all levels; a host of cooperation schemes were established in an uncoordinated manner. [1]

2.1 Continental Level

At the continental level, several attempts have been made to attain the highly ambitious objective of a united Africa, all but one have unfortunately failed, mostly because of such factors as divergent ideologies, different languages, colonial heritage, national interests, and personal rivalries. Notable examples were Nasser's Afro-Asian Peoples Solidarity Organization (AAPSO), Nkrumah's Conference of Independent African States (CIAS), the Pan-African Freedom Movement of East and Central Africa (PAFMECA), the All-African Peoples Conference (AAPC), the Union Africaine et Malagache (UAM), and the Casablanca Bloc. [2] The exception was the Organization of African Unity (OAU), whose agreement was signed in Addis Ababa, Ethiopia, in 1963 by heads of state and government of thirty-two independent countries.

The establishment of Organization of African Unity (OAU), the predecessor of the AU, was a response to the challenges confronted by the problems of the African countries. It was through the endeavours of Emperor Haile Selassie of Ethiopia and President Sekou Toure of Guinea, representing respectively, the Monorovia and Casablanca groups of independent states that a Charter creating the OAU was approved by 32 Heads of states and government at Adis Ababa on May 25, May 1963. It pledge the co-ordination of African economic, diplomatic, defence, education and health policies.

The OAU through its numerous summits, resolutions, declarations and decisions, especially at meetings held at Algiers (1968), Adis Ababa (1970 & 1973), Liberville (1978) and Lagos (1980) kept the continental integration agenda in focus laying stress on its essentiality for the welfarc of the peoples of Africa. OAU was established with the object of promoting unity and international cooperation among African states and for eradicating all forms colonialism from the continent. Another aim was that it should lead almost immediately to the establishment of a 'Union Govt.' of all African states.

OAU has succeeded in speeding the political emancipation of the greater part of the continent. It has effectively presented the African viewpoint on many vital international issues. Its most significant achievement is that it has served as an important stabilizing influence in the continent and assisted in the settlement or containment of many political and other disputes among its members that might otherwise have developed into serious conflicts leading possibly to war. Another respect in which the OAU has justified its establishment is the way in which it has succeeded in maintaining a generally independent stance on important world issues and in consistently refusing to allow itself to be deflected from its main objective of protecting African interests, disputes all kinds of external pressures from the big powers. In this respect, the organization has proved far more effective than any comparable organizations in other parts of developing world.

In spite of persistent and well meaning efforts directed at continental unification during the 38 years of its existence the OAU failed to unify the diverse African continent. It proved ineffective and was at the risk of challenges posed by the emerging regional blocs, liberalization of world trade, rapid technological changes and globalization of world production. Further, the position of the fragmented and vulnerable national African economies in the world economy continued to weaken and the continents marginalization in world affairs kept on growing. [3] For example, the OAU has so far failed to bring to an end civil wars and military conflicts in Angola, DRC the Great Lakes Region and Sierra Leone. Various plans and proposal for African unity such as the Lagos Plan of Action and other remained on paper.

2.2 Abuja Treaty and AEC

In spite of the formation and functioning of the numerous RECs and the implementation of the SAPs, the pace and pattern of the Africans socio-economic development continued to be characterized by declining GDP, food insecurity, unemployment, crippling external debt burden, poverty and unsettled political situation in many African countries.

It was against this background of economic decline leading to marginalisation of the continent on the international scene that the OAU member states adopted the Abuja Treaty (1991). With the adoption of the Abuja Treaty in Nigeria on 3rd June 1991 by the majority of OAU member states, the idea of African unity has assumed new dynamism and relevance. The essence of Abuja Treaty was a proposal to establish an African **Economic Community** (AEC) "in order to foster the economic social, cultural integration of the African continent" According to this proposal, existing regional economic communities such as **SADC, COMESA, ECCAS, EAC, ECOWAS, AMU** justify the creation of AEC and indeed form foundation of the AEC. The Abuja Treaty formally came into existence in May 1994. The Treaty also recommended the establishment of an African Union and a **Pan African Parliament** (PAP). AEC and PAP was scheduled to be established by the year 2025 i.e. over a period of 34 years in six phases – Preferential Trade Area (PTA), Free Trade Area (FTA), Customs Union (CU), Common Market, African Economic Community (AEC) and creation of Pan – African Parliament elected by continental universal suffrage. [4]

It was the first attempt to date that provided a legal framework for realizing the long cherished goal of economic integration across Africa. It clearly articulated principles and objectives of economic integration and prescribed setting up of institutions and mechanisms for implementing the Treaty.

The AEC Treaty assigned a central role to the existing REC sponsoring a new challenge to the continental integration process. Besides, pursuing their specific mandates pertaining to their respective geographic areas, the RECs were to serve as programme executing bodies for the AEC. They were called upon to expedite and consolidate achievements of their stated objectives as they were to serve as a building block of the proposed AEC.

The member states under the Treaty reaffirmed and pledged to adhere to a legal system of the community, peaceful settlement of mutual disputes, promotion and protection of individuals socio-economic, political and human rights and popular involvement through the agency of NGOs. Member-states were asked to harmonize their development strategies and policies and to refrain from adopting measures inimical to the attainment of the objectives of the Treaty. It aimed at replacement of the market-oriented integration approach by the production cantered approach. This called for shifts in the development objectives and priorities of the member-states governments.

2.3 AU: A New Beginning

The persistent adverse political and economic conditions, and dissatisfaction with the ineffective working of the OAU led

African leaders to search for alternative organization resulting in the establishment of AU. This latest and the most ambitious unification dispensation enshrined in the Constitutive Act of the African Union designed on the lines of European Union (EU) identifies the need to set up a number of component institutions and structures in a regional and global environment abounding in integrative arrangements with varying levels of capabilities in terms of managerial skills, materials resources and political will pursuing comprehensive and often overlapping mandates.

The Sirte summit of OAU Libya on March 2, 2001 marked a new dawn emerging in Africa. This summit had unanimously declared the establishment of the African Union (AU) replacing the 38 years old OAU. The AU came into existence on May 26, 2001 after obtaining required ratification of two thirds (i.e. 37) of the 53 Member – states of the OAU. It was formally launched in Durban in July 2002. This event signified a major landmark in the grand old vision for a United States of Africa. The AU is expected to provide a new launching pad for greater continental cooperation and integration. [5]

2.4 Sub-Regional Level

Uncoordinated action at the sub-regional level has paralleled the hasty move at the continental level. The tendency to increase sub-regional cooperation efforts has been due, in part, to the frustration faced at the continental level.

The drive towards regional integration in Africa can be divided into two waves: the first took place during the post-independence period, i.e., in the 1960s and early 1970s, with an extension for Southern Africa to around 1980. The second wave is quite recent; its start might be put around the time of the signing of the Abuja Treaty on the African Economic Community in 1991. Both waves have been influenced by the views and ideology of their respective periods and by events outside the African continent. The formation of the regional integration groupings belonging to the first wave is well documented. [6]

The West and Central African sub-regions have been the most active, whereas North Africa has made less significant efforts. The experience of the East and Southern African sub-region was disappointing before 1981 but has since turned out to be promising

2.5 West African Sub-region

Geo-politically, the West African sub-region [7] consists of fifteen countries, including eight former French colonies, four British colonies, one Portuguese, and one Spanish. [8] The former French colonies have been the most active group in the sub-region and in the continent as a whole, in terms of economic cooperation. Thanks to them, West Africa has become the most active sub-region in terms of cooperation initiatives.

Economic cooperation in the sub-region, as in the other sub-regions, dates back to the colonial era. The Bank of West Africa (BAO) was established in 1901; it served as an issuing institution for all French colonies in West and Central Africa. In 1955 the BAO was split up into two separate issuing institutions: the Bank of French West Africa and Togo (AOF) for West Africa, and the Bank of the French Equatorial Africa and Cameroon (AEF) for Central Africa. In 1959 the first bank was renamed the Central Bank of West African States (BCEAO).

In 1959 Benin, Burkina Faso, Cote d'Ivoire, and Niger signed the Treaty of the Council of the Entente States, to which Togo acceded in 1966. The objectives of this grouping were mostly political in nature. In the same year, the West African Customs Union (UDAO) was established, but collapsed after a short life. The Organization of Senegal River States (OERS) was established. The creation of the OERS was justified on the grounds that it was the offspring of the interstate committee founded in 1963 for the development of the Senegal River Basin. The founders of the OERS therefore requested that their organization be acknowledged as the nucleus of the proposed enlarged community. However, the OERS ultimately failed to achieve its objectives and broke down in November 1971. The

OERS was followed in early 1972 by a new organization: the Organization for the Development of the Senegal River (OMVS), consisting of Mauritania, Mali, and Senegal. The main objectives of the OMVS in terms of trade and development were similar to those of the defunct OERS.

The three member countries of the OMVS, together with Benin, Burkina Paso, Cote d'Ivoire, and Niger, had earlier constituted the West African Customs and Economic Union (UDEAO). Political considerations, which dominated integration dynamics in the continent, led the countries of the UDEAO to expand the union's activities by transforming it into the West African Economic Community (CEAO). The member countries, all French speaking, wanted to assert their common identity vis-à-vis the English-speaking countries in the sub-region; in particular, Nigeria, which was trying to play a leading role in the sub-region, suggested the formation of a pan-West African cooperation arrangement embracing all the countries of the sub-region. The 'CEAO treaty was signed in Abidjan, Cote d'Ivoire, in 1973 and came into force the same year.

The leaders of Nigeria never gave up their dream of leading a comprehensive pan-West African cooperation arrangement embracing all the countries of the sub-region. In May 1975 the Lagos Summit of Heads of State and Government adopted the draft treaty to create the Economic Community of West African States (ECOWAS) on the basis of the Lome proposals. By December 1975 all fifteen signatories had ratified the treaty, and Cape Verde adhered soon after.

Another pan-West African cooperation arrangement, the West African Clearing House (WACH), was established in 1975. The initiative came from *the* Association of African *Central* Banks (AACB) in 1973, when it adopted sub-regional payments systems and required all African sub-regions *to* establish their own clearing-houses. At its operational inception, the WACH had a membership of eight central banks representing thirteen countries: BCEAO (for Benin, Burkina Faso, *Cote* d'Ivoire, Niger, Senegal, and Togo) and the central banks for Ghana, Guinea, Liberia, Mali,

Nigeria, Sierra Leone, and The Gambia. The central banks of Guinea Bissau and Mauritania subsequently joined the WACH in 1978 and 1980, respectively, thus raising the membership of the WACH *to* ten central banks for fifteen countries. In *the* fiscal year 1984/85, the Bank of Mali became *part* of the *West* African Monetary Union (WAMU).

2.6 Central African Sub-region

The Central African sub-region comprises eleven countries, five of which are former French colonies, three Belgian, and three Portuguese. [9] The apportionment of the sub-region among the three colonial powers has undoubtedly had a strong bearing on cooperation efforts among the now independent countries of the sub-region.

As in West Africa, the former French colonies have been the most active group of countries in the sub-region as far as regional cooperation is concerned. Cooperation among them can be traced back to 1910, when the Central African Republic (CAR), Chad, Congo, and Gabon were integrated in what was then called French Equatorial Africa, which had a governorate-general and a high commission in Brazzaville. The governorate-general was intended to undertake a limited range of common services, but it nonetheless followed strong centralizing policies. Because the member countries were not quite satisfied with the way resources were allocated, they decided in 1956 to end the federal system and instead to elect territorial governments. However, although they favoured political independence, the four newly independent states maintained most of their former economic links and in October 1957 established the Customs and Fiscal Convention, which in June 1959 became the Equatorial Customs Union (UDE).

Following the unification of Cameroon in 1961, a convention was signed in June that year providing for progressive integration of the Cameroon market into the UDE and for other forms of cooperation comparable to those existing among the UDE's four member countries. While efforts were being made in the following three years to put this convention into operation, a problem arose concerning the location of a projected oil refinery. This issue drew the attention of the partner countries to the necessity of having a common 'development strategy and sparked off a series of meetings and commissions that finally led to the formation in December 1964 of the Economic and Customs Union of Central African States (UDEAC), which aimed at attaining not only a common market but also the ambitious objective of economic union. The treaty entered into force on 1 January 1966. Two years later, the treaty faced its first crisis when Chad and CAR left the union in April 1968 in a dispute over the distribution of the solidarity fund's resources and the location of new industries. The two countries then joined with Zaire to form the Union of Central African States (UEAC), which was more political than economic, but the relevant treaty has never been ratified. In December 1968, CAR rejoined the union. [10]

The four member countries of the union decided to enlarge it to include the eleven countries of the sub-region. To this effect, they invited the other seven countries to attend the 17th Summit Meeting of the Heads of State and Government of UDEAC, held in Libreville, Gabon, from 17 to 20 December 1982. The meeting agreed in principle to create the Economic Community of Central African States (ECCAS), which will cover a total area of about three million square kilometres and comprise a total population of well over sixty million. The agreement has received the blessing of the OAU and the ECA.

As stated previously, the five French-speaking countries in the sub region, together with the French-speaking countries in West Africa, have, been enjoying a common monetary system that was integrated into the French system from 1901 to 1955. The Bank of West Africa (BAO) was established to serve as an issuing institution for all French colonies in West, and Central Africa, but in 1955 it was split into two separate issuing institutions: the Bank of French West Africa and Togo (A OF) and the Bank of French West Africa and Cameroon (AEF). In 1959 the first bank became the Central Bank of West African States (BCEAO), and the second became the Bank of Equatorial African States and Cameroon, which was reorganized and renamed in 1972 as the Bank of Central African States (BEAC), comprising Cameroon, CAR, Chad, Congo, and Gabon. Equatorial Guinea joined the bank in January 1985. The two central banks of West and Central Africa have continued issuing the same currency, the CFA, which is called "the franc of the African Financial Community" by the BCEAO and "the franc of financial cooperation in Central Africa" by the BEAC. It is important to note that UDEAC and BEAC have been developed independently and on a parallel basis; there has been no coordination between them, which is reflected in the independence of their decision making centres and the presence of Chad in BEAC only.

Another monetary arrangement, the Central African Clearing House (CACH), was created by the six member countries of BEAC as well as Zaire. The agreement was signed in January 1979 and became effective in May 1981 after its ratification by the contracting parties. After some operational difficulties, it commenced operations on 1 February 1982. Its major purpose is to foster trade, mainly between the BEAC member countries on one hand and Zaire on the other; the obstacles related to intra--BEAC trade in terms of payments are eliminated by the use of only one currency, the CFA, in circulation in all the member countries. The former Belgian colonies of Burundi, Rwanda, and Zaire tried to have their own cooperation arrangements. They created the Economic Community of the Countries of the Grand Lakes (CEPGL) in 1976, which was actually a continuation of the old economic union formed in 1925 by the government of Belgium itself. The independence of Zaire (formerly Congo) in 1960 ended the old economic union, but after Burundi and Rwanda achieved independence in 1962, the three countries re-created the union under its present name.

2.7 East and Southern African Sub-region

The story of cooperation is rather different in the nineteen countries of the East and Southern African sub-region (one of which is the Republic of South Africa). [11] Of these countries, there were ten British colonies, three French colonies, and one Portuguese colony. As in West and Central Africa, operation among the countries of this sub-region began as early as 1917, mainly for demonstrative convenience. The former British colonies, not the French ones, took the lead in this sub-region, but unlike the former French colonies in the other sub-regions, they failed to maintain their pre independence relations. Almost all cooperation schemes collapsed immediately before or after each country achieved independence in the early 1960s. Even after independence, they tried in vain to re-establish sub-regional cooperation. It was only in the early 1980s that they managed, in coordination with the other countries in the sub-region, to establish sub-regional arrangements.

Following the original occupation of East African territories by Britain, a de facto common market-the East African Common Market (EACM)-was developed among Kenya, Tanganyika (now part of Tanzania), and Uganda. The three territories share common boundaries and a homogeneous population, but they were each separately ruled by a governor. Common services, particularly for transport and communications, were soon developed, and there were no tariffs or any other restrictions on inter-territorial trade. In 1917 a free trade area was created between Uganda and Kenya, which soon developed into a common market. Tanganyika joined the common market in stages between 1922 and 1927, although the customs administrations were not amalgamated until 1949. The bulk of the benefits of integration was captured by Kenya, a fact that led the other partners to express dissatisfaction with the distribution of the costs and benefits of integration among the three partner countries.

The situation was compounded by political considerations that threatened the very existence of the common market in the aftermath of independence. At that time, Tanzania had a socialist orientation and therefore adopted a radically different economic approach. In 1965, it announced that it was going to have its own central bank with a separate currency, and thereafter it imposed quotas and other restrictions on its imports from Kenya. Uganda followed Tanzania's lead. In an attempt to maintain the common market, the three countries agreed to appoint a committee to assess the situation and submit definite recommendations. Based on these recommendations, a treaty of East African Cooperation was signed in Kampala, Uganda, on 6 June 1967 and came into force on 1 December 1967. The treaty established what is referred to as an East African Community, including a common market. Nevertheless, the subsequent pace of events demonstrated that the differences among the three countries were so great and growing that nothing could have prevented the eventual collapse of the infant community; it broke up in 1977. [12]

British colonial authorities created three common monetary areas in the sub-region: the East African Currency Board (EACB), the Southern Rhodesian Currency Board, and the South African Reserve Bank. The three boards collapsed, however, immediately after the countries of the sub-region gained their independence.

The East African Currency Board, comprising Kenya and Uganda, was formed in December 1919; Tanganyika joined in 1920 and Zanzibar in 1936. During World War II, the authority of the board extended to Ethiopia, British Somalia, and Aden. The board operated only as an automatic money changer and had no control over credit. Ethiopia, Somalia, and Aden left the board in 1945, 1950, and 1965, respectively. Zanzibar later merged with Tanganyika to form Tanzania. The British government intended to transfer the East African Currency Board into a common central bank. From 1955 to 1964 the government made some innovations to this end, including moving the headquarters of the board from London to Nairobi in August 1960 and placing the board under the control of the colonial governments. However, the structure and operations of the board were not considered advantageous to future economic development in the three countries. Therefore, on the eve of their independence, the three individually explored the possibility of establishing a common central bank.

In 1959 Uganda commissioned W. T. Newlyn to make recommendations on the future central banking system of the area, but Newlyn's report was never implemented. Tanganyika in turn entrusted Erwin Blue- mental to investigate the possibility of converting the EACB into an East African central bank. Blumental submitted his report in January 1963, but it was also shelved. In 1964 the three governments invited the IMF to rec-ommend a central banking system for East Africa, but before the IMF experts arrived the three countries had moved toward establishing separate central banks. The three governments appeared to have agreed that a common central bank would not be realistic in the absence of a political union, which could not have been attained given the divergent ideologies of the three member countries at that time. Thus, Tanzania set up its own central bank in December 1965, followed by Kenya and Uganda in May 1966. The Southern Rhodesian Currency Board was established in 1938 to take care of the currency needs of British Central Africa. It comprised Southern Rhodesia (now Zimbabwe), Northern Rhodesia (now Zambia), and Nyasaland (now Malawi). In due course, the British authorities in Central Africa felt the need for a central bank in order to develop the region's financial infrastructure and to encourage monetary stability. The Bank of Rhodesia and Nyasaland was therefore created in 1956. However, the bank suffered from a number of shortcomings that, in conjunction with the political factors of the independence of Northern Rhodesia and Nyasaland, led to the 1964 bank split into the Reserve Bank of Rhodesia, the Bank of Zambia, and the Reserve Bank of Malawi.

In 1921 the South African Reserve Bank was established, and the commercial notes, which had been legal tender in the whole of Southern Africa, were replaced with the South African rand. The new rand also be-came the official currency of Bechuanaland (now Botswana), Basutoland (now Lesotho), and Swaziland. The three countries, along with the Republic of South Africa (RSA), unofficially constituted the Rand Monetary Area, and the financial institutions of the three countries began to comply with the monetary and exchange control directives of the South African Reserve Bank. The three countries continued to use the rand unofficially after their political independence. In 1974 Botswana opted out of the Rand Monetary Area and introduced its own currency, the pula. Lesotho and Swaziland also issued their own currencies, the loti and lilangeni, respectively, which were tied to the South African rand at the rate of 1:1. Each of the three countries now has its own central bank. In addition, all four countries formed the Southern African Customs Union (SACU), whose agreement was revised both in 1910 and in 1969. (The last revision became effective as of 29 January 1970). However, given the geographical setting of the three BLS countries (Botswana, Lesotho, Swaziland) and the surrounding political circumstances, it is difficult to consider the SACU a proper "cooperation" arrangement because it was essentially imposed on "the three countries. The recent political and constitutional changes in the RSA involving, inter alia, the adoption of majority rule had far-reaching implications on the modus operandi not only of SACU but also of SADC and the Preferential Trade Area for Eastern and Southern African States (PTA and COMESA).

This history of failure notwithstanding, the countries of the sub-region did not give up altogether their collective cooperation efforts. It was only three years after the collapse of the East African Economic Community in 1977 that they initiated, almost simultaneously, two ambitious all-embracing cooperation arrangements: the Southern African Development and Co-ordination Conference (SADCC) and the Preferential Trade Area for Eastern and Southern African States (PTA). The member countries seem to have benefited largely from the lessons drawn from the subregion's previous experience with multilateral cooperation.

Unlike traditional cooperation arrangements, which are based on for mal treaties spelling out their objectives, activities, and institutions, SADCC was based on a collective declaration made by the nine founding states in Lusaka, Zambia, in 1980 that set forth its objectives and strategies but not its institutional structure. The ultimate goal of this non-traditional grouping was to reduce dependence of the member countries, especially (but not solely) on the Republic of South Africa, which is political in nature. The establishment of SADCC dates back to April 1980, when the heads of state of Angola, Botswana, Lesotho, Malawi, Mozambique, Swaziland, Tanzania, Zambia, and Zimbabwe met in Lusaka, Zambia, and decided (1) to issue the Lusaka Declaration, according to which the heads of state committed their countries to a program of harmonious and coordinated development, and (2) to approve a program of action that accorded the highest priority to improving transportation and identifying a number of other strategic areas in which activities for economic development could be undertaken on a regional basis.

At almost the same time, preparatory work for the establishment of the PTA was under way. Again in Lusaka, an extraordinary meeting of the sub-region's ministers of trade, finance, and planning was held to consider, among other things, the creation of a Preferential Trade Area for the East and Southern African states. A corresponding treaty was signed on 21 December 1981 by twelve countries: Comoros, Djibouti, Ethiopia, Kenya, Lesotho, Malawi, Mauritius, Somalia, Swaziland, Uganda, Zambia, and Zimbabwe; it came into force on 30 September 1982. Burundi, Rwanda, and Tanzania later signed the treaty as well. After the treaty was signed, the PTA Clearing and Payments Committee, which consists of the governors of the central banks of the PTA member countries, entered into negotiations for setting up the PTA Clearing House. The agreement was approved by the PTA Council of Ministers in December 1983, and the clearinghouse commenced operations on 1 February 1984. The Reserve Bank of Zimbabwe was designated to perform the duties of the clearinghouse as an interim measure, pending the establishment of an autonomous clearing-house. In line with the gradual approach adopted by the treaty, the clearing-house is regarded as a first step toward the establishment of a payments union and eventually of a monetary union that will be an integral part of the sub-regional common market.

2.8 North African Sub-region

The North African sub-region-comprising the seven countries Algeria, Egypt, Libya, Mauritania, Morocco, Sudan, and Tunisia-is by far the least active of all African sub-regions in terms of cooperation initiatives. Only two attempts have been made at the sub-regional level to establish multilateral arrangements. The first was made by the Maghreb countries (Algeria, Libya, Morocco, and Tunisia) when they set up the Maghreb Permanent Consultative Committee (CPCM) in 1964 to advise the Conference of Ministers of Economic Affairs on issues falling within the conference's jurisdiction. The committee proceeded to set up the specialized subcommittees required for planning, statistics, transport and communications, tourism, employment, industry, and agriculture. In 1970 Libya withdrew from the CPCM. Meanwhile, Mauritania attended the meetings as an observer. The CPCM undertook a number of studies relating to common project in the above fields; some of them were considered and approved, but very few have been implemented. Since 1976, though, the CPCM has come to a virtual standstill as a result of the conflict on the Sahara issue between Algeria and Morocco.

The second cooperation attempt was made in 1989 by the same group of countries: a new arrangement called the Maghreb Arab Union (MAU). The union is still in the formative stage. [13]

Some writers have tried to explain the North African sub-region's reluctance to establish multilateral cooperation arrangements. They argue that the countries of the sub-region are divided into two groups: the Maghreb countries (including Algeria, Libya, Mauritania, Morocco, and Tunisia) and the others (Egypt and Sudan). Egypt associates mainly with the Arab Mashreq countries, and Libya desires to associate itself with Egypt. Sudan is inclined to deal with the countries of East and Central Africa, whereas Mauritania belongs more to West Africa than North Africa. The socio-political structures of the proper three Maghreb countries-Algeria, Morocco and Tunisia-underlie their failure in boosting their cooperation.

The reluctance of these countries to have their own multilateral cooperation arrangements can largely be attributed to the "dual identity" of the sub-region. The North African countries belong simultaneously to the Arab / world and to Africa. This double affiliation has substantially influenced intra-sub-regional cooperation, e.g., by retarding the establishment of proper sub-regional arrangements. As signatories to the older Arab arrangements-such as the Arab League (1945), the Defence and Economic Cooperation Treaty (1950), and Arab Economic Unity (1957), to mention only a few-the North African countries probably have not found it necessary to create similar sub-regional ones. In addition, complicated political dynamics, a common phenomenon in the Third World (particularly in East Africa before 1981), have had a strong adverse effect on cooperation initiatives among these countries.

Nevertheless, this does not mean that intra-sub-regional cooperation is absent outside the Arab arrangements. It has in fact been present all along, but at the bilateral rather than sub-regional level. This approach was encouraged and recommended by the North African Sub-regional Committee of the Association of African Central Banks (AACB) at a meeting held in Toronto, Canada, on 8 September 1987 to review the question of monetary cooperation in the sub-region, particularly with regard to the creation of a payments union. As a first step, the committee decided to move in the direction of creating flexible payments arrangements on a bilateral basis be-fore moving on to sub-regional payments arrangements.

2.9 Second Wave of Regional Integration in Africa

The origin of the second wave of regional integration in Africa can be traced to a number of developments outside the continent during the second half of the 1980s. There is no clear definition of the 'new regionalism', but some of its most typical characteristics are : outward-oriented trade strategy with low external tariffs, rather than regional import substitution behind high protective tariff walls; harmonisation of macro-economic policies (monetary and fiscal); standardisation of technical norms and procedures and environmental regulations; liberalisation of trade in financial and other services; facilitation of cross-border investment flows; attention given to the credibility of government policies (the involvement of regional partners diminishes the weight of national pressure groups and may help to avoid policy reversals).

The renewed worldwide drive towards regional integration, together with the long delay before the Uruguay Round agreement could be reached, have stimulated a second integration wave in Africa. In 1991 African Heads of State signed the Abuja Treaty on the establishment of a Pan-African Economic Community (AEC). Even though the formidable practical issues and constraints are not addressed in detail, the treaty can be interpreted as a strong expression of general political desire for more integration in Africa, in view of the increased regionalism in the rest of the world.

In 1992, SADCC was transformed into the Southern African Development Community (SADC.) The new SADC explicitly added a market integration SADCC. In 1993, the member states of the Preferential Trade Agreement signed a new treaty to establish the Common Market of Eastern and Southern Africa (COMESA). The objectives of COMESA are to go beyond the creation of a customs union and include free movement of capital and persons and formation of a monetary union. COMESA includes the possibility of supranational elements in decision-making. Also in 1 993 the ECOWAS Treaty was revised.

Other striking developments took place at the beginning of 1994, following the devaluation of the CFA franc. The West African Monetary Union has been transformed into the West African Economic and Monetary Union (UEMOA), taking on board the responsibilities of the West African Economic Community (Communaute Economique Ouest Africaine, CEAO). In a parallel move, the Central African countries that are part of the Franc Zone also embarked on an Economic and Monetary Union (Communaute Economique et Monetaire d' Afrique

Centrale, CEMAC). It is interesting to observe that the founding of UEMOA was followed by disbanding CEAO.

2.10 Evaluation

In the event, despite considerable (but superficial) effort aimed at achieving it, effective market enlargement through economic integration has not yet occurred in Africa. It has not yielded results by way of enhanced efficiency, or in terms of successful industrialization, market enlargement modernization, sustained development and growth, or competitiveness. Yet African governments remain committed to integration, although they have become slightly more realistic and practical about achieving it.

Integration arrangements in francophone West Africa and in southern Africa have had limited success with customs unions. But attempts at deep economic integration in the rest of Africa between 1960 and 2000 have not yielded discernible benefits. This is clear whatever measures of benefits are employed, whether they involve securing peace and political stability or effective market enlargement. There has been no progressive integration of markets for factors, goods or services. Nor has intra-regional trade expanded. Integration efforts have achieved neither output growth nor the industrial development of member states. Even less has there been any increase in economic convergence, or in the mobility of factors on a sub-regional or Africa-wide basis. No discernible economies of scale have been realized.

Africa has not even attempted to capture the benefits of integration in areas such as tertiary education and high-level health care. Its integration efforts have not achieved much harmonization and co-ordination of standards, legislation, rules and regulations, or of institutions regulating economic interaction. Nor have they helped African governments to secure fiscal and monetary stability.

First-generation integration arrangements in Africa were either legacies from the past (such as the East African

Community) or new arrangements built on the predominant development theories of the day. These advocated industrialization through high levels of protection and the development of closed markets in state-run economies financed heavily by Official Development Assistance (ODA) or sovereign commercial borrowing.

Aid to Africa was driven less by concern about development than by the geopolitical agenda and priorities of donors. The failure of development, and of first-generation integration, was the result both of external influences as well as failure of the post-independence African development model.

That model failed because it was: (a) anti-market-the market being seen by governments and publics as synonymous with inequity, capitalism and colonialism; (b) anti-private sector and anti-property rights; and (c) anti-foreign investment, except perhaps in the minerals and hydrocarbon resource sectors. The emphasis on pervasive state intervention and the implicit (but misplaced) belief in the omnipotence and benignity of the state proved to be a formula for large-scale economic failure.

Attempts at economic integration in Africa between 1965 and 1995 failed for both macro and micro reasons. The macro reasons included:

2.11 Macro Reasons

1. The failure of African governments to translate their commitments in regional treaties and agreements into substantive changes in national policies, legislation, rules and regulations. There was no follow through in translating regional commitments into national actions.
2. The unwillingness of African governments to subordinate immediate national political interests in order to achieve long-term regional economic goals (that would have had much higher pay off for long-term national welfare) or to cede essential elements of sovereignty to regional institutions.
3. An absence of monitoring and enforcement mechanisms to ensure adherence to agreed time-tables on such matters as

tariff and NTB (non-tariff barrier) reductions or in achieving more difficult objectives (such as macroeconomic stabilization).

4. Endemic political instability exacerbated by debilitating conflict in every sub-region of Africa (e.g. Algeria, Ethiopia, Somalia, Tanzania-Uganda, Rwanda, Burundi, Mozambique, Zimbabwe, South Africa, Namibia, Angola, Zaire, Nigeria, Sierra Leone, Liberia, Chad). Conflict made it impossible for integration to work.
5. The pervasiveness of parastatals in almost every sector of productive enterprise. Subjected to continual political interference and bureaucratic intervention in their day-to-day affairs, these organizations functioned with non-commercial objectives and an entirely national perspective in mind. That was inimical to natural cross-border regional interaction, e.g. in electricity, mining, manufacturing, financial services, construction, transport and telecommunications.
6. African antipathy to markets, private enterprise and foreign investment and to more open trade and exchange regimes prevented a higher degree of private sector driven regional integration (through processes such as corporate mergers and acquisitions, and a market-driven quest for investment and operating cost reductions). Africa's development paradigm reinforced the immobility of labour, investment capital, and know-how, thus impeding rather than facilitating integration.
7. Excessive concern on the part of African government about the inequitable distribution of producer gains resulting from regional co-operation and integration and not enough focus on a wider spread of the consumer gains which such arrangements generated.
8. Programmes of debt crisis triggered structural adjustment programmes (SAPs) whose conditionalities did not take account of regional costs and benefits. These proved to be less effective and timely (in terms of results and outcomes) than they might have been if regional rather than national

perspectives in the design of SAPs had been adopted in the first place.

9. Political commitment to African integration being confined to a narrow coterie of political leaders and senior technocrats. The implications, costs, benefits and opportunities of integration were neither fully understood nor supported by all levels of government nor by a sufficiently broad spectrum of public opinion.

2.12 Micro Reasons

Micro reasons for the failure of the first generation of regional co-operation and integration schemes in Africa have been elaborated at as follows: [14]

1. low levels of aggregate demand;
2. low import demand elasticities;
3. relatively large differences in production cost structures;
4. divergent industrial structures and rates of industrial development;
5. low levels of intra-regional trade;
6. poor intra-regional infrastructure linkages;
7. insufficient opportunities for effective intra-industry trade expansion;
8. an absence of effective dispute settlement procedures; and counter-productive obsessions with distributional equity and industrial location policies which resulted in neither being achieved.

This combination of macro and micro reasons goes a long way towards explaining why economic integration did not occur in Africa between 1960 and 2000.

2.13 A New Approach to Integration in Africa in the 1990s

An underlying shift from states to markets, induced to an extent by externally imposed structural adjustment programmes (SAPs) has aimed at revamping the African development model since 1985. That shift has resulted in second-generation integration attempts gathering steam since 1992. In principle, the new approach has abandoned the ossified, static, protected-fortress approach to integration among closed, state-run economies. It lays more emphasis on development of thematic integration (i.e. co-operating to save on large-scale infrastructure costs and achieving economies of scale) and open, rather than protected, market enlargement as a means of consolidating national economic policy shifts towards greater liberalization, market orientation, competitiveness and efficiency.

Second-generation integration relies on achieving these ambitious objectives at the sub-regional or regional level, before attempting to achieve them at the global level, in a world where Africa has yet to overcome a large number of disadvantages in order to compete. If second-generation integration is to succeed in Africa, a number of pre-requisites will need to be met:

- In new arrangements African countries will need to make the right choices of natural partners. In that context the propensity of some integration arrangements in Africa (e.g. The Southern African Development Community–SADC) to widen their memberships for political reasons, rather than to secure and deepen integration in key economic areas where that can be achieved without too much effort, may reflect arguable priorities.
- Economies participating in the new arrangements will need to be stable and sufficiently adjusted, and to enjoy a reasonable degree of macro-and microeconomic equilibrium. In the absence of sufficient adjustment, integration will be impeded by successive adjustment measures that may trigger large attendant shocks (e.g. adjusting exchange regimes), and by structural characteristics that serve to reinforce entrenched non-tariff barriers to trade and market integration.
- There will need to be greater degree of convergence among integrating economies than there was before on key macroeconomic and development indicators, such as inflation rates, interest rates, exchange rate stability, budget deficit control, monetary policy, and a greater degree of coherence and consistency of fiscal structure and policies.

- Mechanisms will be needed for ensuring a modicum of regional equity to ensure that welfare gains from economic integration are derived by all participating members and are not concentrated in just one or two members.
- New attempts at achieving integration will need to be seen widely by publics and investors as being more credible and durable than earlier failed attempts. Integration will not succeed if sufficient political muscle is not applied to make it succeed. Political will needs to go beyond rhetoric, with African leaders being more aware of the national economic and political implications of the regional commitments they make and expending the political capital needed to follow through on such commitments.

And finally, in a continent with Africa's recent economic history, integration arrangements may need to be underpinned with some type of formal arrangements with other established trading blocs, in particular the European Union, to bolster their credibility and durability. [15]

Notes

1. Aly, Ahmad, A.H.M., Economic Cooperation in Africa – In Search of direction, Lynne Reinner, Colorado, London, 1994, pp 1-8.

2. Hoskyns, C., "Pan Africanism and Integration" in A. Hazlewood (ed), African Integration and Disintegration, Oxford University Press, London, 1967.

3. Ndongko W.A., (ed), Economic Cooperation and Integration in Africa, CODESRIA, 1985

4. Mathews K., "Birth of AU", Africa Quarterly, ICCR, New Delhi, Vol. 41, No. 1 & 2, 2001

5. Mathews K., "Birth of AU", opcit

6. Kennes Walter, "African Regional Economic Integration and the European Union", in Danial Bach (ed), Regionlisation in Africa – Integration and Disintegration, Indiana University Press, Indiana, 1999, pp 27-28

7. Asante S.K.B, "Regional Economic Cooperation & Integration: The Experience of ECOWAS" in A. Nyongo (ed), Regional Integration in Africa, 1990.

8. The countries are Benin, Burkina Faso, Cape Verde, Cote d'Ivoire, The Gambia, Ghana, Guinea, Guinea – Bissau, Liberia, Mali, Niger, Nigeria, Senegal, Sierra Leone, and Togo.

9. The Central African countries are Angola, Burundi, Cameroon, the Central African Republic, Chad, Congo, Equatorial guinea, Gabon, Rwanda, Sao Tome & Principe, and Zaire.

10. Jalhoh A.A., "Foreign Private Investments and Regional Political Integration in UDEAC" in W.A. Ndongko (ed), Economic Cooperation and Integration in Africa, 1985.

11. The other eighteen countries are Botswana, Comoros, Dijibouti, Ethiopia, Kenya, Lesotho, Madagascar, Malawi, Mauritius, Mozambique, Somalia, Swaziland, Tanzania, Uganda, Zambia, Zimbabwe, Namibia, and Eritria.

12. Hazlewood A., "Eco Integration in East Africa", in Arthur Hazlewood (eds), African Integration & Disintegration – Case Studies in Economic & Political Union, 1962.

13. Baurename, N., "Integration in the Maghred : Assessments and Prospects" in Nyong'o (ed), Regional Integration in Africa. Opcit.

14. Mistry Percy, "Regional Integration Arrangements in Economic Development : Panacea or Pitfalls ?," in J.J. Teunissen (ed) Regionalism and the Global Economy : The case of Africa, The Hague Forum or Debt and Development, 1996.

15. Mistry Percy, "Africa's Record of Regional Cooperation and Integration," African Affairs, 2000.

References

Aly, Ahmad, *Economic Cooperation in Africa – In search of direction* (Lynne Reinner, Colorado, London, 1994)

Asante S.K.B., *The Political Economy of Regional Integration in Africa: A decade of the Economic Community of West Africa* (ECOWAS), (New York, Preager, 1986)

Bach Daniel C, (ed.) *Regionalisation in Africa – Integration and Disintegration* (Indiana, Indiana University Press, 1999).

Balassa, Bela, *The Theory of Economic Integration – III* (Homewood, Richard Irwin, 1961)

Baurename, N., "Integration in the Maghreb: Assessment and Prospects" in Nyong'o (ed), *Regional Integration in Africa* (Academy Science Publishers, Nairobi, Kenya, 1990).

CACH, *"The Experience of Central African Clearing House"*, in A CMS Seminar on Experience with payments and clearing system in African Countries, (Freetown, Sierra Leone, May 1987).

Chileste, J.H, *The Challenge of Developing Intra – African Trade* (East African Literature Bureau, 1977).

De Melo Jaime and Arvind Pangaria, (eds.) *New Dimensions of Regional Integration* (Cambridge University Press, 1994).

Hazlewood Arthur, *African Integration and Disintegration – Case studies in Economic and Political Union* (Oxford University Press, London, 1962).

Hoskyns, C., "Pan Africanism and Integration", in Arthur Hazlewood (ed), *African Integration and Disintegration: Case studies in Economic and Political Union* (Oxford University Press, London, 1967).

Landau, A., "Multilateralism and Regionalism International Economic Relations" in Daniel C. Bach (ed.) *Regionalisation in Africa: Integration and Disintegration* (Indiana University Press, 1999).

Mistry, P., Regional Dimensions of structural Adjustment in Southern Africa', in J. Teunissen (ed), *Regionalism and the Global Economy: The case of Africa* (The Hague: Forum on Debt and Development, 1996).

Mistry, P., *Regional Integration and Development: Panacea Pitfalls?* (New Delhi, Research and Information system for the Non Aligned and other developing countries, 1995).

Mulaisho, D., *Post Apartheid Implications for SADCC and the Drive Towards Economic Integration* (Institute of Development Management, Gaborone, 1992).

Ndongko W.A. (ed.), *Economic Cooperation and Integration in Africa* (CODESRIA, 1985).

Nyongo, A. (ed.), *Regional Integration in Africa* (Academy Science Publishers, Nairobi, Kenya, 1990).

SADC – EU relations: Looking Back and Moving Ahead, (South African Institute of International Affairs, 2002).

Asante S.K.B., "Structural Adjustment Programme and African Regionalism, *West Africa* (London), October 1991,

Asante S.K.B., "What really is African Union", *West Africa*, 7-13 July, 2003.

Chidzero, B.T. Cr., "The meaning of Economic cooperation in Africa", *East African Journal* (Nairobi), December, 1965.

Davis, R. "Approaches to Regional Integration in Southern African Context", *Africa Insight* (London), Vol. 24, No.1, 1994.

Harsch, E., "Making African Integration a reality", *Africa Recovery*, Vol. 16, No.2-3: Sept. 2000. New York.

Jalloh Abdul A., "Regional Integration in Africa Lessons from past and prospects for the future; *Africa Development* (Dakar), Vol. 1, No.2, 1976.

Mathews K, "Birth of AU", *Africa Quarterly* (Delhi), ICCR, Vol. 41, No.1 & 2: Jan to June, 2001.

Mathews K, "Towards a United States of Africa", *Mainstream*, New Delhi, Vol. 339, No. 28, June 30, 2001.

Mehta S.C., 'African Unification: Past Experience and Future Promises", *Africa Quarterly* (Delhi), ICCR, Vol. 41, No. 4, 2001.

Mistry Percy S., "Africa's Record of Regional Co-operation and integration', *African Affairs* (London), 2000.

3

A Case Study of COMESA

Every continental region has at least one major integration movement such as European Union in Europe; North Atlantic Free Trade Area (NAFTA) in North America; Latin American Integration Association (LAIA) in Latin America; the Caribbean has the Caribbean Community and Common Market (CARICOM); the Middle East has the Council of Arab Economic Unity (CAEU); Central America has the Central American Common Market (CACM); Asia has the Association of South East Asian Nations (ASEAN), and the Asia-Pacific Economic Cooperation (APEC); and finally Africa has three major ones: the Southern African Development Community (SADC); the Economic Community of West African States (ECOWAS); and the Common Market for Eastern and Southern Africa (COMESA).

These regional blocs or economic groupings have the common goals of economic transformation and development, implicitly including eradication or reduction of poverty in the process. In other words, economic cooperation and integration is not an end in themselves, but rather a means towards sustainable economic development. The article focuses upon the experience of one of the three major economic groupings in Africa—the Common Market for Eastern and Southern Africa (COMESA). Size and extent of membership [1] makes COMESA more appropriate for study in terms of relevance and interest as compared to either SADC or ECOWAS

3.1 Historical Developments

At the first and second conferences of independent African States, held in Accra, Ghana, in April 1958 and in Addis Ababa, Ethiopia in June 1960, respectively, economic problems to be faced by independent Africa were discussed. There was a consensus that the smallness and fragmented nature of post-colonial African national markets would constitute a major obstacle to the diversification of economic activity that would comprise modern and internationally competitive enterprises, which would satisfy domestic needs and meet export requirements. It was, therefore, agreed that African countries which had gained political independence, should promote economic co-operation among themselves.

Two options were advocated for the implementation of the integration strategy in Africa: a) a Pan-African, all-embracing regional approach, which envisaged the immediate creation of a regional continental economic arrangement; and b) a geographically narrower approach that would have its roots at the sub-regional levels and build on sub-regional co-operation arrangements to subsequently achieve geographically wider forms of co-operation arrangements. [2]

The majority of the countries favoured the narrower sub-regional approach. Based on this, the United Nations Economic Commission for Africa (ECA) proposed the division of the continent into four sub-regions: Eastern and Southern, Central, West and North Africa. The Commission's proposals were adopted by the OAU Conference of Heads of State and Government. All independent African Sates were enjoined to take, during the 1980's, steps necessary to strengthen existing sub-regional economic co-operative groupings and, as required, establish new ones so as to cover the whole continent sub-region by sub-region and promote co-ordination and harmonization among the groupings for the gradual establishment of an African Economic Community by the end of the century.

3.2 Formation of COMESA

The origins of COMESA can be traced to the mid-sixties. Before the Lagos Plan of Action and the Final Act of Lagos were adopted, the countries of Eastern and Southern Africa had already initiated the process towards creating an Eastern and Southern African co-operation arrangement.

In October 1965, the ECA convened a ministerial meeting of the then politically independent states of eastern and southern Africa to consider proposals for the establishment of a mechanism for the promotion of sub-regional economic integration. The meeting, which was held in Lusaka, Zambia, recommended the creation of an Economic Community of Eastern and Southern African states. To achieve this objective, the meeting also recommended that an Interim Council of Ministers, assisted by an Interim Economic Committee of officials, should be set up to negotiate the treaty and initiate programmes on economic co-operation, pending the completion of negotiations on the treaty.

At the first meeting of the interim Ministerial Council held in Addis Ababa, in May 1966, the Terms of Association to govern the interim arrangements before the signing of the formal Treaty were adopted and signed by Burundi, Ethiopia, Kenya, Madagascar, Malawi, Mauritius, Rwanda, Somalia, Tanzania, and Zambia. In November 1967, a meeting of the Interim Economic Committee of officials recommended an interim programme of action for implementation which would be integrated into the Treaty when approved. Parallel with these developments, two other organizations were established, the Pan-African Freedom Movement in East, Central and Southern Africa (PAFMECSA), and the conference of East and Central African states. Although these were mainly political in their orientation, their membership extended beyond the sub-region and they included in their activities programmes on economic co-operation.

In the 1970's, the need for a sub-regional economic arrangements became more urgent as a result of three major developments. First, the collapse of the federations in Eastern and Central Africa reduced political co-operation among the States of this region. Second, the destabilization of the economies of the southern African States by apartheid South Africa made it necessary to urgently create, a sub-regional organization which would be an economic counterweight to South Africa. Third, despite the failure of earlier efforts to establish a sub-regional economic co-operation arrangement, the countries of Eastern and

Southern Africa recognised that there was no other alternative to reducing their traditional economic dependence on the industrialized countries of the north than through the adoption of self-sustaining development measures in all sectors.

In March 1978 the First Extra-ordinary meeting of Ministers of Trade, Finance and Planning met in Lusaka. The meeting recommended the creation of a sub-regional economic community, beginning with a sub-regional trade area which would be gradually upgraded over a ten-year period to a common market until the community had been established. To this end, the meeting adopted the "Lusaka Declaration of Intent and Commitment to the Establishment of a Preferential Trade Area for Eastern and Southern Africa" and created an Inter-governmental Negotiating Team on the Treaty for the establishment of the PTA. The meeting also agreed on a tentative time-table for the work of the Intergovernmental Negotiating Team.

After the preparatory work had been completed a meeting of Heads of State and Government was convened in Lusaka on 21st December 1981 at which the Treaty establishing the PTA was signed. The Treaty came into force on 30th September 1982 after it had been ratified by more than seven signatory states as provided for in Article 50 of the Treaty.

The PTA Treaty envisaged its transformation into a Common Market and, as such, the Treaty establishing COMESA was signed on 5th November 1993 in Kampala, Uganda and was ratified a year later in Lilongwe, Malawi on 8th December 1994.

3.3 Objectives of COMESA

The aims and objectives of COMESA have been designed to remove the structural and institutional weaknesses of member States by pooling their resources together to sustain their development efforts individually and collectively. The aims are:

- to attain sustainable growth and development of the member States by promoting a more balanced and harmonious development of production and marketing structures;

- to promote joint development in all fields of economic activity and the joint adoption of macro-economic policies and programmes; to raise the standard of living of its peoples, and to foster closer relations among member States;
- to co-operate in the creation of an enabling environment for foreign, cross-border and domestic investment, including the joint promotion of research and adaptation of science and technology for development;
- to co-operate in the promotion of peace, security and stability among the member States to enhance economic development in the region;
- to co-operate in strengthening the relations between the Common Market and the rest of the world and adoption of common positions in international fora; and
- to contribute towards the establishment, progress and the realisation of the objectives of the African Economic Community. [3]

The COMESA agenda aims to deepen and broaden the integration process among member States through the adoption of more comprehensive trade liberation measures such as the complete elimination of tariff and non-tariff barriers to trade and elimination of customs duties; through the free movement of capital, labour, goods and the right of establishment; by promoting standardised technical specifications, standardisation and quality control; through the elimination of controls on the movement of goods and individuals; by standardising taxation rates (including value added tax and excise duties), and conditions regarding industrial co-operation, particularly on company laws, intellectual property rights and investment laws; through the promotion of the adoption of a single currency and the establishment of a Monetary Union; and through the adoption of a Common External Tariff (CET).

By agreeing to the above, member States agreed on the need to create and maintain:

- a full free trade area guaranteeing the free movement of goods and services produced within COMESA and the removal of all tariffs and non-tariff barriers;
- a customs union under which goods and services imported from non-COMESA countries would attract an agreed single tariff for all COMESA States;
- free movement of capital and investment supported by the adoption of common investment practices so as to create a more favourable investment climate for the entire COMESA region:
- a gradual establishment of a payments union based on the COMESA Cleaning House and the eventual establishment of a common monetary union with a common currency;
- the adoption of a common visa arrangement, including the right of establishment leading eventually to free movement of bona fide persons.

Looking at all the objectives and principles of COMESA as outlined above, it is apparent that they encompass ultimate ideals of a free trade area; customs union; common market; economic union; and total economic integration. In a free trade area, countries eliminate all barriers to imports originating from within the region. A customs union involves free trade among partners, but also the establishment of a common external tariff (CET) with the rest of the world (known commonly as third countries). A common market is a customs union with free factor mobility. An economic union involves the adoption of both common external trade policies and the free movement of primary factors of production as well as goods within the union. [4] Finally, total economic integration involves the joint pursuit of all macroeconomic functions by all member states.

Stages of regional integration followed by COMESA are the following:

1. Preferential trade Area (PTA): This is where trade among member countries is conducted on a preferential basis. Each country maintains its own tariffs on goods imported from third country. This was the situation that obtained during the

PTA days from 1982 to 1994, before it was transformed into a Common Market;

2. Free Trade Area (FTA): This stage means member States eliminate tariff and non-tariff barriers on goods and services produced and traded among member States but each Member State maintains its own tariff and non-tariff barriers on imports form third country. In this regard, COMESA has attained the FTA in 31st October, 2000.
3. Customs Union: The next step for COMESA is implementation of a Customs Union by 2004. To that end, a Common External Tariff (CET) has been agreed with a four band tariff structure of 0-5-15-30 percentage points on capital goods, raw materials, intermediate goods and finished products respectively.
4. Common Market: This stage allows for free internal trade in goods and services as well as free movement of labour and capital among member countries, which maintain a common external tariff on goods imported form third country.
5. Economic Community: Establishment of a monetary union, including a single currency issued by a common monetary authority and by common monetary authority and common monetary and fiscal policies for the member countries, free movement of people including the right of establishment and right of residence by the year 2025.

3.4 Achievements of COMESA

Some of the achievements are:

- implementation of tariff reduction for intra-COMESA Trade - Nine countries have zero tariff and others have reduced by 80% and 90% ;
- removal of non-tariff barriers - most of the traditional non-tariff barriers have been removed;
- implementation of the Automated System of Customs Data (ASYCUDA) by most member States customs administration to facilitate trade, implemented in thirteen countries;

- the formulation and adoption of a single COMESA Customs Document, the COMESA–CD. This document replaced at leas 13 other documents and reduced administration;
- putting in place effective measures for transit traffic to facilitate the movement of goods. This includes several instrument including:
  - ✓ The COMESA Yellow Card, Regional Third Party Motor Vehicle Insurance Scheme
  - ✓ The Customs Bond Guarantee Scheme
- the establishment of and provision of capacity building support to, a wholly private sector organisation so as to enable private sector economic operators take full advantage of the benefits arising from regional integration and globalisation of the world economy
- the establishment of independent institutions such as the following:
  - ✓ Regional trade and development bank (the PTA Bank)
  - ✓ PTA Reinsurance Company (ZEP-RE)
  - ✓ Clearing House
  - ✓ Court of Justice
  - ✓ Africa Trade Insurance Agency
  - ✓ Leather and Leather Products Institute

3.5 COMESA Programmes

COMESA programmes of activities are:

1. Trade Liberalisation: Free Trade Area, Rules of Origin, Customs Union, Customs Documents, Common Statistical Rules, Common Tariff Nomenclature.
2. Trade Facilitations
3. Financial and Monetary systems
4. Investment
5. Institutional support
6. Immigrations and Free movement of persons

3.6 COMESA Free Trade Area (FTA)

It was established in October 2000 with nine of its Member states—Djibouti, Egypt, Kenya, Madagascar, Malawi, Mauritius,

Sudan, Zambia and Zimbabwe. Rwanda has joined it in January 2004, making the total membership to ten. Rest of the countries are expected to join it in a few years. It took over 14 years for members to achieve zero tariff.

The objective of the FTA is to create an integrated market for trade in goods and services and to increase the COMESA region's competitive advantage as a production base geared for the world market. The integrated enlarged market should attract investments much more effectively than the much smaller national domestic markets and thus stimulate growth and raise for COMESA member countries, the stakes in one another's purchasing power and economic progress. This, of course, does not mean that investments will necessarily flow into each member economy. Every country must compete for those investments by improving infrastructive, economic policy environment, peace, law, order, governance and labour productivity.

The economies of scale made possible by the larger regional market make for more efficient production and marketing. The FTA fosters competition within the region before regional industries and firms face the inevitable competition brought about by global liberalization. The FTA is serving as a catalyst for greater efficiency in production and long-term competitiveness. In addition, it is giving the COMESA consumers wider choice and better quality consumer products.

The backbone of the COMESA FTA is the planned implementation of the Automated System for Customs Data and Management (ASYCUD) and Euro Trade Systems. These systems will help to simplify and standardise customs operation in the member countries with the ultimate aim being increased trade flows. In addition, the COMESA Customs Document (CD) was introduced in 1997 to assist in the uniformity of customs administrative procedures.

All commodities are eligible for COMESA preferential treatment so long as they satisfy the COMESA Rules of Origin. Goods must be consigned directly from a Member state to another Member state, plus satisfy one of the following conditions:

- be wholly produced;
- import material content of not more than 60% of ex-factory cost;
- value added of at least 25% of ex-factory cost;
- undergone substantial transformation during production.

The elimination of tariffs in the 20-nation Common Market for Eastern and Southern Africa (COMESA) was scheduled to occur in December 2004 but it has been deferred to next year. This has been rescheduled taking into consideration the special needs of some of the members states who had requested more time to prepare.

In 2003, trade among COMESA Free Trade Area countries grew by 48 percent, compared to a growth of 22 percent among COMESA countries as a whole. Intra-regional trade was valued at $5.3 billion in 2003. The formation of the Free Trade Area means that there are no customs duties or tariff barriers to goods that are produced and traded among the participating member states, provided such goods meet the requirements of the COMESA rules of origin.

COMESA sees the creation of the Free Trade Area as the first step towards full regional integration and the adoption of a common currency by the year 2025. Regional integration, in today's world, is the only way to generate sufficient economic activity, improve efficiency, heighten competition, attract investments and thus create jobs. No single nation in Africa can prosper outside the framework of regionalism.

COMESA is also trying to eliminate barriers to the free movement of people within its vast geographical zone, which extends from Egypt in the north to Zimbabwe in the south, but does not include South Africa.

The COMESA will set up a "**common investment area**" to attract foreign investors and boost trade within the region. COMESA is carrying out country consultations on the common investment area with different member states. The common investment area proposal is an excellent suggestion as the world is becoming one market place. However, the proposal is a long-term project that is likely to be accomplished by 2025.

3.7 COMESA vis-à-vis Other Trade Agreements

For Eastern and Southern Africa to reap all the benefits of deeper integration and reduce the risks of trade diversion and agglomeration it will need to address sooner rather than later some of the problems stemming from the conflicting and overlapping regional trade agenda. First, some countries face conflicting obligations. COMESA plans to have a customs union in place by 2004; EAC plans to also have its own customs union and free trade area in place by 2004; SACU is already a customs union; and SADC plans to have a free trade area in place by 2008. As noted, a free trade area implies that imports from one member of the FTA to another member of the FTA are free of duty. On the other hand a customs union implies that all countries belonging to the customs union apply the same tariffs on all imports into the customs union, meaning that if a product imported from outside the customs union attracts a duty of 20 per cent then all the countries in the customs union must apply a duty of 20 per cent on the imported product after which the product can move within the countries of the customs union free of duty. As each member of a customs union needs to apply the same tariff, it follows that one country cannot be a member of two customs unions.

In this situation, members of a future customs union (i.e. COMESA) will not be able to offer preferences to non-members with whom they are partners in another free trade arrangement. If COMESA or EAC become a Customs Union in 2004 as planned, countries in those organizations that are also participating in the SADC FTA implementation program may well be in violation of GATT Article XXIV if they seek to maintain preferential tariffs for imports from the SADC countries. Following the same pattern, for Namibia and Swaziland, their joint membership of COMESA and SACU has become more acute now with the introduction of the COMESA FTA. These countries have been unable to implement preferential tariffs for other COMESA countries and cannot introduce free trade for imports from other COMESA countries in terms of the FTA. The Common External Tariff (CET) of the SACU agreement cannot be broken by some members granting preferences in terms of other FTA regimes, unless all the other members give their consent. Botswana and South Africa have not given their consent to such action by Namibia and Swaziland, because once the CET wall is broken it would be very difficult to prevent goods illegally crossing to other SACU members without payment of duty. This is probably also in violation of General Agreement on Trade and Tariffs (GATT) Article XXIV paragraph 8 (a) (ii). This situation is creating ambiguity over which RTA will prevail in practice.

Second, a further manifestation of a conflicting and confusing regional trade agenda has to do with the rules of origin and customs procedures embedded in the agreements. Different trade agreements have adopted different and also conflicting rules of origin. COMESA's rules of origin apply across the board and are based on minimum value added requiring that local materials constitute at least 35% of the value added in order for the product to be considered as local and therefore, benefit from the preferential tariffs. On the other hand, many SADC rules of origin are sector specific, and include specific requirements for different sectors and products. For example for textiles and garments, SADC rules of origin require a double transformation in order to qualify for tariff preferences –garments must be made from regionally produced textiles, fabric must be made from regional produced yarns, yarn must be made from uncarded, uncombed fibre or from chemical products. Other examples of restrictive rules of origin are Coffee, Tea and Spices where at least 60 per cent by weight of the raw materials must be wholly originated in the region. Such restrictive rules of origin are very difficult to satisfy for most regional garment producers. Some of SADC rules of origin are still pending final ratification by the countries and there are a few sectors whose negotiations are still ongoing. EAC is currently negotiating the rules of origin under its planned customs union based on a combination of COMESA and SADC ones. The rules of origin that are most commonly used at the moment by the operators across the region are those of COMESA, which have the advantages of their simplicity, low verification costs, and low protectionist level. However, once the EAC Customs Union is in place and SADC rules of origin are finalized, potential conflicting and confusing situations may arise over which trade agreement should govern trade operations within the region. On customs procedures, both SADC and COMESA have their own customs documentation, further complicating the situation.

Implementation is difficult for all countries belonging to more than one RTA because of the complexity of obligations and wide variations in rules of origin, tariff structure, non-tariff barriers (NTBs), speed of adjustment, custom procedures, etc., which creates an uncertain business environment that obstructs investment and marketing decisions and elicits corruption and bribery practice at the borders. Moreover, the management and administration of all these trade agreements are becoming a heavy burden on the limited institutional, diplomatic and negotiating capacity and resources in member countries. Solutions to this "spaghetti bowl" are not easy. The necessary rationalization of the regional trade agreements should ensure that they become stepping stones to greater openness and development, rather than vehicles for protection and unintended inefficiency. Rationalization of the current situation through consolidation, possibly in a single arrangement, is something that should be considered. Sometimes political forces against regional integration are very strong and a radical merger may not be possible. However, if merger is not yet politically feasible, countries need to focus on choices of design to minimize the economic costs of the present arrangements. This would include rapid progress on external liberalization and deepening and widening of the arrangements to lessen the risks of inefficient trade diversion and asymmetric benefits. Present inconsistencies need to be eliminated through harmonization of the features adopted by different arrangements, including rules of origin, external tariffs, customs procedures, product standards, and the speed of convergence.

Ultimately, in the long run if all members of the RTAs in the sub-region are to reap the benefits of their membership, they should move beyond trade arrangements, like free trade areas or customs unions, towards deeper integration schemes. In these more advanced ways of integration, static trade liberalization gains would not be the dominant consideration, but rather deeper integration would focus on the potential gains stemming from increased competitiveness through the reduction of administrative and transaction costs, and other barriers to trade of goods, services, and cross-border movements of labor and capital. [5]

3.8 Assessment of COMESA Experience

Trade and market integration can be a very useful strategy to increase investment in member countries through their potential to reduce distortions, enlarge markets, and enhance the credibility of economic and political reforms. Such benefits are most likely when countries or their endowments are small, limiting market size. For countries in Eastern and Southern Africa (ESA) increased amounts of foreign investment are essential in order to receive the transfer of technology and know-how and to create the backward linkages with local industries that will enable them raise their productivity and competitiveness, achieve product diversification, expand trade in global markets and ultimately achieve higher growth. There is evidence that FDI inflows can be induced by regional arrangements in cases where they can obtain access to significant markets and markets of industrialized countries. [6] Smaller countries lacking such links may find themselves increasingly marginalized from international capital flows. Other potential benefits or regional arrangements include stronger commitment to reforms, increased bargaining power, enhanced cooperation, and greater security. But theoretical and empirical analyses show that these benefits are neither automatic nor necessarily large. The bottom line is that regional integration arrangements must be viewed as a means to the end of improving welfare in participating countries—not as an end in themselves.

For all this to happen ESA countries must move from the old regional schemes based on the promotion of industrial development through import substitution behind high tariff barriers towards a new outward-looking regionalism centered on export promotion and integration into global markets.

Regional Trade Agreements in ESA are considered to be South-South Regional Trading Arrangements (RTAs). Recent literature shows that, although South-South RTAs can be particularly effective in encouraging liberalization of domestic markets and removing invisible barriers to trade, they are more likely, if not properly designed and effectively implemented, to lead to trade diversion and asymmetric distribution of benefits and costs, than south-north or north-north agreements. [7] This means that agreements between developing countries comprising a poorer one and another relatively richer, with a more developed manufacturing sector, tend to be more beneficial to the latter than to the former. Typically, following the fall of preferential tariff rates the least developed members increase their imports of manufactured products from the more developed partners, whose firms may not be internationally competitive. The most likely outcome is that prices do not fall and producers from the exporter country capture most of the foregone tariff revenue.

Asymmetric distribution can also be caused by agglomeration effects. Industry and new investments tend to concentrate in the more developed member in the regional block once the trade barriers are removed. If not corrected with a workable compensation mechanism they can generate tensions among members. Indeed, past experiences have shown that perceptions in many countries that gains and costs are very unevenly distributed easily result in the lack of implementation of regional commitments, or in the break up of the arrangements in the most extreme cases. There are signs that such phenomena of trade diversion and asymmetry could be developing in the region particularly in SACU and SADC where as we saw South Africa, the richest country in the region, dominates trade (over 50 percent of total intra-block imports are from South Africa). Misgivings that Kenya is reaping all the benefits from the integration process have also bogged down negotiations on regional trade liberalization within the EAC. This is not completely obvious, since South Africa's ascension as a leading regional exporter has coincided with the end of the apartheid and the associated trade blockade. Therefore, it could be the case that for some products South Africa is indeed the world most competitive exporter.

Given the fact that the establishment of structural funds à la Union Europèan involving massive transfers of funds from the richer to the poorer countries is not something that could be expected among developing countries, a key step to minimize these trade diversion or agglomeration effects is to lower protection against non-members. The lower the marginal difference between world and domestic prices, the less the incentives for trade diversion and subsequent transfers from the poorer to the richer country.

There are a number of problems that continue to plague regional co-operation in eastern and southern Africa. One of them is the multiplicity of groupings. [8] At least nine of the COMESA members [9] are also the members of SADC. Thus, almost half the members of COMESA belong to SADC and almost two-third of the SADC countries belong to COMESA. This has significant implications for any policy prescriptions that two regional groupings make. Similarly, Uganda and Kenya are members of COMESA as well as EAC.

The biggest challenge facing regionalism in East and Southern Africa is the conflict of COMESA and the SADC. The struggle between the COMESA and the SADC secretariat does not augur well for regionalism in the region. The rivalry between PTA/COMESA and the SADC stated due to the manner in which each of the two institutions was established explains the differences between them. The PTA/COMESA was designed by bureaucracy at the ECA as part of a grand plan for an African Economic Community. Its membership is therefore defined more by geography than shared common interest. On the other hand, SADC was established with a political motive, that is, to reduce economic dependence on apartheid South Africa by the Southern African states. It is for this reason that the heads of states of the southern African countries are more personally involved in the SADC than COMESA.

The other more compelling reason for the SADC member states to be reluctant to let the SADC merge with COMESA is that the SADC is project-orientated. The benefits of the projects to member states are direct and therefore more noticeable than the more policy orientated programmes of the PTA/COMESA. Besides, the projects are mostly donor-funded and therefore member states do not want to risk the funds being diverted. The countries of southern Africa have also not been convinced that there are any economic benefits to be had by integrating with many – and economically and politically diverse – nations. For example, some have wondered what common interest Eritrea or Djibouti has with Botswana or Angola. In the more recent past, the southern Africa countries have seen the possibility of a few anchoring on the more powerful and prosperous South Africa as a more viable option of regionalism than COMESA.

The new political realities in Africa also shape the aspirations of regionalism. The treaties of both COMESA and the SADC emphasize guarantee of democratic and human rights of the members' citizens and the rule of law. Countries have been objecting to some regional economic issues on the basis that they would not be politically acceptable in their countries. A case in point is the initial refusal by Zimbabwe to ratify the COMESA treaty before it was accepted by its parliament. The countries of the SADC have used this point effectively against the merger with COMESA. The evolving economic environment-especially the new world trade order associated with WTO-and the increase in regionalism, exemplified by NAFTA, the European Union, the Pacific Rim and AFTA, also explain the conflict between COMESA and the SADC. The SADC believes that a small grouping with credible commitments and well articulated policies and programmes is better placed to benefit from the new world trade order as it is able to negotiate effectively and obtain favorable access to markets for its members. Those who believe in a large community of COMESA argue that the larger the grouping, the more effective it would be to negotiate on behalf of its members.

Duplication in membership with other regional organisations remains problematic, even though the problem between SADC and the COMESA has to an extent been resolved through the creation of joint SADC-COMESA Task Force in May 2001.

Other challenges facing the region are: to spread of AIDS; to strengthen peace and stability; economic cooperation; infrastructural development; liberalise and harmonise the bloc's various transport system; and the establishment of European Union South Africa Free Trade Area (EU-SA-FTA). [10]

3.9 Future Scenario

To continue to tap the huge trade potential, it is important to put in place mechanisms to facilitate and regularize informal trade, design schemes for financing small and medium scale enterprises and for industry to produce high quality products by adopting ISO standards. COMESA therefore promises to be the first regional grouping in post-colonial Africa to achieve a Free Trade Area. It has already demonstrated that through joint action, the region can take its rightful place in the global economy. The other items on the agenda include:

- Expansion of the Free Trade Area: Despite several efforts, only the five states of Burundi, Rwanda, the Democratic Republic of Congo, Namibia and Swaziland have signed up to join before January 2004. While African leaders acknowledge that intra-regional trade among the nine FTA countries, amounting to $370 million, has improved due to the FTA, they note that some members are reluctant to join because they fear domination by neighbours. Another issue impeding expansion, and growth in general, are complicated rules of origin.

- Transformation of FTA into a Customs Union: Creation of a customs union would be a further step in COMESA's quest to achieve economic growth and prosperity through dismantling trade barriers and opening markets. Creation of a Customs Union would enable free movement of goods from one member country to another without being subject to bureaucratic delays.
- Promotion of trade and investment: Low level of intra-regional trade is an important impediment of the region leading to a shallow integration process. The fund, with assistance from the New Partnership for African Development (NEPAD), is also expected to help spur private sector investments in infrastructure.
- Strengthening and liberalization of transport network: At least three quarters of goods within COMESA travel by road and the related cost pose a considerable hindrance to trade between member states.
- Regional stability and security: The issue of regional stability and security is of prime concern. Some members are involved in war while others face internal turmoil. The situation will need to greatly improve, if progress is to be made towards the desired goal of bringing all 20 members into a customs union by 2004 and monetary union by 2025.
- Integrated strategy: Other regional bodies such as SADC should pursue a common approach when negotiating in WTO, with the European Union and the United States under the Africa Growth and Opportunity Act (AGOA).
- Food Security: A common agricultural policy should be developed. Cooperation in agriculture and food security should be high on the agenda. Mechanisms to promote large-scale irrigation projects, reduce dependence on rain-fed farming, and encourage regional specialization should be established.
- Bridging the information gap which remains a real challenge to investors, traders, co-operating partners and stakeholders.

- Stamping out corrupt tendencies and crime which are turning off potential investors.
- Adopting sound and consistent economic policies that do not encourage inflation. A stable financial sector is important in this regard. Central banks should therefore ensure effective commercial banking supervision.
- Doing everything possible to resolve the many regional conflicts that continue to plague the region. If the general populace is economically empowered, the level of poverty and conflict. For, one who has "something" does not want conflict as it endangers his wealth.
- Paying particular attention to, and providing sources for infrastructure development in order to reduce operational costs and to improve competitiveness. Roads, railways, telephones, water and electricity are essential to industrial development. COMESA is therefore vigorously promoting the telephone inter-connectivity and tariff harmonization through the COMTEL project that is moving steadily. With regard to energy, the development of the Inga Dam hydro-electric project in the Democratic Republic of Congo is the most cost effective means to supply electricity to the COMESA Member States.
- Articulating its position, pro-actively and safeguarding its interests in multilateral arrangements. This can be best achieved by working together with other regional groupings under the aegis of the African Union/NEPAD. The African renaissance can then best be demonstrated through unity and joint actions on global issues such as the debt crisis; the World Trade Organization and the ACP/EU trade regime; and
- Adhering to the provisions of the Treaty and resorting to the COMESA Court of Justice for dispute settlement instead of taking unilateral decisions.

3.10 Emerging Global Environment

The future of regionalism in East and Southern Africa is inextricably tied to competing interest among the regional groupings and the consequences of the new political realities emerging in the countries of the region. The evolving global environment, especially the move towards regional trading blocks, also has some bearing on the direction of the development of regional co-operation within the COMESA.

Globalization and economic liberalization have continued to pose challenges to all COMESA Member States. The region has been further traumatized by regional conflicts that threaten to erode the gains already made and undermine investor confidence. Events taking place elsewhere such as the Asian economic crises have their ripple effect felt in the sub-region such as depressed demand for exports, increased and often unfair competition. With increased integration in Europe under the European Union - the traditional market for exports from COMESA - and the end of preferences under the World Trade Organization, the market has become extremely competitive. The signals are clear. Only the most efficient economies will manage under the evolving global economic environment. COMESA Member States must therefore carefully develop and implement their strategies, their options and quickly take advantage of opportunities as soon as they present themselves.

Since the early 1990s, COMESA Member States have enjoyed renewed interest brought about by privatization of State-owned enterprise (SOE) and the improved policy framework that encourages private capital flows into the region. Most of the erstwhile SOE have found it very difficult to operate in the changed environment without State protection or subsidies, thus rendering them uncompetitive. There is also the factor of changed behaviour - consumers are now better informed and therefore demand products that are competitive in quality and price.

The massive redundancies that ensued following privatization of SOEs implied that effective demand was severely reduced as poverty increased. For example, the tourism sector suffered badly as a result of Western holiday makers switching to cheaper destinations in Asia to take advantage of currency devaluations.

Following the recent Free Trade Area between European Union and South Africa (EU-SA-FTA) in 1999, definite concern has arisen amongst the countries within the COMESA as to the impact of this free trade area on their exports into these two markets. It is feared that although many COMESA countries already have preferential access for certain of their exports into both markets, the margin of preference in their favour may be reduced following the new trade agreement.

The economic rationale behind the development of a regional African trade zone is based on the expectation that a free trade area will help ensure regional market access for local producers, thereby enabling the region to develop with a greater degree of economic predictability. It is also a step away from dependency on northern markets, which continue to present African exporters with numerous impediments despite the recent Cotonou Agreement [11] and its predecessor, the Lomé Convention (both preferential access accords with Europe).

Conflicts between member states of COMESA and internal conflicts in member states are the main obstacles for this continental integration. However, in a short span of time COMESA has contributed meaningfully in averting conflicts and removing obstacles. COMESA member states should cooperate with other regional economic communities and sub regional organizations to promote peace and security and good governance. Good governance has become an important issue in Africa and to this end the New Partnership for Africa's Development (NEPAD) [12] has introduced the Peer Review Mechanism [13] to uphold the good governance practices.

With a view to accelerating the process of integration in the continent to play its rightful role in the global economy while addressing multifaceted social, economic and political problems compounded by the general aspects of globalization, the establishment of the African Union (AU) in 2002 can be described as an event of great magnitude in the institutional evolution of the continent. In this changed environment of greater African cooperation and integration, the sub-regional groupings such as COMESA are expected to play the role of harmonizing inter-regional conflicts and trade disputes so as to further the ultimate goal of a larger and a deeper integration process. Narrow bickering and mutual rivalries should give way to enhanced cooperation and continental integration.

3.11 Prospects for Regional Integration under Liberalized Economic Regimes

The pessimistic view of regional integration in sub Saharan Africa is that there are no economic gains to be had from integration. Some even argue that 'regional integration would appear to be a "dead end" in terms of contributing in any substantive fashion to rapid and sustainable growth of sub Saharan African economies.' They further note that: the fact that African leaders, first in the Lagos Plan of Action of 1980 and then in the Abuja Treaty of 1991, have elected to pursue the quixotic goal of an African Common market in spite of their continued failure to begin removing even modest impediments to the flow of goods and services within the region, would suggest that their agenda is driven by political rather than economic considerations, and by domestic rather than regional pressures.

History would tend to vindicate these sentiments, although recent political and economic changes provide a cause for optimism. This is especially true for East African countries and those of southern Africa.

The COMESA and the SADC were formed when the member states faced serious macroeconomic problems. The stated aims of trade promotion therefore faced immediate serious constraints. Non-tariff barriers in the member states resulted mainly from poor economic performance. To design a programme to eliminate the barriers without addressing the cause of poor economic performance was setting a goal beset with difficulties in implementation. No wonder, therefore, that some member states resisted the elimination of non-tariff barriers. The SAPs have been designed to eliminate macroeconomic distortions in many of the countries in the region. Studies have shown that countries in the region have implemented far-reaching economic reforms in the last few years.

Unilateral economic liberalisation, by eliminating distortions in individual countries, facilitates the process of intra-regional trade liberalization. The polarization effects of trade reforms will be minimized as the countries move towards macroeconomic stability. The other problem facing the COMESA is the notion that sheer numbers is the source of strength. The region should have borrowed a lesson from the European Union, which – though formed in 1967 (European Economic Community) – currently has 25 members. These countries have taken time to evolve institutions, notably the council of ministers, the commission, the parliament and the court of justice. Regional co-operation should arise out of shared interest and common objectives. This condition is not fulfilled by the membership in the COMESA. Hence, other sub-groupings exist within the COMESA area.

Regional integration should also allow for 'variable geometry' and subsidiarity. 'Variable geometry' means that the pace of implementation of regional policies would not be dictated by the slowest member as in the past. Those countries that are able to work faster than others should be able to do so. The principal of subsidiarity implies that decisions should be decentralized as much as possible. In this connection in will be important for civil society to be more involved in the debate on decisions that are eventually to be carried out by the sub-regional organizations. At the minimum, policies should be debated and passed in national parliaments. This will make it difficult for heads of states or the sub-regional secretariats to contradict or reverse regional policies.

The above arguments point to the need to rethink regionalism in eastern and southern Africa. The lack of common interest among COMESA members and the conflict with the SADC are not conducive to stable regional co-operation. This is further complicated by the revival of the East African Community (EAC). [14] To promote stable economic grouping, countries in the region should belong to one economic group that fully represents their interests. These sub-groupings should be responsible for sectoral projects and harmonization of macroeconomic policies in their sub-regions. The COMESA however, should remain and specialize in areas that cut across all countries in the region and work towards the unification of the sub-groupings for a future COMESA.

Table 3.1: Regional Trade Agreements in Eastern and Southern Africa

Countries	COMESA	SADC	SACU	EAC
Angola	*	*		
Botswana		*	*	
Burundi	*			
Comoros	*			
D.R. Congo	*	*		
Djibouti	*			
Egypt	*			
Eritrea	*			
Ethiopia	*			
Kenya	*			*
Lesotho		*	*	
Madagascar	*			
Malawi	*	*		
Mauritius	*	*		
Mozambique		*		
Namibia	*	*	*	
Rwanda	*			
Seychelles	*	*		
South Africa		*	*	
Sudan	*			
Swaziland	*	*	*	
Tanzania		*		*
Uganda	*			*
Zambia	*	*		
Zimbabwe	*	*		

Table 3.2: Intra COMESA Trade (Exports and Imports)

S.No.	Member States	Membership of COMESA FTA	Value of Exports (US $ mn)	Value of Imports (US $ mn)
1.	Angola	No	1.62	96.57
2.	Brundi	Yes	8.20	50.52
3.	Comoros	No	0.06	3.64
4.	D.R. Congo	No	61.46	51.31
5.	Djibouti	Yes	10.76	72.53
6.	Egypt	Yes	68.50	236.35
7.	Eritrea	No	0.12	1.56
8.	Ethiopia	No	68.52	47.06
9.	Kenya	Yes	647.97	144.57
10.	Madagascar	Yes	9.79	29.93
11.	Malawi	Yes	79.14	57.83
12.	Mauritius	Yes	119.54	66.94
13.	Rwanda	Yes	--	--
14.	Seychelles	No	3.83	11.39
15.	Sudan	Yes	43.54	108.94
16.	Swaziland	No	51.40	0.47
17.	Uganda	No	112.37	281.43
18.	Zambia	Yes	87.59	139.49
19.	Zimbabwe	Yes	48.83	104.35

Notes

1. As of March 2005, COMESA has 19 member states, namely: Angola, Burundi, Comoros, DR Congo, Djibouti, Egypt, Eritria, Ethiopia, Kenya, Madagascar, Malawi, Mauritius, Rwanda, Seychelles, Sudan, Swaziland, Uganda, Zambia, and Zimbabwe.

2. The CASABLANCA and MONOROVIA groups

3. Article 3 of the COMESA Treaty.

4. Balassa (1961, p.2) and DeRosa (1995, p.9).

5. Robson 1998

6. (Robson 1998, World Bank 2000).

7. World Bank 1999

8. refer to Table-1.

9. Angola, DRC, Malawi, Mauritius, Namibia, Seychelles, Uganda, Zambia and Zimbabwe are members of COMESA as well as SADC.

10. EU-SA-FTA was signed in 1999 and came into operation in January 2000.

11. Contonou Agreement was signed between European Union and the African Caribbean and Pacific (ACP) Group replaces Lome Convention. It aims at gradual integration of ACP into the world economy by entering into Economic Partnership Agreements (EPAs) with the EU, either individually or collectively, taking into account the regional integration processes already in existence.

12. NEPAD is a common programme of economic recovery in Africa. It aims to consolidate democracy and sound economic management on the continent.

13. Peer Review Mechanism is a voluntary system designed to monitor each other's (African States) performance.

14. In 1999 EAC Treaty was revived. It is the revision of the economic cooperation agreement which broke in 1977. The Treaty provides for a progressive regional integration process-beginning with the formation of a FTA and a Customs Union. This will be followed by a common market a monetary union and ultimately a political federation.

References

Balassa, B., *The Theory of Economic Integration*, (Richard D. Irwin, Homewood, 1961).

Danso, K, "The African Economic Community: Problems and Prospects", *Africa Today*, vol. 42, no. 4, 1995.

De Melo, J and Panagariya, A. (eds), *New Dimensions in Regional Integration* (Cambridge University Press, Cambridge, 1993).

DeRosa, D. A., *Regional Trading Arrangements among Developing Countries: The Asean Example* (IFPRI, Washington, D. C. 1995).

Fasano-Filho U., "Economic Policy Making in Sub-Saharan Africa and IMF Involvement", *Quarterly Review of Economics and Finance*, vol. 36, Special Issue.

Green, R.H. and G .K. Krishna, *Economic Cooperation in Africa: Retrospect and Prospect* (Nairobi, Oxford University Press, 1967)

Hazlewood Arthur, *African Integration and Disintegration – Case studies in Economic and Political Union* (Oxford University Press, London, 1962)

Hess R., *SADC versus PTA: Alternatives for Economic Integration?*(SADC Press Trust, Harare, Zimbabwe, 1994).

Hill, C. W. L., *Global Business Today* (Irwin McGraw-Hill, Boston, 1998.

Hoskyns, C., "Pan Africanism and Integration", in Arthur Hazlewood (ed), *African Integration and Disintegration: Case studies in Economic and Political Union* (Oxford University Press, London, 1967.)

Leistner Erich, "Designing Framework for A Southern African Development Community", *Africa Insight*, Vol. 22, No.1, 1992.

Leistner Erich, "Regional Cooperation in Sub-Saharan Africa", *Africa Insight*, Vol. 27, No.2, 1997.

Mawencha, Erastus, I.O., "COMESA Agenda for 1999 and Beyond", *COMESA Bulletin*, Vol. 1, Issue 1, 1999.

Robson Peter, *Economics of International Integration* (London, New York, Routledge, 1998).

SADC – EU relations: Looking Back and Moving Ahead, (South African Institute of International Affairs, 2002.)

Takirambudde, Peter, "The rival strategies of SADC & PTA/COMESA in Southern Africa" in Daniel Bach (ed) *Regionalisation in Africa: Integration & Disintegration* (Indiana University Press, 1999).

World Bank, *Can Africa Claim the 21st Century* (Oxford Press, Washington D.C.,2001)

World Bank, *Regional Integration in Southern Africa: Overview, Challenges and Recent Developments,* Background Paper, Washington, 2001.

World Bank, *Trade Blocs,* World Bank Policy Research Report, Washington D.C., 2000.

4

European Union: A Model for Regional Integration

The world is an ever-changing arena. And the EU is one of the best examples of the dynamics of international relations. [1]

The EU is the result of a process of deep regional cooperation and integration that began in 1951 among Benalux Countries [2] and grew to include Germany, France and Italy. In 1952, Treaty of Paris was signed establishing the European Coal and Steel Community (ECSC). The logic behind this was that, if the two basic industries which had provide the where-withal to make war were placed under joint, rather than national, control, the inclination to resort to force to settle disputes would be thwarted. The power to take decisions about coal and steel industries, in those countries was placed in the hands of an independent, supranational body called the "High Authority".

The ECSC was such a success that, within a few years, their same countries decided to go further and integrate other sectors of their economies. In 1957, these same countries signed the Treaty of Rome which established the European Atomic Energy Community (EURATOM) and the European Economic Community (ECC). A preamble to this treaty defined the ultimate purpose of the great European enterprise as 'ever closer union among the peoples by Europe' – a formula which echoed Jean Monnet's [3] concept of future of the European continent. The member states set about removing trade barriers between them and forming a "common market".

In 1967, the institutions of the three European communities were merged. From this point on, there was a single Commission and a single Council of Ministers as well as the European Parliament. All the above three bodies collectively came to be known as European Community. Amendments were carried out to the earlier treaties by the Single European Act of Luxembourg in 1985.

The collapse of the Soviet Union and the reunification of Germany in 1989 presented European leaders with provable challenges. They realised that the opportunities offered by the end of the cold war reinforced the need for further integration in the Western half of the continent. As a result of these developments, Maastricht Treaty was signed in 1992. It introduced new forms of cooperation between the member state governments and led to the creation of European Union. The treaty was intended to be their response to the seismic developments in the continent. The most eye catching decision was the abandonment of the name 'Community' in favour of 'Union'.

During these 50 years of political, economic and social cooperation, the EU expanded to include 25 members. [4] EU has grown in size with successive waves of accessions. Initially EU consisted of just six [5] countries, Ireland and the United Kingdom joined in 1973 followed by Greece in 1981, Spain and Portugal in 1986 and Austria, Finland and Sweden in 1995. The EU in May 2004 has welcomed 10 [6] countries from eastern and southern Europe. Bulgaria, Romania and Turkey are expected to follow a few years later. To ensure that the EU can continue functioning efficiently with 25 or more members, its decision making system must be streamlined The Treaty of Nice (December 2000) was a response to this enlargement. It lays down new rules governing the size of the EU institutions and the way they work. It came into force on February 1, 2003.

In 1992, the EU decided to go for Economic and Monetary Union (EMU), involving the introduction of a single European currency managed by European Central Bank. The single currency – the euro – became a reality on January 1, 2002, when euro notes and coins replaced national currencies in twelve [7] of the 15 countries of the EU. Having a single currency makes it easier to travel and to compare prices, and it provides a stable environment for European business stimulating Growth and competitiveness.

After 50 years of integration, the Union has drafted a Constitution. The European Union needs simpler treaty – a constitution clearly setting out the EU's aims and values, and saying who is responsible for doing what. To draft this document, a convention was set up in 2002, bringing together representatives of all the member states and candidate countries as well as the EU institutions. The draft of the EU constitution was presented in July 2004, and the European Union Constitution signed on October 29, 2004. It is designed to give the Union a sharper international profile and speed up decision-making in a club now embracing 25 nations.

The treaty was the result of 28 months of sometimes acrimonious debate between the 25 E.U. Governments and now faces ratification in national Parliaments. At least nine E.U. nations also plan to put it to a referendum. This may lead to delay in its adoption as scheduled by the year 2007.

The Constitution foresees simpler voting rules to end decision gridlock in a club that expanded to 25 members in May, 2004 and plans to absorb half a dozen more in the years ahead. It includes new powers for Parliament and ends national vetoes in 45 new policy areas—including judicial and police cooperation, education and economic policy — but not in foreign and defence policy, social security, taxation or cultural matters.

Although it is not binding on individual member states to ratify the Constitution, but the outcome is politically symbolic because Europe's transition from an economic entity into a political union has encountered dogged opposition. While the new Constitution is far from perfect, it needs to be judged against the imperative of evolving political institutions compatible with the unprecedented expansion of economic and technological cooperation. The anti-Europe forces typically prey on the fears of an ill-informed public by raising the bogey of a centralised super-state that will erode the sovereignty of nation-states. The fact is that the European Constitution—to a large extent, a consolidation of prevailing domestic laws—is intended to coexist with national Constitutions. Paradoxically, the resistance has penetrated the very institutions of the EU that embody the spirit of integration, notably the European Parliament.

4.1 Structure of European Union

The European Union is built on an institutional set up which is the only one of its kind in the world. The Member States delegate sovereignty for certain matters to independent institutions which represent the interests of the Union as a whole, its member countries and its citizens. The Commission traditionally upholds the interests of the union as a whole, while each national government is represented within the Council, and the European Parliament is directly elected by citizens. Democracy and the rule of law are therefore the cornerstones of the structure.

This "institutional triangle" of Commission, Council and Parliament is flanked by two more institutions – the Court of Justice and the Court of Auditors – and five other European bodies. In addition, thirteen specialised agencies have been set up to handle certain essentially technical, scientific or management tasks. [8]

4.2 Enlargement of the European Union

Enlargement is one of the most important opportunities for the European Union at the beginning of the 21st century. This phenomenon has considerable social, political and economic ramifications, not only for Europe but also for the world at large. In a world constantly ravaged by war and fear, "Enlargement", is one phenomenon, which stands for peace and prosperity. It is an effort made by the citizens of Europe to share common goals and ideals for stability, economic progress and peaceful co-existence.

After successfully growing from 6 to 25 members, the European Union is now preparing for the next enlargement. As regards the 3 remaining candidate countries, Bulgaria and Romania hope to join by 2007, while Turkey is not currently negotiating its membership.

In order to join the Union, they need to fulfil the economic and political conditions known as the 'Copenhagen criteria', [9] according to which a prospective member must:

- be a stable democracy, respecting human rights, the rule of law, and the protection of minorities;
- have a functioning market economy;
- adopt the common rules, standards and policies that make up the body of EU law.

The EU assists these countries in taking on EU laws, and provides a range of financial assistance to improve their infrastructure and economy.

4.3 Benefits of Enlargement

The benefits of enlargement can be looked at from two perspectives: internal and external. By internal, one implies those benefits that would arise to existing and new members of the EU, while external benefits refer to those that would arise to third countries, like, say, India.

The political, economic, and cultural benefits of enlarging the European Union are as follows:

- The extension of the zone of peace, stability and prosperity in Europe will enhance the security of all its peoples.
- An almost 20% increase in population with the addition of 76 million people, in rapidly growing economies, to the EU's market of 379 million. This will boost economic growth, as GDP of EU 25 will increase by 5% compared to EU 15 GDP and create jobs in both old and new member states.
- There will be a better quality of life for citizens throughout Europe as the new members adopt EU policies for protection of the environment and the fight against crime, drugs and illegal immigration. (To give an example, there will be lower incidence rates on AIDS in the EU 25 than in EU 15.)
- The arrival of new members will enrich the EU through increased cultural diversity, interchange of ideas, and better understanding of other peoples.

- Enlargement will strengthen the Union's role in world affairs - in foreign and security policy, trade policy, and the other fields of global governance.

Already, some of the benefits are visible. For instance, in Central and Eastern Europe, stable democracies have emerged, with democratic institutions and increased respect for minorities. The economic reforms in these countries have led to high rates of economic growth (higher than the EU) and better employment prospects. As a result the Union enjoys growing trade with these countries and this generates employment and growth in the member states.

For third countries, the benefits of enlargement are, among others, the following:

- An even larger market than before: with a population of almost 455 million and a GDP of around €9712 billion, the enlarged EU will account for some 18% of world trade. The new member states are adopting the EU external tariff, which is in average lower than the one applied in most of them individually (3.6% EU vs. 9% in the 10 new countries)
- The current European Union is already the largest single market in the world. There are no internal borders between the Member States and the harmonization of regulations and standards ensures a free circulation of goods and services. Enlargement will extend these characteristics to the acceding countries.
- Third countries will benefit from an increased single market and a simplified and enhanced access to the current acceding countries' markets.

4.4 Trade Policy Impact of Enlargement

Enlargement will extend the EU's trade policy regime to the acceding countries. The current system, featuring a single trade regime for the EU and a different regime for each of the candidates, will disappear. A single set of trade rules, a single tariff, and a single set of administrative procedures will apply not just across the existing fifteen member states but across the enlarged Union of twenty-five.

This will greatly simplify the dealings that third country operators have within Europe. Also, it will strengthen the EU as unique interlocutor representing 25 countries in the WTO. For trade in goods, the new member states will have to adopt the Community Common Customs Tariff (CCT) upon accession. The average weighted industrial tariffs of the acceding countries are in general higher than the 3.6% average for the EU. As far as farm products are concerned, most acceding countries have a lower average rate, though the biggest agricultural economies such as Poland and Hungary have rates that are higher than the average tariff for EU imports of farm goods (10,5%). Thus, in most cases, third countries' business will benefit from lower tariffs in their trade with new member states.

In the case of services, third countries' services providers will benefit from the implementation of the single market in acceding countries, where they will get the same treatment as in the rest of the EU.

For investors, the very high standards of treatment currently afforded by investors in the EU will be applicable throughout the enlarged Union. The national treatment provisions for inward investors as set out in the Treaty of Rome will be extended to the new Member States. For instance, the right of establishment and free movement of capitals entrenched in the Treaty will be applicable to all companies of the new Member States.

As regards technical regulations and their impact on the openness of an economy, the "one standard for all" principle of the single market will be extended to the acceding countries with the obvious advantages to third country suppliers. The advantages in terms of trade facilitation will accrue for the exporters of the third countries with which the Community has concluded Mutual Recognition Agreements (or MRAs) as regards their exports to the new Member States.

There is also the issue of tariff quotas. These are some sectors where the European Union maintains some limited quantitative restrictions with third countries, notably in the cases of textiles and steel. Although the new member states will apply these restrictions as of their accession, the effect on third countries is likely to be limited. Indeed, WTO rules foresee that all textiles and clothing quotas shall be phased out by 31 December 2004. As far as steel is concerned, the two EC agreements foresee quotas run until 31 December 2004 and would disappear if the countries concerned joined the WTO before then. Moreover, a number of issues pertaining to steel are being discussed under the OECD Steel talks where India is also playing an important role on the future of strategy that countries would be adopting in the future.

Third countries will receive enhanced levels of intellectual property rights (IPR) protection in the acceding countries due to their adoption of EU directives in this field upon accession. The Europe Agreements already contain an obligation for the acceding countries to join the relevant international conventions in this area and bring levels of IPR to a similar level to that afforded in the EU.

In terms of the direct impact on market access for third countries, the application of EU public procurement rules, especially directive 93/38 which opened up procurement in the water, energy, transport and telecom sectors, will bring major benefits.

Likewise for subsidies: new member states' subsidies will be brought within EU rules, which are in line with OECD and WTO disciplines. Once again this will benefit third countries by imposing stricter standards than the rules currently applied by the candidate countries. With accession, the new member states will lose their transition economy status and with it the right to obtain exemptions from WTO subsidies disciplines through the use of Article 29 of the Subsidies Agreement.

EU enlargement will bring both opportunities and challenges: awareness and strengthened contacts between the enlarged EU and third countries will be key in contributing to making it a success for all. Nonetheless, the prime objective of ensuring peace and stability on the European continent is beyond doubt as this has been the primary factor behind the creation of the EU in the 50s and its continuous enlargement since then.

The dark pages of history have made it improve present and future prospects and this goes far beyond economic integration. Enlargement and the need to further consolidate integration called for an in-depth review of the EU institutional arrangements. The European convention, which concluded its work in July 2003, brought together representatives from member state governments, (including the future members), parliaments and the European institutions to respond to the following challenges:

- To adapt institutional system to an enlarged EU with 25 members;
- To find agreement on how best to develop existing policies and areas where new powers could be attributed to the Union;
- To clarify and streamline EU legislation so that European citizens know what the EU does and what the member states do.

4.5 Assessment

Europe is a continent with different traditions and languages, but also with shared values. The EU defends these values. It fosters co-operation among the peoples of Europe, promoting unity while preserving diversity and ensuring that decisions are taken as close as possible to the citizens.

The European Union has offered a number of lessons to be learnt for other schemes.

- First, political commitment is necessary: the deeper the integration, the greater the required commitment.
- Second, an explicit commitment to redistribution is useful, even if it is on a small scale.
- Third, there is a danger of becoming inward – looking, and doing so is harmful.
- Fourth, the free internal circulation of goods benefits from, and possible requires, supporting policies designed to prevent or settle disputes.

- Fifth, pragmatism is probably the only way of proceeding, at least in the early stages, national govt. have to be brought along at every step.

The European Union has delivered half a century of stability, peace and prosperity. In the early years, much of the cooperation between EU countries was about trade and the economy, but now the EU also deals with many others subjects of direct importance for our everyday life, such as citizens rights, ensuring freedom, security and justice; job creation, regional development; environmental protection; making globalization work for everyone. It has helped to raise living standards, built a simple Europe – wide market, launched the single European currency, the euro, and strengthened Europe's voice in the world.

EU integration has been rather special. It arose from a sense of mission far beyond the attainment of mere economic benefits. It explicitly sought to go beyond trade preferences to a common market and laid the ground for even deeper integration. The mission continues today and has resulted in a pragmatic attitude towards deepening integration in which every partner is brought along, and in which preserving the fact of integration has been as important as its content.

In an increasingly interdependent world of the 21st Century, it will be even more necessary for every European citizen to cooperate with people from other countries in a spirit of curiosity, tolerance and solidarity.

Notes

1. Speech by President of the European Commission, Mr. Romano Prodi: "EU–India Relations in a changing global matrix" FICCI Auditorium, New Delhi, 29 November 2003.

2. Benalux countries include: Belgium, Netherlands & Luxembourg.

3. Jean Monet was a French public servant, who inspired the process of integration in Europe and he became the first President of ECSC.

4. Austria, Belgium, Denmark, Finland, France, Germany, Greece, Ireland, Italy, Luxembourg, Netherlands, Portugal, Spain, Sweden, United Kingdom. Cypress, The Czech Republic, Estonia, Hungary, Latvia, Luthuania, Malta, Poland, Slovakia and Slovania.

5. Belgium, Netherlands, Luxembourg, Germany, France and Italy.

6. Cypress, The Czech Republic, Estonia, Hungary, Latvia, Luthuania, Malta, Poland, Slovakia and Slovania.

7. U.K., Denmark & Sweden have not yet adopted Euro.

8. For details see Treaty of the European Union.

9. Heads of State and Government from the fifteen member states of the European Union and ten candidates for EU membership met in Copenhagen on 13 December 2002, they reached agreement on a formula for the admission of ten new member states to the Union. Following that historic decision, Cyprus, the Czech Republic, Estonia, Hungary, Latvia, Lithuania, Malta, Poland, the Slovak Republic and Slovenia joined the EU on 1 May 2004, after ratifying the accession treaty.

References

European Union Information Brochure, "Africa and the European Union", May 2003.

European Union, Encyclopedia Article; The Columbia Encyclopedia, VI Edition, 2000.

Gonzalez Felipe, "European Union and Globalization", *Foreign Policy*, Summer 1999.

Ian Black, "The EU's Growing Pains", *Foreign Policy*, March—April, 2001.

L. Alan Winters, "The European Community: A Case of Successful Integration?" in De Melo and Arvind Panagria (eds), *New Dimensions of Regional Integration*, Cambridge University Press, 1994.

Maitland Donald, "The European Union: The Way Ahead", *International Relations*, May 2001.

McCormick, John, *The European Union: Politics and Policies*, Westview Press 1996.

Redmond, J, The Expanding European Union: Past, Present, Future, Lynne Rienner Publishers, 1998.

Treaty of the European Union.

Wallace, H. and William Wallace, Policy making in the European Union, Oxford University Press, 1996.

5

Economic Partnership Agreements

5.1 An Overview

The African, Caribbean and Pacific (ACP) group was founded in 1975 with the signing of the Georgetown Agreement. The ACP group is made up of 78 African, Caribbean and Pacific countries. Following 25 years of four successive Lomé Conventions (the fourth with two financial protocols), the 20-year Cotonou Agreement, [1] signed June 2000, is a framework for a deeper partnership with a view to addressing the major challenges of poverty, conflict and war, environmental threats and risks of economic and technological marginalisation.

The agreement marks a turning point in the objectives, the ways and means to achieve them and the nature of the partnership. It makes a clear association between the political dimension, trade and development and partnership, based on clearly defined performance criteria. In this framework, from the European Development Fund (EDF), [2] the European Union (EU) provides assistance to 77 ACP countries, and to Overseas Countries and Territories (OCTs). Development co-operation shall be pursued through integrated strategies that incorporate economic, social, cultural, environmental and institutional elements that must be locally owned. It shall thus provide a coherent enabling framework of support to the ACP's own development strategies, ensuring complementarity and interaction between the various elements.

The new trade regime envisaged by the Cotonou Agreement represents a radically different perspective for ACP partners. To promote sustainable development and the eradication of poverty, ACP and the EU have agreed to conclude WTO-compatible trade agreements that will progressively remove barriers to trade between them and enhance co-operation in all areas relevant to trade. This commitment will take the form of negotiations on

Economic Partnership Agreements (EPAs) starting in September 2002 and to be concluded by December 2007.

The ACP-EU Partnership is centred on the objective of reducing and eventually eradicating poverty, consistent with the objectives of sustainable development and the gradual integration of the ACP countries into the world economy. Dialogue plays a key role in the success of development co-operation activities and is at the heart of the ACP-EU relationship. It is conducted within and outside the institutional framework at national, regional or ACP level, in order to encourage the introduction of all sections of society, including the private sector and the civil society organisations, into the mainstream of political, economic and social life.

Respect for all human rights and fundamental freedoms, democratic principles, good governance and the rule of law are essential elements of the partnership and transparent and accountable governance is an integral part of sustainable development. A participatory approach, by including civil society and economic and social actors in the ACP-EU partnership, will help define strategies and priorities that were previously the exclusive jurisdiction of governments. The idea is not just to involve these actors (civil society, the private sector and local authorities) in implementing projects but to bring them into the political dialogue and procure their participation in defining and evaluating development strategies and programmes. Decentralised co-operation, based on this principle of participative management, is thus destined to become an essential aspect of the ACP-EU partnership.

5.2 New Spirit of Development Co-operation

The Cotonou Agreement defines a general strategic framework reflecting international commitments and simultaneously taking into account the political, economic, social, cultural and environmental components of development. Co-operation strategies will reflect international commitments including conclusions of UN conferences and the OECD

(Organisation for Economic Co-operation and Development) Development Assistance Committee's strategy. Priorities are established on a country-by-country basis and focus on poverty reduction. Development strategies promote local ownership of economic and social reforms.

In past Lomé Conventions, trade co-operation was based on generous preferential tariffs. The new ACP-EU Agreement aims to support the mutually reinforcing effects of economic and trade co-operation and development aid. The objective of integrating the ACP countries into the global economy involves enhancing production, supply and trading capacity as well as increasing ACP capacity to attract investment, to formulate strong trade and investment policies, and to handle all issues related to trade. Economic Partnership Agreements (EPAs), integrated with development assistance including Trade Related Technical Assistance, will progressively remove barriers to trade between the ACP and the EU and enhance co-operation in a wide range of trade-related areas.

The EU's development co-operation gives great importance to regional integration and co-operation. It is based on the principle that this approach fosters economic and social development, raises and locks-in improved governance as well as promotes stable and peaceful relations among nations. It also better enables countries to meet cross-border challenges, particularly in the area of the environment and the management of natural resources.

5.3 Rationale of Economic Partnership Agreements

The Economic Partnership Agreements are an integral part of the Cotonou Partnership Agreement signed in 2000 between the 15-member European Union and the 77 members of the Africa-Caribbean-Pacific community of states. The 20-year Cotonou Agreement replaces previous 5-year agreements (first called Yaounde and then Lome Conventions) in governing cooperation between the two blocs. These agreements were mainly based on a dual approach: non-reciprocal preferential and in most cases free access for ACP products to the EU market (with the specific protocols for sugar, bananas, beef and rum) and financial assistance to ACP countries comprising traditional grant aid and export earnings stabilization mechanisms (STABEX and SYSMIN).

The new trade arrangement (EPAs) under the Cotonou agreement results from the acknowledgement that the previous approach did not work: in 2000 only 3 per cent of EU imports originated in ACP countries against 6.7 per cent in 1976. Furthermore, 65 per cent of those imports were raw materials. In addition, the Lome regime of preferential access to some products was declared "non compliant" by the World Trade Organization. A complaint against the Banana regime brought to the WTO by the US and some Latin American countries resulted in its envisaged dismantling by 2006; the Lome trade regime was granted a waiver until 2007. Finally, the previous regime did nothing to overcome the sort of market fragmentation that has stifled foreign investment in ACP countries and regions.

Cotonou has, at its core, the central objectives of poverty reduction, sustainable development and progressive integration of ACP countries into the world economy. The agreement attempts to promote those through a comprehensive and integrated approach including a political dimension, a focus on participatory approaches, a strengthened focus on poverty reduction, reform of financial cooperation and a new framework of trade cooperation, of which EPAs are a central components.

As a trade instrument, EPAs are basically free trade agreements between the EU and ACP sub-regions where an internal free trade arrangement has already been or is being negotiated. Said like this there is not much difference between that and what is being done as part of the FTAA or any other Free Trade Agreement. However, there is indeed a substantial difference, for EPAs are fundamentally an instrument for development: they are to be negotiated in the comprehensive context of Cotonou, where there is assistance envisaged for regional integration, improved governance, social development, regulatory upgrading, environmental sustainability, and trade negotiation capacity building.

Moreover, EPAs are about flexibility, about negotiating as ACP regions get ready for it, at their own pace (EPA negotiations only have to be concluded by 2008), with transitory periods that may exceed 10 years, with those countries that so wish and with the possibility of asymmetry. It means that the EC will liberalize substantially all imports from ACP regions while the latter may still maintain tariff protection for sensitive products.

The main advantages for the Caribbean of negotiating an EPA lies in broadening access to EU markets for basically all ACP products (including agriculture). It will reinforce ongoing regional integration schemes like the CSME. It will promote foreign investment, as markets will no longer be fractured in the context of regional integration and as integration-related reforms are "locked in" in an international context. It will lower the price paid for capital and intermediate goods, fundamental for local industries. Ultimately, it will promote more competitive, better-governed and more credibly regulated economies, again fostering investment and growth.

Criticisms raised thus far relating to disadvantages caused by the EPAs tend to be two-fold: EU products and firms will sweep the field once they gain unhindered access to ACP markets and ACP fiscal imbalances will worsen as import duties are slashed.

There the answer is perhaps tough but inescapable: trade liberalization giving easier access to "a priory" more competitive firms and products will take place anyway. The CSME and to a larger extent the FTAA and the WTO-round are quickly imposing a rather tight expiry date on sheltered economies (on top of what history has taught regarding inward-looking export-substitution models), uncompetitive industries and excessive reliance on import duties for revenue. This is a message that Caribbean leaders have been hammering in the context of the CSME: small, uncompetitive economies that do not reform will struggle to survive. Integration is inevitable and it better happen soon, particularly for very vulnerable, small countries like most of those in the Caribbean. In that context, tax reform (from import duties to income and value-added tax) is not an option, but a necessity that a number of countries in the region have already undertaken or are seriously considering.

All that will probably happen with or without an EPA. The big difference is that, through an EPA, and in the framework of the Cotonou Partnership Agreement, those inevitable processes will not happen in a "Darwinist" environment, but will be assisted, nurtured and modulated to the needs and the pace of the Caribbean.

EPA negotiations began in September 2002. It was decided to divide the negotiations in two phases: a first one with all ACP countries where issues of interest to all would be addressed and a second one with individual ACP regions. Negotiations with West and Central Africa got started in October 2003, with South and Eastern Africa following suit in February 2004. Negotiations with the CARIFORUM began on 15 April, 2004.

5.4 Instruments of Support

The Cotonou Agreement has rationalised the wide range of instruments that existed under previous Lomé Conventions. Available grant resources to support long-term development are channelled through National and Regional Indicative Programmes and the Investment Facility, a revolving fund aimed at stimulating investment and strengthening the capacity of local financial institutions, which is managed by the European Investment Bank. Development finance co-operation is implemented on the basis of objectives, strategies and priorities established by the ACP partners at national and regional levels. This co-operation will promote local ownership and a partnership based on mutual rights and obligations. It recognises the importance of predictability and security in funding and is flexible to address individual situations. Support is provided through sectoral programmes, budgetary support, investments, rehabilitation, training, technical assistance and institutional support.

Each ACP country and region receives an indication from the European Community of the volume of resources available over a five-year period to finance activities included in the National or Regional Indicative Programmes (NIPs and RIPs). The access of non-state actors to these funds has improved with Cotonou. The resources available to non-state actors form part of the allocation granted to each ACP State or region. Once a Country (or Regional) Support Strategy has been agreed to in consultation with the stakeholders, the EU Member States and bilateral and multilateral donors, it is developed and implemented through a work programme. This programme serves as a blueprint for all ongoing and intended EC activities in the country or region, broken down by sector and by instrument and following a defined timeline.

To help alleviate the debt burden of ACP countries and their balance-of-payment difficulties, resources are provided to contribute to debt relief initiatives agreed to at international level. Support is provided for macroeconomic and sectoral reforms. Within this framework, the parties ensure that adjustment is economically viable as well as socially and politically feasible.

The agreement on additional support in case of fluctuations in export earnings recognises a partner's vulnerability resulting from high dependence on export earnings from the sectors of agriculture and/or mining. Eligibility is linked to whether the loss jeopardises overall macroeconomic stability and in principle will be used to finance the national budget.

A redefined policy framework on decentralised co-operation places the actors at the heart of development co-operation and supports programmes initiated by non-state actors. This approach funds programmes that support decentralisation to foster the emergence of efficient systems of local governance, local development initiatives and political and social dialogue.

Recognising the important role of markets and of the private sector as engines of economic growth, the Cotonou Agreement provides for an integrated approach that involves the private sector in most areas of ACP-EU co-operation. Emphasis is placed on building the capacities of representative private sector organisations to engage in this dialogue. Domestic and foreign investment is promoted through a support package in linked forms of investment: promotion at national and regional levels, finance and support, guarantees and protection.

Technical co-operation assists ACP partners in developing national and regional manpower resources and the sustained development of institutions critical for development success.

5.5 ACP-EU Joint Institutions

5.5.1 ACP-EU Council of Ministers: The ACP-EU Council of Ministers is composed of a representative from every ACP and EU country and a representative from the European Commission, who meet once per year.

Its mission is to:

- engage in political discussions;
- adopt policy directives;
- take decisions regarding the implementation of Agreements on cooperation between the ACP and EU.

5.5.2 ACP-EU Joint Parliamentary Assembly: The ACP-EU Joint Parliamentary Assembly was created out of a common desire to bring together the elected representatives of the European Community - the Members of the European Parliament - and the elected representatives of the African, Caribbean and Pacific states ("ACP countries") that have signed the Cotonou Agreement. It is the only international assembly in which the representatives of various countries sit together regularly with the aim of promoting the interdependence of North and South. Since the entry into force of the Treaty on European Union and EU enlargement it has acquired a more prominent role. A substantial part of the work of the Joint Parliamentary Assembly is directed towards promoting human rights and democracy and the common values of humanity, and this has produced joint commitments undertaken within the framework of the UN conferences.

5.5.3 Composition and Working Methods: The representatives of the 78 ACP states, who, under the Cotton

Agreement, must be members of Parliament, meet their 78 European Parliament counterparts in plenary session for one week twice a year. The Joint Parliamentary Assembly meets alternately in an ACP country and an EU country. The institution is governed by common, democratic rules.

Two co-presidents who are elected by the Assembly direct its work. Twenty-four vice-presidents (12 European and 12 ACP) who are also elected by the Assembly constitute the Bureau of the Joint Parliamentary Assembly, together with the two co-presidents. The Bureau meets several times a year in order to ensure the continuity of the work of the Joint Parliamentary Assembly and to prepare new initiatives aimed notably at reinforcing and improving cooperation. It also considers topical political questions and adopts positions on all human rights cases.

5.5.4 ACP-EU Committee of Ambassadors: The Committee is composed of representatives from all EU Member-States, Heads of Mission from every ACP Embassy to the EU, and a member of the European Union.

It meets once per month to:

- monitor the implementation of cooperation agreements ; and
- participate in meetings of the ACP-EU Council of Ministers.

5.6 Centre for the Development of Enterprise (CDE)

The mission assigned to the CDE under the Cotonou Agreement is to contribute to poverty reduction by fostering wealth creation by lending support to the various types of operator that make up the private sector in the ACP countries; in this role it draws extensively on the capabilities of enterprises in EU countries.

It lends support, in a variety of forms, to:

- the creation and development of ACP enterprises
- intermediary institutions such as trade and/or sector organizations, combining its
- operations with those of PRO-INVEST and other EU and bilateral programmes
- firms of consultants

It grants SMEs subsidies to meet part of the costs of support and advisory services (diagnostic analyses of businesses, feasibility studies etc.) before, during and after an investment. It does not finance the investment itself but may help enterprises to find suitable sources of funding and set up financial engineering.

5.7 Technical Centre for Agricultural and Rural Cooperation (CTA)

The Technical Centre for Agricultural and Rural Cooperation (CTA) was established in 1983 under the Lomé Convention between the ACP (African, Caribbean and Pacific) Group of States and the European Union Member States. Since 2000, it has operated within the framework of the ACP-EC Cotonou Agreement.

CTA's tasks are to develop and provide services that improve access to information for agricultural and rural development, and to strengthen the capacity of ACP countries to produce, acquire, exchange and utilise information in this area. CTA's programmes are designed to: provide a wide range of information products and services and enhance awareness of relevant information sources; promote the integrated use of appropriate communication channels and intensify contacts and information exchange (particularly intra-ACP); and develop ACP capacity to generate and manage agricultural information and to formulate ICM strategies, including those relevant to science and technology. CTA's work incorporates new developments in methodologies and cross-cutting issues such as gender and social capital.

Notes

1. For details see Appendix 3 of this book.
2. For details see Appendix 5 of this book.

6

European Union-Africa: Towards True Partnership

At present Africa is home to about 70 per cent of the world's least developed countries, to many of the world's conflicts while it also faces relatively new disasters such as the HIV/AIDS pandemic and growing environmental degradation. Yet while such crises are particularly manifest in Africa their root causes lie in the wider world. Undoubtedly African solutions to Africa's problems should be supported and nurtured. At the same time we need to build and reinforce the African relationship with the European Union (EU) which has so far been neglected.

In a globalising world where capital flows far outstrip the flow of goods and services, and where comparative advantage in economic terms is increasingly knowledge based, sub-Saharan Africa's prospects for economic development will remain bleak as long as the provision of and access to health, education and other services is denied to the bulk of its people. Unless such a scenario is overturned talk of freer trade or market access will remain academic to many. Therefore it is vitally important to work within the Union for a transformation of Europe's relationship with Africa, from one that is marginal to one which recognises the achievement of the EU's twin development co-operation goals of sustainable development and poverty eradication in Africa as a central aspect of its external relations.

This chapter describes the context in which the EU-Africa relations can be further strengthened and explored. The importance of the EU - both actual and potential - as a global player is clear. The EU is the world's largest trading bloc, its single largest economic bloc (since the introduction of the EURO) and, together with the bilateral programmes of its Member States, it is the largest provider of development assistance. In its function as a development actor the EU's key role is evident particularly in light of the development goals enshrined in the Amsterdam Treaty [1] and the International Development Targets to which the EU and its Member States have committed themselves.

In this regard, this chapter goes on to examine some of the major barriers in Africa to the attainment of these development goals, particularly those relating to poverty eradication. The issues it examines, trade, debt and adjustment policies, good governance, HIV/AIDS conflict resolution/prevention, peace building and development assistance, are assessed in relation to the EU's own commitments to sustainable development and poverty reduction. They are examined from the viewpoint of current European development policy which is now the subject of a review and consultation process, and from the perspective of the momentous global changes of the 1990s which have impacted on development policy and practice.

In this context this chapter concèntrates necessarily on the relations between the rich and powerful countries of the European Union and the contribution that they can make to sustainable development and poverty eradication in Africa. It is however, acknowledged that development is a mutual undertaking and there are many things those governments and civil society in poor countries can do for themselves without reference to the international systems of which they are a part. They must take the initiative in issues of governance and equity, such as land reform, taxation and the delivery of pro-poor services.

At present there are two distinct EU approaches to the African continent. On the one hand, sub-Saharan Africa is dealt with under the Lomé Convention [2] (and its successor - the new Partnership Agreement), which is essentially a development instrument. By contrast, the countries of North Africa form part of the Euro-Mediterranean Partnership governed by the Barcelona process, which has been described by the Commission as a *"high profile geo-political project"*. [3] The links between these should become clear as the EU is currently in the process of formulating an overarching development policy covering all regions of Africa and indeed the developing world.

The EU has a range of inter-linking relationships with countries across the African continent (Libya excepted), but there are three main arrangements which underpin EU – African relations. The first, and most well known, is the Cotonou Agreement linking 48 countries of Sub-Saharan Africa with the EU. Secondly, South Africa and the EU recently established a wide-ranging Trade, Development and Cooperation Agreement. Thirdly, four North African countries (Algeria, Egypt, Morocco and Tunisia) belong to the Euro-Mediterranean Partnership. In order to understand the rationale behind each relationship, a consideration of the three agreements will now be given.

The Cotonou Agreement signed in June 2000, and enacted in April 2003, is the most recent of a long line of arrangements between the EU and Sub-Saharan Africa. The relationship was first established in 1957 when the African colonies of France and Belgium were associated with the newly established European Economic Community (EEC). When African states gained their independence, the link with the EEC was sustained through the Yaoundé Conventions of 1963 and 1969, and then from 1975 through the first of four Lomé Conventions (which also included former European colonies in the Caribbean and Pacific). The Lomé Conventions contained a number of specific non-reciprocal trade provisions (preferences and protocols) and aid commitments to encourage African, Caribbean and Pacific (ACP) development. However, through the 1990s the provisions of the agreement came under attack as a result of the pressures of neo-liberalism and globalisation, and because of a perception that the development aspects of Lomé were not working. The ACP's trading performance actually declined over the period of the four Lomé Conventions, with the ACP's share of total EU imports falling from 6.7 percent (1976) to 2.8 percent (1999). Further, the ACP's high dependence on a few commodities did not improve, with nine products representing 57 percent of total ACP exports in 1999.

In order to address the perceived failings of Lomé, the succeeding Cotonou Agreement was radically different and the basis of the EU-ACP relationship is now to encourage 'the smooth and gradual integration of the ACP countries into the world economy...thereby promoting their sustainable development and contributing to poverty eradication'. To facilitate this, the signatories to the agreement have committed themselves to conclude WTO compatible free-trade Economic Partnership Agreements (EPAs) by December 2007 at the latest. In addition, the non-trade aspects of the Agreement were revised in an attempt to improve aid disbursement and political cooperation.

The EU's relationship with South Africa is slightly more complex than with the other countries of Sub-Saharan Africa. When South Africa emerged from apartheid in 1994, the country was completely isolated with regard to international trade policy. As a consequence, the new South African government had to negotiate trading regimes with the world's major economic blocs including the EU. However, EU policy-makers were reluctant to allow South Africa to benefit from the non-reciprocal Lomé trade preferences due to the country's internationally competitive manufacturing sector. As a consequence, South Africa became a signatory to the Lomé Convention in 1998 and subsequently the Cotonou Agreement, but was excluded from the trade chapters. Instead, a specific Trade, Development and Cooperation Agreement were agreed between South Africa and the EU. The Agreement includes an asymmetrical Free Trade Area (FTA) to be phased in over twelve years. It will result in the EU liberalising 96 percent of its imports from South Africa, and South Africa liberalising 86 percent of its imports from the EU. The agreement is the first fully reciprocal FTA to be signed between the EU and an ACP country, and is seen as a model for the EU-ACP EPAs being negotiated at the present time.

The relationship between the EU and the countries of North Africa is a long-standing one based, as it is, on deep historical, cultural, political and economic links. The first formal ties between the two regions were instituted in the Treaty of Rome, which allowed France to maintain its special relationship with her former colonies of Morocco and Tunisia (Algeria was still a French department in 1957). During the 1960s, Association Agreements were signed with a number of North African countries, and then, in the early 1970s, the EEC established a Global Mediterranean Policy that deepened political and economic cooperation with the region. The present relationship between the two regions was established after the accession of Spain and Portugal to the European Community in 1986 and the changed geo-political climate in Europe at the beginning of the 1990s. The result was the Euro-Mediterranean Partnership Programme (MEDA) [4] or Barcelona Process agreed towards the end of 1995. The Partnership agreement includes every North African state with the exception of Libya, and a number of other non-EU countries and territories that border the Mediterranean Sea, including Israel and the Palestinian Authority. The Barcelona Process calls for a multilateral and bilateral relationship, with an emphasis on peace and security, creating an area of shared prosperity (through the achievement of a FTA by 2010), and social, cultural and human exchange.

As can be seen the nature of the relationship between the EU and the countries of Africa is complex, multi-dimensional, and long-standing. The great advantage of such political, economic and social cooperation is that there is a permanent and clearly demarcated institutional framework to facilitate improved relations and understanding. As a consequence, a number of important initiatives have been established, including:

- Increasing EU engagement in conflict demobilisation and reconstruction programmes, in cooperation with pan-African bodies such as the Lusaka Peace Process, the Inter-Congolese Dialogue, and the Ethiopia/Eritrea Mission.
- EU support for the newly established African Union, and the related initiative entitled 'New Partnership for Africa's Development which is a sustainable development programme based on the principles of African ownership and leadership.
- A range of EU programmes and budget lines to assist African countries to deal with the HIV/AIDS crisis. Most recently €10

million was disbursed to South Africa for a HIV/AIDS awareness and education programme.

- The Euro-Mediterranean Parliamentary Forum, launched in 1998, which brings together parliamentarians from all 27 partners, and provides a space for civil society to debate the goals and priorities of the Barcelona Process.
- The TEMPUS [5] programme on cooperation in higher education that was extended to the MEDA partners in 2002.
- Despite the many positive aspects of EU-African relations, the overall perception of the relationship is seriously damaged by a number of issues related to EU trade policy and aid disbursement. The unequal balance of power within these aspects of the relationship has drawn accusations that the Union is being extremely parsimonious in its attitude towards African development. Indeed, rather than improving the economic potential of African states, the policies and intransigence of the EU are severely damaging the continent's productive output. Two of the most important issues are highlighted here: the damage caused by the EU's Common Agricultural Policy (CAP) [6] to African agriculture, and the unbalanced use of the EU's financial aid budget, less than half of which is actually disbursed to the world's poorest nations.

The principles and instruments of the CAP were contained within the Treaty of Rome [7] in 1957, reaffirmed the following year at the Stresa Conference, and enacted in 1962. Originally developed to ensure security of food supplies in Western Europe, the CAP is now highly expensive to maintain, encourages overproduction by farmers, and seriously distorts the international trade in agricultural produce. Although the EU continues to emphasise the important role of liberalised trade in reducing poverty in the developing world, the majority of its annual €41.5 billion agricultural budget is spent on trade-distorting subsidies. For example, Europe's white sugar production costs are among the world's highest at €760 per tonne, compared to around €320 per tonne in Malawi and Zambia. Nevertheless, EU producers have a 40 percent share of the white sugar export market. A combination of export subsidies and high EU prices under the CAP, together with prohibitive import tariff rates mean that farmers in developing countries, including Africa, suffer from low prices, lost market share and unfair competition. The subsidies are particularly damaging, resulting as they do in export dumping, whereby agricultural products are exported at prices below the cost of production and undercut more efficient producers in the developing world. It is estimated, for example, that Mozambique loses €120 million a year as a result of the EU's sugar policy. One mitigating factor in all this is that a small number of ACP countries do benefit from high EU sugar prices through the Sugar Protocol. However, the vast majority of the benefits go to only five ACP countries, none of which are categorised as Less Developed. The net effect of the CAP's sugar regime, therefore, is to seriously damage the interests of the majority of poor developing countries. Indeed, it is suggested that substantial reform of the CAP could provide an additional income of between €28-€45 billion a year for developing countries.

Reform of the CAP has been on the EU's agenda for a number of years, but little progress was made due to the significant resistance on the part of EU Member States and European farming interests. However, as part of the Doha Declaration, that defined the parameters for the present World Trade Organisation (WTO) negotiations, there was a commitment to initiate discussions aimed at 'reductions of, with a view to phasing out, all forms of export subsidies' and substantial reductions in other 'trade distorting' agricultural subsidies. The EU was party to the declaration, and, as a consequence, has come under significant pressure to reform the CAP. At the end of June 2003, EU Member States agreed to limited reform of the CAP, which weakened the link between subsidies and production. However, the reforms will not start until 2005 or 2007 depending on the position of each Member State.

In addition, the reforms failed to consider sugar and made little progress with the dairy sector. The tepid reform undertaken of the CAP has serious implications for the future of the Doha

WTO round of negotiations, and for the EPAs that are currently being negotiated between the EU and ACP. Any agreement on the latter without fundamental CAP reform could well place the ACP countries in a worse trading position than they are at present. ACP markets would be liberalised, while the EU would retain restrictions on its agriculture – a sector that holds the greatest export potential for the developing world. An indication of the hard fight to come can be seen within the context of the EU's 'Everything but Arms' (EBA) initiative introduced in 2001. The EBA was originally intended to provide immediate free-market access for all non-military exports from the Least Developed Countries. However, market liberalisation of the crucial sugar and rice sectors has been delayed until 2009 – a clear indication of the EU's reluctance to open up its own agricultural market.

The EU's aid policy towards the developing world, and Sub-Saharan Africa in particular, has also come under scrutiny. Although the development aid budget managed by the European Commission amounted to €7.7 billion in 2001, only 43 percent was distributed to the poorest countries or regions of the world. In 1987, the proportion was just under 70 percent. During the last decade or so there has been a dramatic reorientation of aid flows from ACP countries to Central and Eastern Europe, the Balkans and to a lesser extent the Mediterranean. Therefore, although the EU claims that poverty reduction is a key objective of its development cooperation policy, a majority of its development budget is attributed to better-off developing countries and to those states that have important geo-political links with the EU. Pressure for change, however, is coming from a number of EU Member States who maintain their own aid budgets, while also contributing to EU funds. In particular the UK government has committed itself to allocate 90 percent of its bilateral resource to the poorest countries by 2006, and is putting pressure on the EU to do the same.

However, it can be argued that a complex set of relationships has been established between the EU and Africa. In many respects the links between the EU and the various regions of Africa have been, and continue to be beneficial. For example, the ever-deepening political cooperation, the collaborative demobilisation and reconstruction programmes undertaken in Sub-Saharan Africa, and the various health and education schemes, are positive indicators of a mutually supportive relationship between the two regions. However, such benefits are significantly outweighed by the trade and aid policies that the EU follows at the present time. The Union's aid budget must be refocused so that the resources can effectively target poverty reduction. Further, and even more importantly, the EU's discriminatory trade policies, particularly the CAP, must be overturned. The situation whereby every cow raised in the EU receives $3 a day subsidy, compared to the 40 percent of Africans who live on less that $1 a day must be reversed. Reform of the CAP is vital as EU support for its agricultural sector is equivalent to double the aid budgets of the European Commission and EU Member States combined. The possibilities for deeper and more productive partnership between the EU and Africa are apparent, but the parsimonious attitude of the EU with regard to trade and aid must be overcome. [8]

6.1 Global Context of EU-Africa Relations

At the global level following facts about the EU-Africa relations can be highlighted: [9]

- A chronic and crippling debt burden which current multilateral and bilateral debt initiatives are only partly addressing. Despite widespread human deprivation in terms of access to health and education, debt servicing continues to exceed spending on health and education in 23 sub-Saharan African countries.
- European integration and enlargement continues to push development concerns into the background. Over the period 1992-1997 aid from OECD countries fell by 21 per cent in real terms, representing a decline to 0.22 per cent of their combined Gross Domestic Product and only rising marginally to 0.23 per cent in 1998. The overall share of official development assistance to GNP levels for the EU was still

less than half the 0.7 per cent UN target or 0.34 per cent.

- The adoption of a set of International Development Targets for the year 2015 - including halving the proportion of people living in extreme poverty. However, in the case of sub-Saharan Africa, taking current and projected growth rates, there is virtually no hope that these targets will be reached without a sharp reversal in development assistance trends combined with a coherent set of policies which promote sustainable development and poverty eradication.
- The alarming increase in the number of complex emergencies and human rights violations in Africa caused to a large extent by a new type of post cold war civil conflict and in which EU member states and European companies played a role. In response, the EU has been grappling with strategies to enable Africa to prevent, manage and resolve conflict.
- The huge flow of people from Africa to Europe over the past two decades.
- The efforts made by many African countries during the last decade to create a multi-party political system, accountable to its citizens, and a democratic environment. This has happened with varying degrees of success across the continent.
- The realisation by the EU that civil society has an important part to play in economic, social and political development in Africa. This is reflected in its policy of Decentralised Co-operation. Strengthening of African civil society is seen as a precondition for development and for holding African governments responsible for pro-poor development policies.

6.2 European Union Development Policy

Whilst development co-operation has a long history in the European Union, it was first given a legal base in the 1992 Maastricht Treaty. Title XVII of the Maastricht Treaty (now Title XX of the Treaty of Amsterdam) spells out the objectives of Development Co-operation which are to:

- foster sustainable economic and social development in developing countries, particularly the most disadvantaged;

- ensure the smooth and gradual integration of developing countries into the world economy; and to
- campaign against poverty in developing countries.

Development co-operation should, under the Treaty, also contribute to the general objective of developing and consolidating democracy and the rule of law, and that of respecting human rights and fundamental freedoms. Moreover, the objectives of development co-operation should be taken into account in all policies which are likely to affect developing countries.

In the 1990s considerable efforts were made to put flesh on the bones of the Maastricht Treaty. However, these have fallen short of what was needed prompting an OECD peer review of EU aid to state that: *There is no coherent Commission-wide development strategy or statement on development co-operation and the policies on country macro-economic and sector approaches, project and programme identification, implementation, procurement and evaluation lack Commission-wide consistency and coherence.* Furthermore, the May 1999 EU Development Council tacitly acknowledged this, stating: *The Council stresses the need for an integrated and strategic up-to-date statement on development policy based on the broad goals set out in the Treaty of the European Community.* It has therefore called on the Commission to prepare an overall statement on EU development policy for consultation and for adoption at the May 2000 meeting of the EU Development Council. Unfortunately the timeframe provided for consultation on this paper has been extremely short.

In agreeing an effective development policy with poverty eradication as a central objective there is clearly a need for a common EU understanding and interpretation of poverty. Yet despite the urgent need for consensus on this issue there remains no clear EU definition of what constitutes poverty. The crude benchmark for absolute poverty of a dollar a day is a useful but rather limited tool. Poverty measurement must take into account social indicators such as education, health, and access to services and infrastructure. Moreover, less tangible aspects also need to be covered such as livelihood insecurity, social exclusion, absence of choice and powerlessness. Unless the EU defines the problem in all its complexity, 'solutions' can at best be of only limited value.

At the same time the campaign against poverty is only one of the EU's development objectives and among Member States the priority given to the issue of poverty varies widely. The EU as a whole needs to give greater priority to its campaign against poverty. Whilst the language used by the EU emphasises the centrality of poverty reduction and eventual eradication (for example, in the new ACP-EU Partnership Agreement), the reality of its dialogue with its developing country partners suggests otherwise. Indeed conceptual problems arise, such as poverty alleviation versus poverty eradication, terms which are frequently used interchangeably (even occurring in the UNCTAD X Plan of Action of February 2000). This conceptual ambiguity is a critical obstacle to a clear, coherent development policy.

To overcome this is needed is not merely a safety-net approach, which focuses on poverty alleviation, but a comprehensive empowerment approach, which is focused on the elimination of poverty. Central to this is support for civil society participation in economic as well as political decision-making, a theme which has been a consistent aspect of advocacy and development work of CIDSE and its member organisations. From the perspective of sustainable human development, poverty eradication, not alleviation, must be the overarching goal of EU.

6.3 Development Assistance

Whilst the EU reiterates its commitment to the UN's official development aid target of 0.7 per cent of GDP, and continues to emphasise the International Development targets, there is a veritable chasm between the rhetoric and reality of EU aid policy. Most EU Member States are very far from the 0.7 per cent target (Belgium 0.31 per cent, UK 0.26 per cent, France 0.45 per cent, Finland 0.33 per cent, Germany 0.28 per cent, Austria 0.26 per cent, Luxembourg 0.55 per cent, Italy 0.11 per cent, Ireland 0.31

per cent, Spain 0.23 per cent, Portugal 0.25 per cent). All but 4 of these countries (Luxembourg, Spain, Ireland and Portugal) have shown a decline in aid in the decade 1986/7 and 1997. And those who increased did so from a relatively low base. Moreover, those EU Member States, which have exceeded the 0.7 per cent target (Sweden 0.79 per cent, Netherlands 0.81 per cent and Denmark 0.97 per cent), have, with the exception of Denmark, also shown a decline in the same period (4).

With regard to funding from EU Member States to the least developed countries, taking the top 10 aid recipients of each Member States' assistance, the picture is a very varied one: Germany none, Austria 1 LDC, France and Spain 3, Finland 4, Portugal, Denmark, Italy and the Netherlands 5, Belgium, the UK and Luxembourg 6, Ireland and Sweden 7. In terms of aid to sub-Saharan Africa, an analysis of recent OECD statistics point to the following: in Austria, 19.9 per cent of its aid goes to sub-Saharan Africa, Germany 20.88 per cent, Spain 23.56 per cent, Netherlands 26.72 per cent, Sweden 32.92 per cent, UK 33.13 per cent, Finland 34.7 per cent, Denmark 40.27 per cent, Belgium 40.3 per cent, Italy 40.36 per cent, France 47.85 per cent, Luxembourg 50 per cent, Ireland 70.68 per cent and Portugal 97.5 per cent.

According to 1999 OECD statistics, in terms of overall EC development assistance 37.2 per cent of funds was allocated for programmes in sub-Saharan Africa. At the same time the top ten recipients of EC aid (Poland, Morocco, Egypt, Russia, Bosnia and Herzegovina, Tunisia, Former Yugoslavia, Palestine, Bulgaria and Romania) are as much a reflection of EU Member States geopolitical concerns as development criteria.

Two major problems hamper the efficiency of the Commission's aid management. The first is gross understaffing which, despite numerous appeals from the Commission and the European Parliament, has not been addressed. According to the OECD, USAID had a total staff of 7,488 for a budget of $6.9 Billion while the Commission had a staff of only 1,947 for a similar sized budget. Put differently the level of Commission staffing is less than the municipal staff capacity of the city of Amsterdam. Thus there is a large element of self-fulfilling prophecy in Member States' complaints about the lack of effective management of aid programmes.

The second is that staff capacities are further limited by servicing committees, comprised of civil servants from EU Member States, of which there are over 400. This comitology procedure, designed to oversee and determine Commission spending, is extremely bureaucratic and expensive.

Particularly important for sub-Saharan Africa is the European Development Fund (EDF). The EDF is not budgetised. This means that it falls outside the financial perspectives which the Heads of State of the European Union determine for themselves on a five-year basis; it depends entirely on voluntary contributions decided upon by Member States and it is outside the scrutiny and accountability structures of the elected European Parliament. Decisions on the EDF are determined largely by the EDF committee which, like other committees in the comitology framework, is made up of civil servants from EU Member States. The European Parliament, the ACP, the Commission itself and the NGO community have for many years urged that the EDF be brought within the European Union budget so that is does not depend entirely on the largesse - or otherwise - of EU Member States. Yet the European Council has always refused this. In this regard it is to be welcomed that the Recent European Commission Communication on guidelines for Community Development Policy recommends budgetisation of the EDF.

The importance of this issue cannot be overstated. The current proposals for the 9th EDF represent a 2.8 per cent increase over the already inadequate 8th EDF package, a figure which does not even keep up with inflation, bears no relation to needs and goes against the EU's stated commitment to help the world's poorest countries and to meet various International Development Targets. Indeed it has been estimated that these figures represent a 3 per cent decline in real terms. This amount is even more disappointing when one realises that, unlike previous five-year financial protocols, the 9th EDF is to cover the period 2000-2007 (with the amount supplemented by unspent funds from previous EDFs).

In addition, the introduction of 'rolling programming' imposes further conditions on EDF disbursement. Under rolling programming, amounts to be allocated to National Indicative Programmes will be purely indicative (as opposed to contractual, as was the case until 1995). Monies will continue to be released in tranches based on an assessment of need and performance criteria. It is extremely difficult to know how these criteria will be assessed and balanced against each other and how this arrangement will be implemented in practice. A certain scepticism with regard to the needs criterion seems justified since past allocations to the EDF do not seem to have taken this much into account. With regard to performance criteria, the tendency is likely to be for administratively stronger ACP countries to fare better whilst administratively weaker countries get less and/or for countries to look for large and/or quickly implemented programmes in order to access additional financing. And this could well be at the expense of more effective and better planned long-term development programming.

6.4 Debt and Adjustment

According to the UNDP Human Development Report 2004, the debt burden has undermined growth, health and education especially in Africa. Debt service payments exceed annual expenditure on health and education in 9 Heavily Indebted Poor Countries (HIPCs) and exceed health and education spending in 29 countries, including 23 in sub-Saharan Africa.

In September 1996, the Interim Committee of the Development Committees of the IMF and the World Bank launched the then much-vaunted HIPC initiative. By a fairly complicated and somewhat arbitrary set of criteria, 41 developing countries were classified as HIPC countries (2). Although all but 12 of the 41 HIPC countries are Least Developed Countries(3), 20 countries officially considered by the UN as LDCs are not included. In Africa, these are Cape Verde, Comoros, Djibouti,

Eritrea, Gambia and Lesotho

The total debt of developing countries is about $2.2 trillion of which about $200 billion is owed by countries eligible for debt reduction under HIPC. The majority of these countries are African. Just prior to its last AGM an IMF paper stated: *It has been well recognised that the external debt situation for a number of low-income countries, mostly in Africa, has become extremely difficult. For these countries, even full use of traditional mechanisms of rescheduling and debt reduction - together with continued provision of concessional financing and pursuit of sound economic policies - may not be sufficient to attain sustainable external debt levels within a reasonable period of time and without additional external support.*

Moreover, HIPC as a creditor instrument completely glosses over the fact that much of Africa's debt is not legitimate debt: some was based on lending to dictators like former President Mobutu, some based on irresponsible lending for badly designed projects and some was lent to promote the exports of creditor countries. A significant proportion is capitalised interest on arrears; money never lent in the first place. While the HIPC initiative ignores such factors at the same time it introduces governance requirements for indebted governments to receive debt relief and these have been expanded over time. Yet governance issues should operate on both sides and should apply to creditor responsibility for loans made.

Following discussions on HIPC at the G7 meeting in Cologne in June 1999, the IMF and the World Bank agreed at their autumn meetings to speed up, to broaden and to deepen the HIPC Initiative, and at the same time to transform the Enhanced Structural Adjustment Facility (ESAF) into a poverty-based facility, based on country-owned Poverty Reduction Strategy Papers. ESAF was renamed the Poverty Reduction and Growth Facility (PRGF).

Among the changes agreed were:

- deeper debt relief through lower debt sustainability targets, lower qualifying thresholds, and calculations based on earlier actual data rather than projections; and

- faster debt relief, including through the earlier provision of front-loaded assistance to free up resources for poverty-focused spending, such as investment into health and education.

Despite some limited improvements, the HIPC initiative remains an instrument for reducing rather than cancelling debt. Its focus has been more on making countries 'good debtors' in terms of meeting agreed debt repayments rather than 'good developers' in terms of prioritising and releasing resources for urgent human development and other needs. Given that the debt, which is being reduced under the HIPC initiative, includes those debts that debtor countries were already failing to service – about half their due debts – much of the debt reduction provided will not release new money into government budgets. And even where it does, countries such as Zambia whose debt repayments are expected to halve will still be spending more on debt than on health and education combined.

One of the central reasons for outcomes such as that of Zambia is that poverty and human development needs are not used as criteria for assessing the amount of debt cancellation countries should receive. HIPC initiative calculations on debt sustainability are mainly based on debt in relation to a country's export earnings rather than on how much debt cancellation a particular country needs in order to invest adequately in human development. Yet the potential benefits of a human development centred approach to debt relief, which would free up resources for social sector investment are enormous, particularly in sub-Saharan Africa where human deprivation is particularly acute. The UNDP has calculated that a 1 per cent increase in the portion of government budgets spent on health and education would reduce child deaths by 24 per cent.

In terms of the EU's contribution to current international debt initiatives in October 1999 the European Commission proposed that the Union should provide a contribution of between 900 Million - 1 Billion EURO towards the enhanced HIPC initiative.

This allocation is to come out of previous unspent European Development Funds, that is from resources already committed to development though not disbursed, and as such does not therefore represent genuinely additional resource flows to these countries. Indeed responding to the question of whether HIPC debt relief can take the place of development assistance, the November 1999 OECD review of EU aid provides an emphatic 'No', stressing that HIPC debt relief can only be fully beneficial if it is accompanied by previous rates of development assistance. Moreover, citizens groups across Europe, and Churches in particular, have been actively calling for debt cancellation with Jubilee 2000 committees working in most member states.

At the same time given that the EU finances 64 per cent of the costs of structural adjustment programmes in Africa while it has only a cumulative voting weight of 27 per cent in the IMF, it has a particular responsibility in ensuring that the structural adjustment policies which accompany debt initiatives are transformed to place poverty eradication and sustainable development at their core. At present, many countries in Africa are in the process of preparing Poverty Reduction Strategy Papers and doing this in consultation with their civil societies. Yet the final decision on approval of these papers rests with the Boards of the World Bank and IMF. Given these organisations poor record in terms of poverty reduction and in promoting local ownership, and the fact that EU member states are key financial players in these bodies, the EU should press for an independent arbitration process for deciding on the merits of such papers.

6.5 Trade

In terms of trade volume, in 2004 the EU's share of world exports was 37.9 per cent, compared to 13.7 per cent for the US and 7.1 per cent for Japan. By contrast, the share of all developing countries' total exports was 18.6 per cent and, of this, sub-Saharan Africa's share was a mere 1.5 per cent. If one excludes South Africa and Nigeria, the two largest markets in sub-Saharan Africa, the share of sub-Saharan Africa was a mere 0.8 per cent.

In terms of EU Foreign Direct Investment (FDI) into sub-Saharan Africa this declined in the period 1992-1995 from 3 per cent to just 1 per cent. Over the same period, FDI from sub-Saharan Africa was so negligible that it does not even register and appears as a zero in official EUROSTAT statistics.

At the same time, the pattern of financial flows from North to South has changed dramatically over the period 1988 to 1996. In 2004 non-market flows (development assistance, including that from NGOs) amounted to 68.5 per cent of total net resource flows. By 1996 non-market flows had fallen to 23.8 per cent of the total, with just over 76 per cent of net resources in the form of market flows (direct investment, international bank lending, bond lending, other private flows at market terms).

6.6 Generalised System of Preferences

As the Generalised System of Preferences (GSP) regime will only be revised in 2004, it is impossible to predict what 'enhanced GSP' will or could look like. The first important difference between GSP and the Lomé Convention/new Partnership Agreement is a political one. The Lomé Convention is a legally binding, contractual agreement, which is negotiated between the ACP countries and the European Union in a spirit of solidarity and partnership. GSP, in contrast, is non-negotiable, non-contractual (and can thus be withdrawn at any time) and depends on the largesse or otherwise of the European Union. The structural shift from a Convention to a GSP regime would therefore undermine the partnership nature of EU-ACP relations, which has been of fundamental importance since the first Lomé Convention in 1975. It would also compromise the political dialogue aspect of the relationship along with the political identity of the ACP.

The second major difference is economic. Towards the end of April 1999, EU and ACP experts conducted a joint analysis of the consequences for the ACP of applying GSP. Given the special treatment envisaged for LDCs, these were excluded from the study. Thus, the analysis was restricted to the 31 ACP non-LDCs (excluding South Africa).

Among the key findings were:

- On the basis of actual trade in 1996 and of duties to be applied in the year 2000, the additional cost to the ACP countries resulting from tariff protection under the current GSP would be 301 Million EURO - an overall loss in the margin of preference of 1.9 per cent. This does not include the Lomé protocols - sugar, banana, rum, beef and veal - which are of major economic importance to some ACP countries.
- For some ACP non-LDCs, GSP would entail high additional duties. Even with the application of the GSP's special incentive clause (which is not at all certain), the countries in Africa which would face high additional tariffs are: Seychelles 21 per cent, Botswana 6.3 per cent, Namibia 5.5 per cent, Mauritius 5.2 per cent, Zimbabwe 5.1 per cent and Kenya 3.5 per cent. This could have a significant impact in those sectors where these countries have not achieved a sufficiently high level of competitiveness in global terms.
- The current GSP would provide only 9 ACP non-LDCs with a margin of preference 'globally equivalent' to that granted under Lomé. Only 4 of these 9 are in Africa: Ghana, Congo, Nigeria and Gabon.
- There would be high preference losses in certain sectors: in addition to the commodities covered by the Lomé protocols, these include dairy produce, fish preparations, products of the milling industry, meat, preparations of vegetables and fruit, cereals, tobacco, live plants and cut flowers, clothing and edible vegetables. These sectors make up about 20 per cent of the ACP non-LDCs' exports.
- More than half of Lomé trade preferences, the most valuable ones, would be lost.

Under current WTO rules the needs of economically vulnerable landlocked and small island states are not taken into account (the Enabling Clause does not allow for differentiation between non-LDC developing countries) yet such needs are extremely important. Thus the current GSP system is only a viable option for a handful of countries - only 4 of them in Africa. And it would need to be enhanced beyond all recognition if it is to be of benefit to ACP non-LDCs.

6.7 Regional Economic Partnership Agreements

REPAs are essentially reciprocal free trade arrangements between the EU and a Lomé country or grouping of countries. Discussions on this issue have been difficult from the outset. These started with six studies released by the European Commission on the impact of REPAS on particular regional groupings. The logic of the studies was unclear from the outset, some groupings were not included and a total of 19 African Lomé countries were excluded from the studies. The study on the SADC region, for example, explicitly excluded South Africa, the largest economy in the region and a member of SADC. Another excluded country was Africa's most populous state, Nigeria.

The studies raise fundamental questions around the implications of EU support for regionalisation as a springboard for the smooth and gradual integration of the ACP countries into the world economy. For example, the SADC study concludes that it would be very difficult to introduce a REPA with SADC because the region is not ready. The bilateral agreement between the EU and South Africa extends *de facto* to the other countries in the Southern Africa Customs Union (SACU) - Botswana, Lesotho, Namibia, Swaziland. Thus these countries could not be party to a separate Free Trade Area with the EU through SADC. In addition, given that half the 14 SADC members are LDCs, they are effectively already covered by special access for this group of countries. Another option could be an agreement with Mauritius, Seychelles and Zimbabwe - but this, the study points out, may not achieve the objective of regional integration.

Even under current arrangements, there would be little interest - if indeed it were even feasible - for LDCs to embark on a regional or bilateral free trade arrangement. This is even more so the case given that the new Partnership Agreement has committed itself (Article 16.9) to allow, at the latest by 2005, *"duty free access for essentially all products from LDCs".*

Consequently countries have nothing to gain by such negotiations. In the East African Co-operation (EAC), Kenya is the only non-LDC. In the Union Douanière et Economique de l'Afrique Centrale - Communauté Economique et Monétaire de l'Afrique Centrale (UDEAC-CEMAC), Cameroon is the only non-LDC, and in the Union Economique et Monétaire Ouest Africaine (UEMOA) only Côte d'Ivoire is a non-LDC. It is therefore not surprising that the term REPA has been replaced by Economic Partnership Agreement (EPA). This is also indicative of a growing 'bilateralisation' of the EU's relations with its ACP partners.

6.8 Special Treatment for LDCs

There is no disagreement regarding the need to accord LDCs special treatment and the EU commitment to allowing duty free access "*to essentially all products from all LDCs*" by the year 2005 is to be welcomed. Yet the Union needs to go further particularly in terms of the interests of African nations who make up the majority of this group of countries. In light of the almost complete marginalisation of the LDCs in the world trading system, all products should be covered and the 5-year implementation waiting period should be substantially cut. At the same time efforts should be increased to provide trade development measures to enable these countries to participate to their advantage in global trade relations.

6.9 Coherence between Aid and Trade Policies

About 50 per cent of the total EU budget is devoted to the Common Agricultural Policy which is a contentious issue at international trade fora. In this regard, the Cairns Group - a grouping of 18 countries committed to freer, fairer and more market-oriented conditions and to placing trade in agriculture on the same footing as trade in other products - is pressing for the elimination of export subsidies as well as trade distorting domestic supports, and for a major expansion in market access for agricultural products. At their last annual Ministerial meeting at the end of August 1999, the Cairns Group of Trade Ministers pointed out that "*Trade in agriculture remains subject to profound and costly distortions. Protectionist policies have severely hampered economic growth and damaged employment.* Undoubtedly, such distortions have increasingly undermined already fragile agricultural systems and economies in many parts of Africa as the examples of beef dumping on West and Southern African markets have amply illustrated.

6.10 Conclusion and Recommendations

6.10.1 Trade

- The EU has proposed duty free access of essentially all products for LDCs by the year 2005. In light of the almost complete marginalisation of the LDCs in the world trading system, among which African states make up the vast majority, all LDC products should be covered and the 5 year implementation waiting period should be substantially cut. At the same time efforts should be increased to put in place trade development measures (manufacturing, processing, diversification) to enable these countries to produce more tradable goods.
- It is critical that those African states, who in 2004 do not feel in a position to engage in an Economic Partnership Agreement, use the provisions under Article 36 of the New Partnership Agreement to consult on all possible alternatives which would assure Lomé equivalence.
- It is equally critical, given the shortcomings of existing REPA studies, that those developing countries contemplating an EPA with the EU conduct their own studies assessing the impact at national, sub-regional and regional levels, and that the EU sets aside resources to support such studies.

6.10.2 Debt and Adjustment

- Recognising the limited potential of the revised HIPC initiative the EU should press for all creditors to move towards the cancellation of unpayable debts.
- Linked to this the EU should ensure that civil society has a

stake in decisions on the allocation of the money freed up.

- Given the EU's long-term commitment to the campaign against poverty and in support of sustainable development the EU should maintain an active stance in ensuring that human development is not jeopardised or undermined by insistence on unrealistic macroeconomic and financial conditions under structural adjustment policies tied to debt relief. Given that the EU as a whole finances almost two thirds of the total cost of structural adjustment programmes in Africa it has a particular responsibility in this regard.
- The EU should allocate the necessary resources to support African governments and civil society organisations in their consultation on the design, implementation, monitoring and evaluation of debt and anti-poverty strategies. The current process of developing Poverty Reduction Strategy Papers (PRSPs) provides an opportunity for doing this. As part of this clear and measurable targets should be identified by the EU for the allocation of resources towards capacity building.
- At the same time the EU should work to ensure that the PRSP process does not become yet another factor in delaying debt reduction as has already happened in the case of Mozambique.
- Furthermore, given the poor record of both the IMF and World Bank on tackling poverty and supporting local ownership of programmes, and the EU's special partnership with African states under successive Lomé agreements, the EU should challenge and question the current dominant position taken by these institutions as the final arbiters of decisions on the PRSP process and on international debt initiatives. Instead alternative, independent and more democratic institutional arrangements such underpin such initiatives which would in turn add to their credibility.
- The EU should explore the possibilities for the establishment up of an international debt arbitration procedure which would provide an independent mechanism for deciding which external debts should not or cannot be paid and which should

be serviced. Such a mechanism would also act as a protective device against future 'bad' debts as creditors and debtors alike would share responsibility for loan policies and practices.

6.10.3 Good Governance

- The debate on good governance requires a broader debate and greater clarity and consensus on the definition of good governance. A clear differentiation should be made between bad and weak governance. In the latter case, the inadequate remuneration and poor training of public service workers should be recognised as a contributory factor to weak governance.
- Bribery does not entirely explain corruption but should be accorded the same rigorous scrutiny and action as given to corruption. In this regard, businesses should be made aware of the OECD Anti-Bribery Convention and the criminal penalties accompanying it. EU member states should pass legislation modelled on the US money laundering Act 1999 which seeks to prevent the US being used as a money laundering safe haven for corruptly and illegally acquired funds.
- In cases where government is non-existent, as is the case in Somalia, it is crucial that the people of that country are not additionally penalised by having all development assistance withdrawn. Rather, where appropriate, development finance should be channelled through other routes, in particular through civil society actors.

6.10.4 Peace Building and Conflict Resolution/Prevention

- The principles enshrined in various EU documents on conflict prevention, management and resolution should be translated into a set of operational and implementation guidelines. The EU should use its position as a major international player and historic partner to persuade African governments to peacefully solve conflict, involving all parties involved.
- The EU should continue and reinforce its support for African mediation efforts, especially those of the OAU, in situations of crisis or conflict on the continent. These support measures

should be linked with the strengthening of local governance. It is also necessary to put resources into strengthening civil society (trade unions, civic associations, churches, peasant movements and NGOs) so that national and regional processes towards social and economic change can be negotiated without conflict.

- There should be greater coherence within the European Union in relation to conflict in Africa. This relates not only to the arms trade but also the role of development assistance in conflict prevention, management and resolution either through direct programmes or indirectly through poverty eradication programmes. Resources are necessary to develop and strengthen independent media in Africa, and the local judicial systems that can ensure persecution of war criminals and offenders of violations of human rights.
- The EU's Code of Conduct on Arms Exports and its efforts to combat the spread of small arms and light weapons must be carefully and systematically monitored, with serious sanctions to punish transgressors and operated according to the principles of transparency and accountability, along the lines of prior parliamentary scrutiny as in Sweden. We call for an arms embargo for countries in conflict areas.
- The role of mining and other companies from European countries in fuelling conflict in Africa needs to be investigated and made subject to extra-territorial EU legislation, following the example of sex offences by European nationals with children in developing countries.
- Recognising that legal and illicit trade often maintains and exacerbates conflicts in Africa there is an urgent need for concerted EU action to end illicit trades (e.g. the illegal trafficking in diamonds), and effective sanctions to prevent its reoccurrence.

6.10.5 HIV/AIDS

- A multi-sectoral pro-poor approach to Health and HIV/AIDS should be fully supported and backed up by increased resources, both human and financial.

- The EU should support governments in formulating and implementing effective preventive strategies and should support governments in monitoring the spread of the epidemic and to assess the impact of preventive strategies.
- The EU should play its part in ensuring greater international co-ordination of and coherence between HIV/AIDS policies and programmes.
- The EU should expand the resources it provides towards developing appropriate vaccines and microbicidal products which in turn are accessible and affordable to the widest possible range of people, particularly the poorest. The same is true for the provision of generic medicines to treat opportunistic diseases, such as tuberculosis.
- The EU Heads of Government should endorse Article 31 of the TRIPs Agreement, which allows the compulsory licensing/parallel importing in situations of national emergency so that local production and distribution of cheaper AIDS drugs in African and other developing countries is possible. The United States has brought bilateral pressure to bear on states to desist from compulsory licensing. What is required from EU Heads of Government is a political statement of support for the compulsory licensing option.

6.10.6 Development Assistance

- Given the multiple humanitarian, rehabilitation and development needs of sub-Saharan Africa the EU should ensure that the 9th EDF is at least 10 per cent greater, in real terms, that the previous one.
- The EDF should be budgetised and thus made more transparent and accountable.
- The current staffing levels and capacities in the European Commission should be augmented to enable effective management of the EU development co-operation programmes. This will improve the quality of aid.
- Given ongoing delays in disbursing funds under various EDFs, and in order to maximise the financial resources available, consideration should be given by the Member

States to transferring agreed commitments (possibly on a yearly basis) to a special interest-bearing account. The interest accruing should be regarded as an ACP reserve fund, the expenditure of which can be jointly determined in various areas such as humanitarian assistance and long-term development programmes.

- At the same time, adequate resources must be provided by the EU in crisis situations and towards efforts to support recovery and rehabilitation as well as longer-term development need to be both strengthened and integrated, most recently in the case of Mozambique.

Notes

1. The Amsterdam Treaty, agreed by the European Union's political leaders on 17 June and signed on 2 October 1997, is the culmination of two years of discussion and negotiation in a conference of member state government representatives. The aim of the treaty is to create the political and institutional conditions to enable the European Union to meet the challenges of the future such as the rapid evolution of the international situation, the globalisation of the economy and its impact on jobs, the fight against terrorism, international crime and drug trafficking, ecological problems and threats to public health.

2. The **Lome Convention** is an international aid and trade agreement between the ACP (African Caribbean and Pacific Countries) group and the European Union aimed at supporting the "ACP states' efforts to achieve comprehensive, self reliant and self-sustained development. Four such Conventions have been signed to date. The first Convention (Lome I) was signed on February 28, 1975. Lome II and III were signed in 1979 and 1985 respectively. The fourth Convention , the LOME IV covered the period from 1990 to 2000. The successor agreement, the **Contonou Agreement** covers 2000-2020 but can be changed every five years. It emphasizes gender equality, environmental sustainability and removal of trade barriers. The EU & ACP countries have five years to set up Economic Partnership Agreements (EPAs) according to the Contonou Agreement which would help in the removal of trade barriers between the member countries and enhance cooperation in all areas relevant to trade.

3. The Barcelona Process is a unique and ambitious initiative, which laid the foundations of a new regional relationship and which represents

a turning point in Euro-Mediterranean relations. The Euro-Mediterranean Conference of Ministers of Foreign Affairs, held in Barcelona on 27-28 November 1995, marked the starting point of the Euro-Mediterranean Partnership (Barcelona Process), a wide framework of political, economic and social relations between the Member States of the European Union and Partners of the Southern Mediterranean. The latest EU enlargement, on 1st May 2004, has brought two Mediterranean Partners (Cyprus and Malta) into the European Union, while adding a total of 10 to the number of Member States. The Euro-Mediterranean Partnership thus comprises 35 members, 25 EU Member States and 10 Mediterranean Partners (Algeria, Egypt, Israel, Jordan, Lebanon, Morocco, Palestinian Authority, Syria, Tunisia and Turkey). Libya has observer status since 1999.

In the Barcelona Declaration, the Euro-Mediterranean partners established the three main objectives of the Partnership:

- The definition of a common area of peace and stability through the reinforcement of political and security dialogue. (Political and Security Chapter).
- The construction of a zone of shared prosperity through an economic and financial partnership and the gradual establishment of a free-trade area (Economic and Financial Chapter).
- The rapprochement between peoples through a social, cultural and human partnership aimed at encouraging understanding between cultures and exchanges between civil societies (Social, Cultural and Human Chapter).

4. The MEDA programme is the principal financial instrument of the EU for the implementation of the Euro Mediterranean Partnership. The programme offers technical and financial support measures to accompany the reforms of economic and social structures in Mediterranean partners.

5. Tempus is one of the member European Community programme designed to help the process of social and economic reform and for development in the partner countries. The partner countries currently included are the Western Balkhan countries, East European and Central Asian Countries and the Mediterranean Partners. The Tempus programme focuses on the development of the higher education system in these countries through cooperation with institutions from the member states of the European Community. The programme is based on the understanding that higher education institutions are of particular importance for the social and economic transition process as well as

cultural development, they are also pools of expertise and of human resources and provide training of new generation of leaders.

6. The Common Agricultural Policy, is a complex system of subsidies paid by the EU to farmers. Member states have to contribute to a central pool, which the EU then divides, as it sees fit. Some of these subsidies are actually paid to farmers to stop them farming their land, in order to keep the amount of food on the market low and therefore maintain a good price for food.

7. The Treaty of Rome refers to the treaty which established the European Economic Community (EEC) and was signed by France, West Germany, Italy, Belgium, the Netherlands and Luxembourg on March 25, 1957. Its original full name was Treaty establishing the European Economic Community -- however the Treaty of Maastricht amended it and among other things removed the word "Economic" from the name of both the community and the treaty. The treaty is therefore now generally called the Treaty establishing the European Community or the EC Treaty. Another treaty was signed the same day establishing the European Atomic Energy Community (Euratom) : their conjunction is known as the Treaties of Rome (plural). Both came into force on 1 January 1958.

8. The preceding section was an extract from Peter Clegg, European Union - African Relations: Partnership or Parsimony?, August 2003 .

9. This is based on CIDSE position Paper, “Towards True partnership: EU Africa Summit”, March 2000.

7

European Union-COMESA Relations: Country-wise Analysis

Over the years, the African countries have been devastated by a vast number of conflicts, many of them of an intractable and prolonged nature. Millions of lives have been lost and human rights abused. Entire population has been forced to abandon their homes and take refuge in neighbouring countries. The economic cost of these countries have been crippling, reversing the development of countries and communities already exposed to extreme poverty.

The realization has grown in Africa over recent years that the continent's leaders have to take collective responsibility if they wish to ensure a significant reduction in the number of conflicts. This realization has led the continent to work towards the economic integration, if they want to achieve the long term goal of economic prosperity and stability. Regional integration, in today's world, is the only way to generate sufficient economic activity, improve efficiency, heighten competition, attract investments and thus create jobs. No single nation in Africa can prosper outside the framework of regionalism.

As Africa takes up the challenge of economic instability and insecurity Europe is at its side. The EU's speedy endorsement of the regional integration programme in Eastern and Southern Africa acknowledges the credibility and authority with which COMESA is working towards this goal.

The EU has taken the lead in supporting the African efforts to promote the cause of economic integration in the continent. It contributes to the task of addressing the root causes of insecurity in Africa through a wide range of instruments. Partnership and ownership are fundamental to ensuring both the effectiveness of cooperation and the coherence of EU's external action, the most important feature of which is the permanent character of its partnerships as well as their global coverage.

The EU has concluded structured legally binding partnership and cooperation agreements with different areas of Africa. At the same time, the EU is in daily contact with the United Nations through the joint crises management group. A dynamic and reinforcing partnership has developed between EU and the Eastern and Southern countries of Africa. This provides a foundation for a crucial area of cooperation and dialogue between the two regions of the world.

The European Union, through its own regional vocation has assisted COMESA in many ways and the impressive progress made in regional integration by COMESA is partly attributable to the support given by the EU.

At the national level, nearly all COMESA countries were party to the trade and development agreement - the Lome Convention - between the ACP-EU which lasted a quarter of a century. The Convention was critical for the development of specific industries and economies in COMESA. The greatest impetus for the evolution and expansion of trade from ACP to EU countries was the non-reciprocal and preferential market access accorded to ACP countries over all other suppliers to the EU.

The non-reciprocal arrangements of the Lome Convention are now being replaced with the new Cotonou Agreement, which foresees the establishment of Regional Economic Partnership Agreements (REPAs) between the EU and African, Caribbean and Pacific (ACP) countries, in preparation for free trade arrangements in the longer term.

The EU is co-operating with COMESA through a number of projects and programmes aimed at strengthening regional integration. Co-operation is most pronounced in the formulation of sound economic policy both in the areas of trade and investment directly through the Regional Integration Project at the COMESA Secretariat and at the national level through the Regional Integration Facilitation Facility (RIFF).

Other institutions of the European Union, namely the European Investment Bank and the Centre for the Development of Enterprises (CDE) have, and continue to, contribute and enrich materially this partnership.

The Common Market for Eastern and Southern Africa (COMESA) and the European Union has signed an $8.6 million agreement to support the second phase of regional integration programs in Eastern and Southern Africa.

The funds would also be used to monitor trade liberalisation programmes in the region and support cross-border trade initiatives in COMESA member countries.

The contribution by the EU was one way of encouraging COMESA to further its ambitions to achieve a free trade area and make a significant impact on the economies of member countries. The EU in 1994 contributed 2.1 million euros for the first phase.

COMESA has further signed an agreement in Lusaka on January 22, 2003 with the European Union on behalf of the Inter Regional Coordinating Committee comprising East African Community (EAC), the Intergovernmental Authority on Development (IGAD), the Indian Island Commission (IOC) and COMESA, for a grant of Euro 1,950,000 or US$ 2.4 million for capacity building in the region to negotiate a new Trade Agreement with the EU from a more equal footing.

The old development-oriented conventions between the EU and ACP countries are to be replaced by Economic Partnership Agreements (EPAs). However, the worry has been that with global trade becoming ever more complex, African countries would be at a disadvantage in the negotiations.

COMESA has led a coordinated response, not only to EPAs but has also contributed significantly to negotiations on WTO issues. As a result of these initiatives, 16 of Eastern and Southern African States (ESA) have joined together to negotiate an EPA with the EU.

The, launch of the negotiations will herald a series of workshops and seminars designed to make the region's negotiators more conversant with the intricate economic and legal requirements (and impact) of global trade. In order to better advise the negotiators, a series of research studies will be carried out and mechanisms established to ensure that the press and, most importantly, the private sector are kept well informed and consulted.

The actual Economic Partnership Agreement will commence in 2008.

The project will be managed within the COMESA Secretariat by the Inter Regional Coordinating Committee comprising East African Community (EAC), the Intergovernmental Authority on Development (IGAD), the Indian Island Commission (IOC) and COMESA.

Currently, virtually all African countries have entered into contractual preference arrangements with the European Union (EU). Because of historical colonial ties, the EU accounts for greater than two-thirds of total African trade. The following section gives an overview of EU's relation with the COMESA member-states and the country strategy adopted by it for individual states. It also provides an insight into the main development projects and priorities for co-operation. Furthermore, EU's support under European Development Fund (EDF) has also been provided to have an understanding of the financial support provided by the European Union.

7.1 Angola

Relations between Angola and the EU are good. The EU's objectives and priorities vis-avis Angola are stated in the conclusions of the General Affairs and External Relations Council of 13th October 2003. These envisage the regular conduct of a political dialogue (Art. 8, Cotonou Agreement). Furthermore the EU undertakes Government of Angola (GoA) to:

- Assist GoA to strengthen democratic institutions and practices as to hold free and fair elections;
- Provide assistance to develop pluralistic democracy, foster dynamic participatory civil society and reinforce overall administrative capacity;

- Assist GoA's efforts to reform the economy through co-operation with the IMF and the fight against corruption, to encourage and assist GoA in its efforts to prepare a PRSP;
- Continue to contribute to the efforts to improve the humanitarian situation;
- Assist GoA in reconstruction of the country, encouraging its intention to convene an international donors' conference with EU support.

Economic and trade relations between the EU and Angola are important, mainly due to the engagement of European companies in the oil sector. Angola in 2002 exported goods worth 2.265 M€ (oil products 73,1%, diamonds 23,1%) to the EU, while imports from the EU were worth 1.375 M€. In 2001 the EU was Angola's main trade partner for imports and the second trading partner for exports behind the US and before China. A new EC/Angola fisheries agreement was signed on 30 June 2002 for a 2-year period (August 2002—August 2004).

Country Strategy: The European Commission's strategy for cooperation with Angola, signed on January 28, 2003 is in line with the objectives defined in the above mentioned Council conclusions of 13th October 2003. An important priority for the EC is to support measures to promote peace and conflict resolution in Angola and in the region. It is also a necessary step towards the central objective of poverty alleviation. Furthermore the EC will contribute to the dialogue with the Government, with particular emphasis on the issue of rule of law (human rights and judicial sector reform), which is the keystone of social and economic revival.

The cessation of hostilities has not, however, meant the resolution of the humanitarian crisis, but it does offer the possibility of resolving it in a more sustainable manner. The support strategy for Angola, therefore, fits into the framework of, and pursues the link between, relief, rehabilitation and development (LRRD), aiming to take advantage of synergies between the different financial instruments. This LRRD strategy proposes short- medium- and longer-term interventions to contribute to:

- the furtherance of the 2002 peace process, national reconciliation and the consolidation of democracy, including the creation of conditions for free and fair elections;
- good governance and development of civil society;
- poverty alleviation, through a gradual concentration of the EC's aid on the focal areas of food security and social sectors.

In the immediate and short term, and in line with its Plan of Action to support the peace process adopted by the General Affairs Council of May 13th 2002, EC funds already earmarked are being used to reinforce the areas of humanitarian assistance and post-emergency aid. Funds previously earmarked for projects which do not fall within the focal areas and have yet to be launched have also been rapidly reallocated to address those areas. This support can also include, if need be, making available funds for the critical processes of disarmament, demobilisation and reintegration and initial resettlement of populations, as well as to help create the conditions for free and fair general presidential and legislative elections.

Also in the short term, the EC is ready to initiate support to good governance, in particular with regard to the judicial sector and the reform of the public administration. In this context, the EC attaches great importance to promoting the development of Angolan civil society, in particular in relation to democracy and human rights. The EC fully acknowledges that good governance constitutes a pre-requisite for more sustainable development interventions in Angola.

In the medium and long term, and in order to support its objectives of poverty reduction, the EC plans to gradually increase the focus of its support in accordance with the analysis of the preceding chapters, by progressively concentrating aid on the development and implementation of adequate national policies for the social sectors and for food security. In order to address the very serious problems which affect the delivery of social services in Angola, the very high degree of food insecurity, and shortcomings in the management of the country's substantial resources, support for these focal areas needs to be delivered in an uninterrupted manner, with the phased link between relief, rehabilitation and development firmly in mind, and the transition between one phase and the next supported by different types of funding. Furthermore, the EC has relatively more experience and greater capacity in these areas and can, by dint of its technical capacity and financial resources, contribute to a gradual reversal of the negative trends. These areas receive less funding from other donors, but absorb about 65 per cent of the EC's non-emergency aid. Moreover, the EC is aware of the great potential of the social sectors and food security in terms of poverty alleviation. The impact of any support in these areas, and the timing of the transition between one phase of LRRD and the next, will, however, be influenced by the unfolding of the political process subsequent to the cease-fire, by the degree of increase in budgetary allocations and execution within the sectors, and by the effective re-establishment of the administration's functions in the country as a whole.

For this reason, it is proposed that good governance be treated as a focal cross-cutting issue, in the short, medium and long term, and that parallel actions to promote democracy and human rights, reform of public finance management, the development of civil society, political and economic integration at regional level, and sensible use of natural resources also follow the phased LRRD approach, in tandem with other donors.

Priorities for Cooperation: The overall indicative allocation for the 9th EDF amounts to EURO 146 million from which EURO 117 million under the envelope A and EURO 29 million under envelope B.

Focal Areas of Concentration: 63-79%

- food security 0-2.5%
- health 42-51%
- education 21-25.5%

Non-focal Areas

- Development of civil society 2.5 %

- Good governance (cross-cutting issue) 0–12.5%
- DDRR, social sectors (if necessary) 6.5–34%

Uncommitted balances of around €64m (7th and 8th EDF) are already or will be used to fund the EC's short-term programme of support for the peace process, good governance issues plus a water/sanitation project in Luanda.

EC budget lines could be used to finance specific operations, in particular for the food security focal sector, for humanitarian aid, for peace-building measures and for human rights and democracy. Finance from these instruments - provisionally estimated at around €40m as far as food security is concerned - will, however, be decided in accordance with the Community's procedures for the budget lines concerned and will depend on availability.

Focal Areas

A. Food Security: The EC's specific objective in the area of **food security** will be to reduce dependence on food aid in kind, and food insecurity. In the specific case of Angola, there is a real prospect of linkages with the relief and humanitarian interventions described above. In 2002, the EC and the Government will study such linkages in detail, and decide on the type of support to be provided to develop them. A multi-annual food security programme, to be launched as of 2003, may be part of that support. Areas likely to be covered include capacity building, training, technical assistance for legislation, support for the development of private services in agriculture, and agricultural pilot projects. A significant number of such actions will be developed with the participation of civil society. At this stage, it is thought that an amount of €40m will be required for food security actions. The Medium-Term Action Plan for Food Security, which will be completed in 2002, will give details of the financing needs as well as specific objectives, activities and indicators.

The main policy measures the Government will consider as its contribution to the response strategy in this sector are: robust handling of the issue of food insecurity and resettlement of displaced persons within the framework of the I-PRSP; positive dialogue with civil society and the donor community on the resettlement strategy and on the guarantee of access to land for displaced persons and other peasants; and the development, approval and implementation of food security policies that are coherent with the poverty reduction strategy.

B. Health: The 9th EDF framework will continue to support the **health** sector. Preparation will start early in 2003 of a programme for around **€50-60m** to complement the 8th EDF health programme. The main thrust of health sector interventions are institutional strengthening, the physical rehabilitation and equipment of basic health units, including municipal hospitals, blood safety, support for a national pharmaceutics policy, development of human resources and supply of essential and nutritional services to the focal provinces.

The main policy measures the Government will consider as its contribution to the response strategy in this sector are: to devise, by the end of 2002, the strategic guidelines of the national health policy; to adopt, by the end of 2003, a position on the financing of the health system, including cost recovery and a medium-term financing framework; to increase the annual budgetary allocations to the health sector in order to reach around 10% of the State budget by 2003, and to take the necessary measures to increase budget execution to 100% in 2004; to define roles and responsibilities at central and local level, as well as the roles of the different partners in the health sector; and to approve and implement national pharmaceutics and blood policies.

C. Education: In partnership with other donors (namely the WB and the ADB), the EC will continue to increase its support for the **education and training** sector, with the specific objective of improving the level of education and access to employment through better quality general education, improved school infrastructure and professional training.

The main interventions foreseen are: to provide continuity and sustainability to primary teacher training projects, and extend training to second and third level teachers; to train new primary teachers; to provide professional training, including in agriculture, to make for sustainable actions already implemented with 7th and 8th EDF financing; to build and rehabilitate first-level schools, including equipment and educational material; to reintegrate street children into general education; to provide institutional support for the formulation and implementation of policies to improve general education and develop education.

The main policy measures the Government will take as its contribution to the response strategy in this sector are: to increase annual budgetary allocations to the education and training sector in order to reach around 10% of the State budget by 2003, and to take the necessary measures to increase budget execution to 100% in 2004; to define roles and responsibilities at central and local level, as well as the roles of the different partners in the education sector; to devise, approve and implement policies for the development of the sector; and to implement the development plan for the sector approved by the Government in September 2001.

Non-focal Sectors of Co-operation

D. Good Governance: An indicative amount of between €20m and €35m, from the 8th EDF with the remainder coming from the 9th EDF if necessary, is planned to be allocated for the promotion of good governance, through interventions launched in the short term to support the peace process, and continuing through the medium term to respond to the LRRD approach. Activities in the Justice sector, the improvement if management of public finances and public sector reform could be envisaged.

E. Civil Society: The development of civil society, including the private sector, will be funded through a programme of capacity building for civil society and a programme of support for small- and micro-enterprises, financed from the 9th EDF. Feasibility studies for these two programmes will be carried out in close collaboration with civil society and private sector representatives, and will identify implementation methods. The capacity-building programmes for civil society may well be administered by a Protocol to facilitate the direct access of beneficiaries to the programme.

Main Development Projects

Examples of ongoing projects funded by the EU (7th and 8th European Development Fund)

- Emergency Programme in Support of the Peace Process
- Programme in the Support of reconstruction (PAR)
- Micro-Projects Programme III
- Water Supply for the Town of Tombwa
- In-service training of primary education teachers
- Project for post-emergency health
- Project for the Support of the National programme for Physical Rehabilitation
- Transition programme for the Support of Displaced Populations
- Institutional Support to the National Assembly
- Institutional Support for the National Statistical Institute

9th EDF Financial Data

	Allocation (A-envelope)	% of overall allocation
Focal area		
Social sectors • Health • education	 50-60 M€ 25-30 M€	 42-51% 21-25.5%
Food security/rural development	0-3M€	0-2,5%
Non-focal areas		
Civil society	3M€	2,5%
Good governance	0-15M€	0-12,5%
DDRR, social sectors	7,6-39,8M€	6,5-34%
Total	117M€	100%

The amount shown above accounts solely for EDF (European Development Fund) allocations – programmable aid.

7.2 Burundi

Relations with the EU: The Commission suspended co-operation with Burundi in January 1997. Following the successful peace negotiations, the Commission started providing, like other donors "enhanced humanitarian aid" through a €48m rehabilitation program (resettlement/reintegration of displaced people, actions for justice and reconciliation, funds earmarked for demobilisation programs) and a €2m institutional support programme to the Ministry of Finance. During the Paris Conference further €150m were pledged to be programmed or committed in 2001. It included a €43m STABEX FMO (signed in Paris), the ECHO plan for 2001 (€20m), a €25m grant for the UNHCR Plan for the return of Burundian refugees in Tanzania and the revival of a €5,3m health project.

A €65m new *National Indicative Programme* (NIP) (which includes €40m not committed from the 6th and 7th EDF, as well as €25m from the initial allocation under the 8th EDF) has completed the pledge. The 7th EDF NIP was signed in November 2001, once the transitional government had been put in place and the IMC moved from Arusha to Bujumbura.

Currently, aid already available to Burundi accounts to €285m, to which ads the €115m of the 9th EDF NIP, which will be signed in 2003. Focal sectors for the 9th EDF are rural development, infrastructure, and institutional capacity building as well as macro-economic support. Besides, Germany, Belgium, Austria, Italy and the Netherlands are amongst the most important donors in Burundi

In the current context of Burundi, one of the European Commission's main focus is to ensure the transition from relief aid to rehabilitation and sustainable development (Linking Relief Rehabilitation and Development - LRRD).

Yearly ECHO programs in Burundi represented €19.75m in 2001 and €17.5m in 2002. Under ECHO's Global Plan for 2003, Burundi will receive €15m. This amount will be managed by UN agencies, NGOs and the Red Cross. ECHO and its partners are addressing humanitarian needs in health and nutrition and assisting the rehabilitation of the returning refugees.

Donor co-ordination in Burundi needs to be improved and an overall international framework for supporting the transition from war to peace needs to be developed. The newly-established *Inter-Agency Cell for Post-Conflict Rehabilitation and Reconstruction* is supporting better planning and co-ordination among UN agencies but there is still some work to be done linking their activities with those of bilateral and multilateral donors and international NGOs. Nevertheless, the elaboration by the government of the *Cadre Strategique Interimaire de la Relance Economique et de la Lutte Contre la Pauvrete* and its adoption as the major donor reference document already contributes to improve the analysis of the situation and harmonises the donor responses. Certain Burundian ministries have also created co-ordination services to improve the planification of development operations.

A consultative process including the national administration, the civil society and the donor community marked the preparation of the Commission's 9th EDF Country Strategy Paper and National Indicative Programme. This has also contributed to building a solid ground for future development co-operation.

Country Strategy: Based on the following criteria and principles, a structured package of interventions under the 9th EDF NIP in Burundi at macro, sector and micro level has been identified.

- Sustainable economic and social development, the reduction of poverty and conflict prevention are the overarching goals of the Response Strategy.
- Bearing in mind that poverty is largely a rural phenomenon in Burundi, the focus of the Response Strategy is in the rural sector. The strategy therefore ultimately aims at transforming the largely subsistence agriculture to a more market oriented agricultural production and in general at diversifying the economic activities in the rural milieu.

- Good governance will be addressed at all levels and in all sectors of the Response Strategy. As emphasised in the Cotonou Agreement, focus will be on human rights, democracy and justice and support to local reconciliation initiatives thus constituting an important conflict prevention aspect of the strategy
- Co-operation with the donor-community will be actively promoted to ensure coherence and efficiency. In order to improve the co-ordination process on the part of the Burundian administration, the EC will provide Burundi macro-economic and budgetary support, as well as technical assistance for its implementation.

Priorities for co-operation

9th EDF - A Envelope (€115m)

Focal Areas

- Rural development (€56.75m - 49.34% of overall envelope)
- Good governance (€17.25m - 15% of overall envelope)
- Macro-economic support (€31.5m -27.39% of overall envelope)

Non-focal Areas (€12m- 10% of overall envelope)

- Capacity building of the civil society (€9.5m - 8.6% of the overall envelope)

Focal Areas:

A. Rural Development (€56.75m - 49.34% of overall envelope): Burundi is largely a rural country, with 90% of the population engaged in agricultural activities. All economic development must thus be channelled through the rural productive sector. The transformation of the rural sector will be done through an increase of agricultural production, aiming to improve food security and thus contribute to poverty eradication. The emphasis is on export promotion, diversification of production and the development of the private sector. The promotion of micro-enterprises and micro-credit are also envisaged.

Rural development also requires an improved transport infrastructure. An adequate transport network that reduces travel costs and time is one of the key factors to ensure economic growth, trade investment, population integration and inter and intra-co-operation in Burundi and the Great Lakes Region.

The improvement of the living conditions of the rural populations also entails the rehabilitation of health and education structures, as well as increased access to drinking water and sanitation.

Particular attention will be given to the economic and social reinsertion of the displaced populations, while protecting natural resources and particularly targeting the needs of women.

B. Good Governance (€17.25m - 15% of overall envelope): The promotion of peace and good governance constitutes the second central axis of the Strategy Response in Burundi. It also constitutes the main objective of the transitional government. The Arusha Peace Agreement includes a three-year transition period starting on the 1st November 2001. This period should permit the installation of a new political, economic, social, cultural and juridical order. The end of this period will be marked by presidential elections aiming to install a democratic government. In the meantime, legislative and local elections are to be held in 2003.

C. Macro Economic Support (€31.5m - 27.39% of overall envelope): Burundi is one of the least developed countries with regards to social, economic and political structures, weakened by the crisis and on-going conflict of the last decade. Budgetary aid will permit higher levels of allocations to priority sectors, such as rural development and the social sector, than without such support. The budgetary support will focus on maintaining macro-economic stability, reducing the external debt and covering the running expenses of certain public services.

Non-focal Areas

D. Capacity Building of the Civil Society (€9.5m - 8.6% of the overall envelope): A four-pronged approach is suggested:

- Component aimed at supporting institutional development contributing to an improved civil society structure.
- Component targeted at reinforcing the management, analysis, negotiation and intervention skills of civil society

organisations (CSOs) in order to help them gain influence in decision-making and access to development opportunities.

- Identification of areas of dialogue at the local, regional and national level.
- Component focusing on enforcing the dialogue between the state and non-state actors. This component will be financed through funds managed by the EC Delegation in Burundi.

Financial Data: 9th EDF Co-operation Programme

Burundi	% NIP	Amounts M€	Financing decision
A Envelope	-	115	-
Focal Sectors	-	-	-
I Rural Development	49.34%	56.75	2004/1st semester
II Good Governance	15%	17.25	2004/1st semester
III Macro-economic support	27.39%	31.5	2003/2nd semester
Non-Focal Sectors	8.26%	9.5	2004/1st semester
B Envelope	-	57	-
Total	**100%**	**172**	-

7.3 Comoros

Relations with the EU: EC-Comoros co-operation was governed by a Council Decision of 14.2.00 (Article 366 bis consultations), taken in response to coup d'état of April 1999. By the terms of Decision, EC aid – until democratic elections were held – was limited to support to democratic process, humanitarian aid, and actions directly in favour of populations. A € 4.5 m micro project programme ongoing + € 1.99 m project in support of return to democracy.

Following cancellation of second tranche (€ 8.25 m) of the 8th EDF National Indicative Programme, Comoros' 8th EDF amounts to € 19.25 m. At present € 8.35 m of the allocation has been committed primarily to infrastructure development and environment protection (the political crisis of the last 2–3 years having prevented the preparation of many of the projects initially envisaged).

Country Strategy: The cooperation strategy between the Comoros Islands and the European Community is based on the general objectives of Community development cooperation policy as defined in Article 177 of the Treaty on European Union. More specifically, it involves the fight against poverty by encouraging the country's sustainable social development, the main obstacle to which is the low level of the population's education, which prevents genuine democratisation of society, which is traditionally over-hierarchical, and where social, economic and political decision-making powers are limited by cultural, financial and educational factors. Thus, the Community strategy proposed for the Comoro Islands meets two of the six priority fields for development cooperation, namely support for the sectoral programmes in the social fields and institutional capacity building.

The Community policy will seek to contribute to the general aim of development and consolidation of democracy and the rule of law by encouraging respect for human rights and more particularly the rights of the child. The partnership with the Comoros Islands, as promoted by the Cotonou Agreement for the ACP countries, will thus focus on the aim of poverty reduction by promoting sustainable development centred on the human person (who is the principal stakeholder and recipient), as well as promotion of a political and institutional environment respectful of human rights. In agreement with the part III of the Cotonou Agreement, cooperation with the Comoros Islands will concentrate on human and social development, of which education in many respects constitutes the most important sector.

Priorities for Co-operation

Focal Sector: Education

With a view to the active and productive involvement of the population in the national and regional development process, priority must be given to strengthening human capital. Indeed, without a critical mass, there cannot be development based on local stakeholders/beneficiaries. To meet this priority, the education system as a whole must be addressed because in its current state the Comorian Government cannot take up the challenge of the social, democratic an economic integration of Comorian youth in the associative, professional and national political fabric. This is a particularly difficult challenge because past efforts have not always produced the hoped-for results.

In order to guarantee the training of human resources with a view to consolidation of the rule of law and the implementation of sustainable development policies for the benefit of the people, the aim for the focal sector is to develop a good quality education system by promoting its accessibility to the whole of the Comorian population. An examination of the determining factors of access to the education system and the evidence of an inverse relation between women's education and fertility, also advocate a strengthening of girls' education. In order to clear the bottlenecks that emerge at the end of the primary and secondary cycle, to ensure a linear performance of the Comorian education system and to provide the productive system with the skilled labour that the country needs for the sustainability of its economic development, Community cooperation will be based on a sectoral approach. The support programme for the education sector will focus on increasing school capacities, improving the quality of learning by strengthening national skills, the fight against gender disparities, community-based management, vocational guidance and informal education. This sectoral approach will complement the programmes of UNICEF, the World Bank and UNDP. The objectives defined in the focal sector are in line with the measures and guidelines laid down by the Government in the Master Plan 1997-2001, which came out of the 1994 General Assembly. These objectives are reiterated in the education recovery policy, for which the Council of Ministers adopted measures to improve the system's performance by means of an increase in capacities, school enrolment rates and the quality of the learning process.

With a view to updating the Master Plan, the Ministry of Education, Vocational training and Human rights set up an advisory national Council of education, an instrument for regulating and implementing national education policy, as well as a technical Committee. An activity timetable for the revision of the Master Plan and the preparation of the national Plan of Education for Ali has already been proposed to the various partners. To implement the plan, scheduled for the beginning of 2003, a cooperation and coordination structure composed of the various donors will be set up. This structure will carry out the necessary analyses of past experience, seek to tailor training to the practical needs of the country especially as regards vocational training, enhance human resources to encourage people who have been trained to stay (essential problem of the brain drain), create synergies between the training provided in the Indian Ocean region (creation of reference centres) and examine the means to allow education to become an intersectoral tool. The objectives of the education/training programme in terms of civic-mindedness, the creation of local capacities and professional integration will guide the choice of activities carried out. The implementation requires the effective participation of the national authorities and civil society for the success of this programme.

Non focal Sector: Decentralised Co-operation

In order to promote the decentralisation process - mainstreamed in the new constitution – a decentralised cooperation programme is envisaged aiming at the emergence of legitimate and effective local governance systems and support for local development initiatives and trends. Federal-type projects for the people of the Comoros archipelago could support different categories of initiatives defined, for example, according to territorial criteria (village-based initiatives, island-wide initiatives, inter-island initiatives) in order to:

- develop information and capacity-building activities for decentralised stakeholders,
- support structuring and environmental actions at inter-island and/or regional level.

Depending on the progress made in the rule of law, good governance and the adoption of transparent budgetary procedures, it will then be possible to envisage budgetary support that would consist of supporting the decentralisation of the Ministry of the Education and related reforms. According to the performance indicators for the implementation of the measures to improve the social services, administrative expenditure connected with the Master Plan for Education and wage arrears could receive budgetary support.

9th EDF Financial Data

	Allocation	% of overall A allocation
Focal sector: Education	20 M€	84%
Non focal sector: decentralised co-operation	4 M€	16%
Total	24 M€	100%

Main Development Projects funded under 6th, 7th and 8th EDF

- Development of food production and seed support
- Mutsamudu/Sima/Pomoni Road
- Promotion and development of small enterprises
- Sea access to Mohéli
- National Mutsamudusima – pomoni road repairs
- Waste management project
- Support to electoral processes in Comores
- Support to the national television

7.4 Djibouti

Relations with the EU: Djibouti continues to benefit from a special relationship with France, who maintains a large military presence (2,700 troops) and provides substantial, though declining, and foreign aid. France is also the only Member State being represented in Djibouti and the most important EU trading partner. The EC Delegation in Djibouti was transformed into an Office in 1996.

The 9th EDF and CSP were signed on 23 September, provides a total amount of 34,8 M€ (29 M€ A-Allocation and 5,8 M€ B-Allocation). The 29 M€ A-allocation will be used for water and sanitation a macroeconomic reform programme and to support for the implementation of the peace agreement. The B-Allocation will be used for additional support in the event of external crisis.

Since 1996 in the aftermath of the civil war, the EC has provided support to 3 IMF approved structural adjustment programmes amount to approx M€ 33. Most of these funds were allocated for the demobilisation of surplus army and police forces recruited at the time of the civil conflict, for support to the social sectors, for operational and investment expenditure; and for debt repayments to public and private firms and clearance of internal arrears.

Country Strategy: The Community cooperation response strategy is based on the general framework arising from the PRSP process. It aims to support the country in implementing its economic, structural and sectoral reforms connected with reducing poverty. It will also help to implement the peace agreement signed in May 2001. On the whole the strategy satisfies the EC's cooperation objectives, thus emphasising in particular the objective of reducing poverty in Djibouti.

In order to ensure maximum effectiveness and efficiency as regards support, the strategy identifies a single focal sector, Water and Sanitation, in which the EC has quite a comparative advantage based on its experience.

Because of the weakness of sectoral policies, there are limited possibilities for offering direct budget support, which is one of the objectives of the Cotonou Agreement. The only exception is the macroeconomic support provided for in the strategy, a domain in which the EC will continue to play an important, active role.

The response strategy does not focus only on the package of aid available under the 9th EDF. It seeks to establish an integrated approach that brings the country allocation into line with the other resources available from the EC, notably EIB funding, regional cooperation funds and aid provided under budget lines.

Particular attention will be paid to the following crosscutting issues in every action to be implemented: gender issues, the environment and capacity building which will form an integral part of every area of intervention in order to improve impact and sustainability.

Priorities for co-operation

Focal Areas

- Water and Sanitation (44% of 'A' Envelope)
- Macro-economic Support (46% of 'A" Envelope)

Non-focal Areas

- Support to the peace agreement (10% of the overall envelope)

Focal Areas

A. Water and Sanitation: Access to drinking water is an absolute priority for the population and, together with sanitation, has been recognised as a prime factor in reducing poverty. Both aspects were included as such in the PRSP. Given the dry climate and scarce natural resources, plus the fact that the exploitation and management systems are at their limit, it is obvious that drinking water supplies have become a vital concern in both urban and rural areas. The implications for the rural economy, dependent on stock farming and agriculture, are clear, however the indirect impact on urban commerce also needs reliable, quality systems.

Ensuring drinking water supplies is also a major constraint in terms of improving living conditions. In most cases, this is an especially long and tedious task, almost exclusively carried out by women and children. In addition, water-borne diseases and poor sanitary conditions due to the lack of hygiene seriously affect those in the country without access to sufficient drinking water. Women, who traditionally perform domestic tasks and must play a major role in preventing illness in the family, are therefore the main ones concerned by easier access to drinking water. The Commission has traditionally been involved in the water and sanitation sector in Djibouti. It has been active in this respect since the beginning of its relations with this country.

In the context of the overall objectives of increasing drinking water supplies, improving access to water at affordable prices and protecting the environment, the EC action aims more specifically to help renovate the urban water system in Djibouti city and the district capitals, renovate rural water supplies, support national sanitation plans and environmental protection projects and explore alternative drinking water resources, mindful of the government policy on diversifying energy sources (geothermal science and wind power).

Approximately €13 million has been earmarked for this sector. In addition there will be a contribution under the programme to rehabilitate/rebuild local infrastructure affected by the civil war, from the non-focal component "implementation of the peace agreement and decentralisation". This aims in particular to repair rural hydraulic systems. The EIB might perhaps provide funding to sectors once the arrears owed to it have been fully repaid.

B. Macroeconomic support: macro-economic and institutional support to implement the strategy to reduce poverty (44% of the global allocation):

The background to the EC support is a tough macroeconomic situation with low growth and a high budget deficit. The amount of previous arrears is a major hindrance to growth in GDP. Therefore the settlement of Government arrears and the placing of public finance on a sound footing are the main objectives of the reform programme concluded with the IMF. The objective of macroeconomic support under the 9th EDF is to underpin the implementation of the strategy to reduce poverty in Djibouti by means of budget and institutional support. The EC's specific objectives are to:

- bring the public finance situation under control by settling the State's internal arrears and possibly continuing with support for demobilisation if the evaluation of the previous programme identifies further needs;
- improve the quality, efficiency and transparency of public finance management;
- effectively implement policy in the basic health and education sectors.

The financial package granted should amount to approximately €12.8 million. Programming for this will last three years (2002-2004) to bring it into line with the timeframe of the PRSP and the support from the World Bank and the IMF. The programme will consist of three annual tranches, the amount of which will depend on performance.

Macroeconomic support under the 9th EDF might be applied as follows:

- Direct budget support (non-targeted) with indicators in the areas of basic health and education.
- Budget support geared to settling part of the State's internal arrears consisting of payments owed to private companies and public enterprises, and salaries owed to employed. These arrears will have to be audited beforehand. Only those that are approved will be covered.

- Short and long-term institutional support for statistics, the macro-economy, public finances, trade policy and the consolidation of the rule of law in the business sector, as well as for implementation of EDF actions. Training schemes in the relevant sectors.
- Support to finance demobilisation premiums for the army and police may be granted provided that the evaluation shows that there are additional needs in this respect.

Non-focal sector of Co-operation

Support for the peace agreement (9% of the overall envelope)

Rehabilitation and Reconstruction: The main objective of EC support is to consolidate peace in the country and hence to contribute to regional stability. The peace process is dependent on the creation of a framework for reconciliation, the involvement of the people in this and an upswing in economic growth. The Reform and Civil Peace Agreement recognises the imperative need to proceed rapidly with the restoration of social and economic infrastructure destroyed by the war. The rehabilitation and reconstruction programme already started some years ago will be continued. The EC will contribute to rehabilitation and reconstruction in the three districts affected, namely Obock, Tadjourah and Dikhil. The action to be financed by the EC will be evaluated beforehand. All aid will be coordinated with the other donors that are supporting the peace agreement. The actions to be financed are contained in the Framework Paper for the Rehabilitation and Compensation Programme (June 2001) and will focus essentially on water. More precisely, the aim is to build water supply systems and wells, as well as reservoirs and underground basins, and to rehabilitate water holding systems and water distribution equipment.

Decentralisation: A second objective is to help develop democracy at local level as well as good governance by supporting the establishment and operation of decentralised institutions on which democracy would be based. These new institutions would eventually allow greater participation by the population in managing local affairs and development operations. The strategy to be followed involves supporting the establishment and operation of local institutions, particularly the Regional Assemblies and their executive bodies, in the three districts. Possible activities include: helping to raise awareness of the need for the population to take part in the election of regional representatives and in the decentralisation process in general, supporting the establishment and capacities of the Regional Assemblies and their executive bodies.

9th EDF Financial Data

	Allocation (A envelope)	% of overall allocation
Focal area		
• Water and sanitation • Macro-economic reform programme	13.0 M€ 12.8 M€	46% 44%
Non focal area		
• Implementation of peace agreement	3.2 M€	10%
Total	**29 M€**	**100%**

Major Development Projects

Examples of ongoing projects funded by the EU (7th and 8th EDF)

- Roads project and the sewerage project "Quartier 4" of Djibouti-ville
- Restoring and maintaining pumping stations, sinking wells and building surface water stations.
- Programme for Urban Development
- Rural water and sewage projects

7.5 Ethiopia

Relations with the EU: The EU is Ethiopia's main trading partner in terms both of imports and exports. Around 38% of all Ethiopian imports originate in the EU, while around 45% of Ethiopian exports are destined for the EU. Exports are mainly made principally of coffee (70%), hides and skins and gold. Imports consist mainly of capital and consumer goods and petroleum.

There is very little European private sector investment in Ethiopia. The country is only slowly opening up to a market-oriented economy after years of a state-controlled economy under the previous Derg regime and there remain many constraints to private sector development, ideological and other. Foreign participation in the banking and insurance sector, in particular, is not permitted.

Ethiopia has for many years been the foremost beneficiary of EC development assistance amongst ACP States. More than € 2.3 billion has been allocated to the country since 1975, of which some 38% has been in the form of food aid. During the border conflict with Eritrea some EC assistance was temporarily suspended. However since the signing of the peace agreement, the EC, in common with most other bilateral and multilateral donors, has resumed full co-operation with Ethiopia. EC assistance to Ethiopia under the 6th, 7th and 8th EDF has focussed on roads, water, human resources development, food security, and democratisation and institution-building.

Ethiopia's 9th EDF Country Strategy Paper/National Indicative Programme was signed in Addis Ababa on 27th February 2002, and provides for an "A" allocation of € 384.2 m and a "B" allocation of € 153.7 m. The sectors of concentration foreseen are transport (rehabilitation and upgrading of the road network) (€ 211 m); food security (€ 54 m) and macro-economic support (€ 96 m). Capacity building for governance, civil society and conflict prevention are foreseen as non-focal sector activities (€ 23 m).

The **European Investment Bank** funded projects amounting to € 54.7 m under the 4th Lomé Convention. Such projects include telecommunications, airlines, support to the textile industry and a global loan for the private sector.

Ethiopia has also benefited significantly over the years from the NGO co-financing facility, EIDHR budget line and the food security budget line.

ECHO has been active in assisting internally displaced populations and victims of deportation in both Ethiopia and Eritrea since the outbreak of the conflict (€ 13.7 m). In addition, it has made a contribution of € 2 m to ICRC for the distribution of supplementary food rations in Southern Ethiopia. Since March 2000, ECHO has launched 4 emergency funding decisions and allocated or pledged a total of € 8,765,000 for emergency drought-response programmes in Ethiopia. A € 4 m programme for the victims of the 2002/03 drought was approved in November 2002.

Priorities for Co-operation

Focal Sectors:

- Transport
- macro-economic support and capacity building for economic reform
- food security

Non-focal Sectors:

- capacity building for governance and civil society

Focal Sectors

Transport: The upgrading and expansion of Ethiopia's road network remains a top priority for the Ethiopian Government and has a noticeable, though longer-term, effect on poverty alleviation. Improved accessibility of rural areas, including the main agricultural production centres, constitutes a significant element in the fight against poverty and food insecurity. Furthermore, the opening up of isolated pockets will allow for the gradual economic, social and political integration of thus far excluded segments of the population. The success of central components of the country's development agenda depends on an improved infrastructure. This holds true for the development of functioning markets, the utilisation of social services as well as the rapid and cost effective provision of humanitarian aid if required.

The major interventions foreseen are:

- the rehabilitation of two existing, but degraded, roads, that are part of RSDP's 2nd phase (Harrar-Jijiga, 102 km and Mieso-Dire Dawa, 155 km),
- the provision of training, technical assistance and surveys destined to strengthen ERA's capacity in managing the RSDP,
- support for the implementation of some transport policies, studies of which have previously been funded by EC (e.g. road safety, axle load, transport regulation).

  The government is expected to make an important effort to improve the maintenance of existing roads, primarily by reducing the backlog of periodic maintenance and by increasing the involvement of private contractors in carrying out maintenance works.

Macro-economic support and capacity building for economic reform: During the 1990's Ethiopia has received considerable amounts of macro-economic support in the framework of consecutive Stabex and Structural Adjustment Support programmes. In this manner the EC has significantly contributed to macro-economic stabilisation in Ethiopia. Through capacity building projects the EC has also supported the economic reform effort in several areas.

The EC will remain an important provider of macro-economic support and will become a financial contributor to the implementation of the PRSP (Poverty Reduction Strategy Paper).

7.6 Kenya

Relations with the EU: The EC is one of Kenya's largest cooperation partners. Annual EC aid finances over 10% of GoK's development budget. EC assistance, under the 6th, 7th and 8th EDFs has totalled €920 million, covering programmable (€412 m) and non-programmable aid (€508 m). The latter comprises STABEX, EIB loans, structural adjustment and emergency aid. In addition, Kenya has received support under EDF Regional Programmes and from the Community Budget, mainly NGO programmes and food aid.

After the 27 December 2002 general election the GoK and the Commission decided to review the existing CSP proposal (for the 9th EDF) in order to take into consideration the political and economic changes. The new CSP/NIP should be approved in June/July and enter into force immediately afterwards.

In trade related areas, the EU is a very important partner for Kenya (31% of imports, 35% of exports). Kenya is a leading player in the EU-ACP discussions on trade in the framework of the Cotonou Agreement. In line with WTO guidelines, the end of non-reciprocal trade preferences in 2008 will need specific EPA negotiations. Despite this important issue, the real challenge for Kenya is more likely to be non-tariff barriers such as standards, regulations, SPS, etc.

Kenya is also the most important "client" of the EIB in sub-Saharan Africa. At present the bank has a portfolio of some 216 M€ in the country of which 62% come from the Banks' own resources. The balance provides from EDF (82.9 M€) in the form of risk capital.

EDF Financial Data

All EDF

	6th EDF	7th EDF	8th EDF
Allocation Million €	135 M€	141 M€	136 M€
Focal Sectors	Agriculture and Food security	Rural Development, Natural Resource Conservation, Social Infrastructure	Productive Sector Strengthening, Public Sector Reform/Capacity Building and Governance, Poverty Reduction and Social Support, Private sector / Tourism/Trade

* The amounts shown above accounts solely for EDF (European Development Fund) allocations – programmable aid. A further €508 in non programmable assistance has been provided since the beginning of Lome IV via mechanisms such as STABEX, EIB loans, structural adjustment, emergency aid and community budget lines .

Main Development Projects funded under 6th, 7th and 8th EDF

- Northern Corridor Rehabilitation Programme -linking the port of Mombasa with the landlocked countries of the Great Lakes Region (Uganda, Rwanda, Burundi, Eastern Congo):

✓ "Mai-Mahiu-Naivasha-Lanet Road" (96km)

✓ "Sultan Hamud-Mtito Andei" (132km)

- District Health Services and System Development programme
- Kenya Family Health Programme
- AIDS/STD Control Programme
- Community Development Programme
- Tourism Diversification and Sustainable Development Programme
- Establishing a Sustainable Tourism Development Base in Kenya
- Bio-diversity Conservation Programme
- Farming in Tsetse control areas (FITCA)
- Cereal sector reform programme
- Support to KIPPRA
- PRBS1 (Public sector reform Programme)
- Democratic Governance
- Capacity Building /Support Services Programme
- Technical Education Support Programme
- Micro-Enterprise Support Programme
- Trade Development Programme
- Revival of the Swahili Culture
- National Museums of Kenya Support Programme (NMKSP)

7.7 Madagascar

Relations with the EU: The EU as a whole, and France in particular, is Madagascar's most significant trade partner. In 2001, 69% (607M€) of Malagasy exports went to the EU mainly fisheries products (prawns), garments, coffee, and vanilla, and 44% (431M€) of the country's imports came from the EU (mainly intermediate manufactures and capital goods).

In 1999, the EU became Madagascar's most important donor, followed by the World Bank. Virtually all of the instruments of EU-ACP co-operation have been employed in Madagascar.

The main areas of concentration under the 6th (€ 125 m), 7th(€ 133.2 m) and 8th (€ 188.5 m) EDFs were transport infrastructure, support to social sectors (health, education), rural development. The 9th EDF Strategy Paper and Indicative

Programme for Madagascar was signed on 19 July 2002. It involves a total amount of € 327m (allocation A: € 267m and allocation B: € 60m). Main sectors of intervention are: Transport (€ 135m); Rural Development and food security (€ 60m); Macro-economic support (€ 60m) and Good Governance (€ 12m).

- Madagascar also benefits from the **Regional Indicative Programme** for the Indian Ocean, which includes the regional EDF-funded PRIDE (Programme Régional Intégré de Développement des Echanges) project, an environmental programme and a programme for the University of the Indian Ocean.
- A € 70m "Programme d'appui budgetaire d'urgence" was approved by the Commission in December 2002 in order contribute to the budget deficit and to support the recovery of the country. A first instalment of € 35m has already been disbursed.
- As a **Stabex** beneficiary, Madagascar was allocated some € 48 under Lomé IV and IV bis for loss of export revenues, notably for coffee, vanilla and cloves. For the years 1997-98-99 a new Stabex commitment of € 19 m was granted.
- A **Structural Adjustment Support Programme** of € 56.8 m (NIP funds € 20 m, Structural Adjustment Facility + ITF € 36.8m) aiming at improving health and education services, was signed between Madagascar and the EC in October 1999. This programme was audited in June 2000 and has been disbursed. It included an instalment depending on the evolution of a series of indicators, mainly social ones, which was considered positive.
- The country is a member of the **Beef and Sugar Protocols** annexed to the ACP-EC Convention (but under Community embargo since 1997 for health reasons).
- **EIB**: Between 1979-1998 the Bank allocated some € 113.3m in EIB risk capital, for the benefit of various sectors (aquaculture, small and medium-sized enterprises, etc). Food Security Programme: Since 1996, Madagascar has been one of the Community's "test" countries of the budget line for the

implementation of its new food security policy. In this context, the country has benefited from a total amount of € 58.5 m of financing, including food aid.

- **ECHO**: Since 1994, Madagascar has received ECHO financial assistance 13 times. In 2000 the Commission approved a sum of € 1.5 m to help the country after the disaster due to cyclone Eline and the tropical hurricane Gloria (February and March 2000). A further € 0.9 m was later approved for work carried out through MSF-F, GAA and CARE-F. A sum of € 1-m is foreseen to address the consequences of the locust plaque.
- **Electoral observation and assistance**: An EU observation Mission was deployed from November 2002 to January 2003 to observe legislative elections held on December 15. An assistance programme to the electoral process was also provided.

Fisheries Agreement: A Fisheries Agreement (in respect of tuna) was signed on in March 2001, covering the period 2001-2004. The Agreement allows 80 European boats to fish in Malagasy waters in return for financial compensation of € 2,475,000. In addition, amounts are made available for scientific programmes (€ 240,000); vessel monitoring (€ 801,000); study grants and training courses for sailors (€ 300,000) and assistance to traditional fishing (€ 210,000).

Country Strategy: The strategy of co-operation between the Republic of Madagascar and the European Commission for the next partnership takes account of all of the following considerations :

- it is founded on the objectives of co-operation of the union, notably the fight against poverty;
- it conforms to the political agenda of the Government, who have made the reduction of poverty their a principle objective;
- it complements the strategies of other donors ;
- it focuses on a small number of sectors chosen a) because of their impact on the reduction of poverty for the selected

populations and b) from the 6 areas in which the European Commission has a comparative advantage.

Priorities for Co-operation

Focal Areas

- Transport (50% of 'A' Envelope)
- Rural development and food security (22% of 'A' Envelope)
- Macro-economic support (22% of 'A' Envelope)

Non-focal Areas

- Governance (12% of 'A' Envelope)

Focal Areas

A. Transport

The following objective will be pursued :

- To assure a high level of human and economic accessibility and to improve the performance of the roads sector. From the indicative programme around 135m has been reserved for this sector. The main activities foreseen are as follows:
- Rehabilitation of sections of the RN6 (North) ;
- Improved accessibility to two provinces in the South.

The principal measures, in terms of sectoral policy, taken by the Government as a contribution to the response strategy in this sector are:

- Pursuit and achievement of institutional reforms foreseen in the sectoral policy for transport;
- Stabilisation of other factors that influence the costs of transport (principally fuel);
- Consolidation of the Roads Fund.

B. Rural Development and Food Security

The objective is as follows:

- To improve, in a manner that is sustainable, the supply and demand of food and exported agricultural products, in particular in the provinces of Fianarantsoa and Tuléar. From the indicative envelope, around 60m will be reserved for this sector. The main activity foreseen is:
- Support to the "Action Plan for Rural Development" (PADR) in the South.

- The principal measures, in terms of sectoral policy, taken by the Government as a contribution to the response strategy in this sector are:
- Maintaining or improving the system of relative prices ;
- Facilitating access to land for producers ;
- Promoting ownership PADR process among a significant number of rural producers ;
- Ensuring effective decentralisation and deconcentration of autonomous provinces(skills, human resources, finances);µ
- establishing a national funds for repairing damage resulting from natural catastrophes

9th EDF Financial Data

	Allocation (A envelope)	% of overall allocation
Focal area		
Transport Rural development and food security Macro-economic support	135 M€ 60 M€ 60 M€	50% 22% 22%
Non focal area		
Good governance	12 M€	6%
Total	**267 M€**	**100%**

The amount shown above accounts solely for EDF (European Development Fund) allocations – programmable aid.

C. Macroeconomic Support

Macro-economic support will be provided in the framework set out by the PRSP and the PPTE initiative. Around 60m has been reserved for macro-economic support.

Non-focal sector of Co-operation

Good Governance

Consolidating the state of law and judicial reform are central to the poverty reduction strategy. Around € 12m has been reserved for this sector.

Examples projects co-funded by the EC

- Support programmes for structural adjustment
- Rehabilitation of the RN6 between port Bergé and Ambanja
- Rural micro-finance projects
- Development of cattle breeding in the South West
- The Bemaraha Programme
- Support to PADR and to Rural Initiatives
- Support to Rural Development education

7.8 Malawi

Relations with the EU: The EU maintains a generally good and close relationship with Malawi. In 2002, total EU imports from Malawi amounted to € 176.8 million as against € 195.0 million in 2001. In 2002, tobacco was the predominant export article to the EU (66.1%), followed by tea (14.5 %), sugar (14.4%), and coffee (1.9 %). Malawi is partner to the Sugar Protocol with the EU and has an agreed quantity in each 12 months period of 20,000 metric tons of white sugar. Malawi can also benefit from the recent "Everything but Arms" initiative of the European Union, which eliminates all EU tariff and quota barriers to trade with Least Developed Countries. Similarly, Malawi can benefit from the new EU-ACP trading arrangements, as foreseen in the Cotonou Agreement, by participating in an EPA.

There is an established framework for donor community and lending agency co-ordination with regular meetings chaired by selected missions taking the lead role in each of the key sectors (Education: Denmark/Ministry of Education; Health: UK;

Agriculture: UK (and EC); Transport: EC; Economy WB). The EU (Commission and MS) is the major donor in Malawi with € 267.0 million foreseen for 2003.

Several donors provide budgetary support. Five donors (Denmark, Sweden, UK, Norway and EC) are now co-ordinating their macro-financial support and the Common Approach to Budgetary Support group (CABS) was created. The discussions of the CABS group with the Government were deepened throughout 2002, and are welcomed by both sides. Not only through their regular reviews, but also through agreement on their own matrix of measures, the CABS group has tried to nudge Government towards a more transparent and pro-poor implementation of the budget. Although results were mixed, it is encouraging to see that the GoM is taking the concerns of the CABS group, and of the stakeholders in the PRSP, into account. The European Commission and the CABS group continue to link their disbursements closely to progress in the implementation of the PRSP and to the achievement of its indicators.

Malawi has been a partner of the European Union since 1976. As a landlocked LDC, Malawi has received quite significant EDF contributions €1,051 Million since 1976. Both the 7th and 8th EDFs are largely committed and projects financed from them are under execution.

The main sectors of concentration under the 8th EDF are transport infrastructure, health and conservation of natural resources, including agriculture. Since the early 1990s Malawi has also received substantial assistance from the Structural adjustment facility (119.4 M€). Beyond EDF support, significant allocations are also being made through the EC food security budget line (± 189 M€ from 1991-2001). Outside the focal areas, activities ranging from construction of buildings for customs & excise to training of journalists have been undertaken. Assistance to the democratisation process has been provided through the Rule of Law project in order to provide for a better access to justice and to the National Initiative for Civic Education (NICE) for voter education activities in the 1999 presidential and parliamentary elections and civic education thereafter. Support to the business private sector has being channelled through the Malawi Confederation of Chambers of Commerce and Industry (MCCCI) and income generating activities and modest credit facilities for women through intermediaries such as National Association of Businesswomen (NABW).

All three micro projects programmes have supported poverty reduction through the provision of small infrastructures mainly in the education, health and transport sectors. With an overhead averaging only 10%, the programmes have been very efficient. Stabilisation of export earnings (STABEX) funds have been utilised in providing assistance to the Tea Research Foundation, providing tea and coffee clonal plants to smallholder farmers, rehabilitating district feeder roads and support to smallholder tea and coffee growers through a small venture capital fund. The Country Strategy Paper and National Indicative Programme for the period 2002-2007, signed by the Government of Malawi and the Commission in August 2002, guides the development cooperation between Malawi and the EC. The CSP identified the main problems facing the country and it was agreed that future EC co-operation efforts in reducing poverty reduction should be focused on two sectors – agriculture/food security/natural resources and transport and infrastructure. Macro-economic support is also to be provided, which will focus on health and education.

Country Strategy: The choice of focal sectors is a direct and logical result of comparing:

- The objectives and strategy of Malawi's own national development policy agenda
- EU development priorities
- Relative strength of past and ongoing EC interventions in Malawi in the various sectors
- Complementarities to EU Member States interventions and the search for lead donors.

After consultation with government, representatives of the private and NGO sectors, civic society and other donor and lending partners, the National Authorising Officer (NAO) and Delegation have concluded that co-operation efforts should be concentrated on poverty reduction efforts through interventions in the following two focal sectors:

- Agriculture & Natural resources
- Transport Infrastructure, focussing on road maintenance

The EC together with Member States is conducting a sector policy dialogue on agriculture and natural resources with the Malawi government. In the future it is envisaged that these discussions will take place in the context of MASIP. Institutional capacity at all levels inputs and marketing as well as land policy issues will form part of this dialogue. Furthermore dialogue for the sector. Policy dialogue in the transport sector has been going on already for a number of years and has e.g. resulted in the establishment of the National Roads Authority and the commercialisation of the road transport sector. This policy dialogue will continue and will be especially focussed on policy implementation. As far as road maintenance is concerned this will entail specific attention to the periodic adjustment of the fuel levy in relation to the maintenance targets

Institutional strengthening will be an essential and crosscutting element of the EC response strategy.

Moreover, macroeconomic support aiming at sustaining the flow of resources needed by Malawi to improve its macroeconomic stability and implement the priority policies chosen is foreseen. In the non-focal areas, continued assistance will be directed to the micro-projects programme, to civic education in support to the democratisation process and support to non-state actors, in particular for capacity building.

Priorities for Co-operation

Under the EDF 9, Envelope A of € 276.0 million, which is to cover long term development operations the indicative allocation is as follows:

- agriculture and natural resources 60 million;
- transport and infrastructure 90 million;
- macro-economic support 70 million and

- other programmes (micro-projects and governance/Non-State Actors) 56 million.

The envelope B of € 69.0 million will cover unforeseen needs as indicated in the Cotonou Agreement, Annex IV, Article 3.2 (b).

Focal Areas

A. Agriculture and Natural Resources: In line with the Malawi government's own analysis that development of the agricultural sector can only go hand in hand with a supportive macro-economic environment as well as social development through investment in human capital, no single option in itself is considered sufficient to meet the national goals in the long run. The removal of structural constraints that impede development is therefore the main objective of the proposed EU intervention in agriculture/natural resources. 85% of Malawi's population is living in rural areas where most poverty is concentrated. Increased household income and improved food security in rural areas can only be achieved through:

1. support for the creation of an institutional enabling environment for improving the livelihoods of the rural poor.
2. support for improving and diversifying income earning opportunities in rural areas;
3. improvement of economic and environmental sustainable management of natural resources in intervention areas;
4. provide support to safety net interventions.

Area 1 will to a large extend be covered by various donors and is intended to be channelled through MASIP. Area 4 will largely be co-ordinated by the UK (DFID) with contributions from the EC and, in the future, possibly other donors. The EC will therefore concentrate on areas 2 and 3 as well as complementing area 1. For the realisation of this complex and broad scheme of interventions, permanent co-ordination will be held with the other major donors involved in the sector, especially DFID, DANIDA and GTZ. In particular in line with the objectives of the interim PRSP, general EC co-operation objectives in agriculture and natural resources are: to improve national food security and household food self-sufficiency; increase and diversify rural incomes; managing natural resources in a sustainable manner, specifically geared to environmental measures like soil conservation and halting/reversing land degradation. The EC will furthermore assist with the maintenance of rural feeder roads and the provision of safety nets for the poor. The development of a SWAP will be supported while assistance to this sector will be provided through classical programmes and, if and when appropriate, through budget support. Cross-cutting issues, notably environment, growth and institutional capacity are crucial to this sector and will be central to the preparation and implementation. Specific objectives taking into account past experiences will be worked out in connection with future appraisals and in line with the on-going PRSP exercise.

B. Transport and Infrastructure: Transport services are crucial for poverty alleviation and economic development. Access is a prerequisite for poverty alleviation. At present, many rural areas are cut off from the outside world during the rainy seasons, hampering economic development by lack of infrastructure and non-availability of public transport. Access is crucial to delivery of social services and to support economic growth, e.g. markets and reliable delivery of inputs. Lack of transport infrastructure results in price increases in imported items and decreases the competitiveness of Malawi exports. The effects of the above are felt more by those who entirely rely on small-scale agriculture and who are living below the poverty line, as they already are highly vulnerable. Road transport is the only mode of transport that reaches the most remote areas of the country (with the exception of some areas along the coast of Lake Malawi) and that serves the widest variety of users. Maintenance of roads is a major contributor to the provision and affordability of transport services. The European Community has, for a long time, been the single major donor in road transport development in the country, and has been instrumental in the setting up of the National Roads Authority. A continued Community presence in this sector as a leading donor will be essential to implement the National Transport Policy and to consolidate past achievements as few other donors are or will be active in the sector (notably the Word Bank and Denmark) providing only limited financial support. In the transport infrastructure sector, the EC's objectives are to: maintain and upgrade the road network through the NRA; upgrade and maintain the rural feeder road network through a high labour intensity Public Works programme, and improve the infrastructure providing links between Malawi's internal, regional and global markets. Support to the NRA and the Road Fund will continue while assistance will also be provided for the establishment and operation of Roads Authorities at district level.

Furthermore institutional support to key institutions operating in the transport (MoTPW, NRA and NCIC) will become a pivotal element of EC support to the sector. It is anticipated that the EC financial support will allow for a reduction by 30 % of the backlog maintenance/rehabilitation requirements over a 5-year period. This has to be seen in the light of the government's overall objective of achieving self-sufficiency/auto financing of all maintenance requirements within the next 10 years. Support to the revitalisation of transport routes likely to lower the international freight costs will be considered. Studies have shown that an efficiently operated Nacala corridor, following its full rehabilitation could result in a 50 % reduction of transport costs to Malawi. The possible EC contribution to the rehabilitation of the corridor aims at supporting the government of Malawi's intentions of achieving this objective.

Both in the implementation of programmes and in institutional support, due attention will be given to HIV/Aids in the form of implementation of awareness campaigns. This concerns not only backlog maintenance and rehabilitation but also rural roads.

C. Macro-economic Support: Malawi has ventured out on the development of sector programmes and thus of budget support versus the classical types of projects. Sector Investment Programmes (SIP's) and Sector Wide Approach Programmes (SWAP's) have been or are being developed for sectors like transport infrastructure, health and education. The EC is already providing budget support under the Food Security and Structural Adjustment Programmes, targeting recurrent account expenditures in health, education, (local) debt repayments and road maintenance. In line with EU development policy objectives, this support is to continue while at the same time supporting a sound macro-economic framework. Institutional weaknesses in the public sector are seriously hampering implementation of government policies. It is therefore only consequent that institutional strengthening and capacity building in each of the focal sectors will be provided for.

9th Financial Data

Focal area	Allocation (A envelope) (€ million)	% of overall allocation
Agriculture and natural resources	**60.0**	**22**
Transport infrastructure	**90.0**	**33**
Macro-economic support	**70.0**	**25**
Non-Focal area		
Governance Governance Micro-projects	**56.0**	**20**

Macro-economic support will be provided in the context of the CABS framework and in line with the overall agreements concluded with the Bretton Woods institutions and with due regard to the PRSP process. The establishment and application of Medium Term Expenditure Frameworks (MTEF) will be encouraged and supported as will the Public Expenditure Reviews (PER) of the various sectors. Macroeconomic support will be focused towards the fulfilment of the financial requirements needed to implement the government's poverty reduction strategy. Ideally it will take the form of direct un-targeted budgetary support. However, depending on the prevailing conditions at time of implementation, the support may also focus on social sectors in the context of a sectoral programme. A pre-requisite for such programme(s) will be an acceptable financial management structure. A set of agreed performance indicators will constitute a key element in designing the budgetary support.

D. Non-Focal Sectors: It is envisaged to reduce the plethora of small, time-consuming interventions in the non-focal areas and to concentrate on other areas where can be built upon past successes: micro projects, good governance and civic education in support of democracy and human rights.

Major Development Projects

Examples of major ongoing projects funded by the EU (7th and 8th EDF) are:

- promotion of soil conservation and rural production (proscarp)
- capacity building for economic management and policy co-ordination
- road management support programme
- limbe – muloza- thyolo road
- urgent repair to roads and bridges
- road management support programme
- golomoti – monkey bay road
- lakeshore road infrastructure programme
- national initiative for civic education
- rule of law programme
- support to health reform and decentralisation
- support to the health reform and decentralisation supplementary funding for chiradzulu district hospital

- malawi blood transfusion service
- physical assets management project
- structural adjustment facility (saf) iv
- automated system custom data (asycuda) phase ii
- government of malawi / European union public works programme
- food security programme (budget line: food security)

7.9 Mauritius

Relations with the EU: Mauritius' main trading partners are the U.K. and France, which together account for 53% of its exports (sugar and textiles). The EU as a whole absorbs 67% of Mauritius' exports, and 27% of its imports originate in the EU. EU Member States also account for 53% of tourist arrivals, with an-other 15% coming from the French DOM Réunion.

Mauritius derives great benefit (+ € 150 m annually) from the ACP-EU Sugar Protocol and the Special Preferential Sugar Agreement.

Aside from the EDF allocations (outlined below) other, non-programmable aid: European Investment Bank (€ 114 m since Lomé III).

Fisheries Agreement: € 1.24 m (1999 – 2002). The 2001 Joint Annual Review was held in Port Louis in October 2002.

Country Strategy: European Community development policy is part of an international strategy adopted by the Development Assistance Committee of the OECD, in which the Community takes part. The guiding principles behind these initiatives are ownership by the developing countries of their own development process and increased attention to the social dimension of growth and development. Emphasis is given to poverty reduction, with a view to its eventual eradication. Attention will consistently be given to human rights, to the environmental dimension, to equality between men and women and to good governance.

The OECD International Development Goals are now accepted by all donors as the targets to aim for in the coming 20 years. Other initiatives go in the same direction as the EU's Development Policy: the World Bank Comprehensive Development Framework, or the IMF/World Bank Poverty Reduction Strategy Papers.

In accordance with the provisions of the new ACP-EU Partnership Agreement, signed in Cotonou on the 23rd June 2000, Mauritius and the EU accept the key role of political dialogue as a means of addressing all issues of mutual concern and of ensuring consistency and increased impact of development cooperation. In this respect, the integration of the private sector and of civil society has been duly encouraged and consultations with them have been effected during the drawing up of the CSS, the 9th EDF work-programme and the EU response strategy for Mauritius.

Priorities for co-operation

Focal Sectors:

- Environment (85% of overall A allocation)
- Decentralised Co-operation Programme (15% of overall A allocation)

The effect of Mauritius' impressive economic growth over the past two decades has been to greatly raise the standard of living of the majority of its population. This has been achieved largely through its own initiative and through the perspicaciousness of successive governments in seeing, and capitalising on the various opportunities for growth that arose.

A major challenge now facing Mauritius is to sustain what has been achieved, in the face of certain threats posed by economic development and demographic growth. One of the major threats is pressure on the environment, which – if not properly managed – will have a negative impact on both the standards of living already achieved, particularly in terms of health, and on important economic sectors such as tourism. Another challenge is to enable those who have missed out on the benefits of the general improvement in living standards to benefit from them, by providing them with the means by which to improve their human condition and future prospects.

After due consideration, it was concluded that the environment sector – and specially the waste water sub-sector – was the area to which the bulk of the EC's support could most usefully be directed, with some 15% of funds going to actions directly aimed at poverty alleviation.

As Mauritius's biggest donor, its grant resources (€ 33m for the 9th EDF) are capable of making an impact in the sector to which they are allocated. In the case of the chosen focal sector, the provision of grant funds for high-cost social infrastructure will allow GoM to undertake necessary investment which might otherwise have been unaffordable, or which would have placed additional strain on the national budget. The conditionalities laid down by donors and lenders in previous projects – such as the requirement to strengthen the capacity of the Waste Water Management Authority and to increase its financial autonomy – have enhanced the sustainability of all investments in the sector.

Focal areas:

A. Environment – Waste Water Sector (85% of 'A' Envelope): Given the EC's experience of working in the environmental sector under the 8th EDF and the high priority assigned to the environment by both the Government of Mauritius and the EU in their development policies, the environment – in the sense of environment to serve human needs – is what has been proposed as the sole focal sector for Mauritius' 9th EDF programme. The waste water sector, in particular, needs considerable investment – as outlined in the 1994 National Sewerage Plan. The presence of a number of donors and lenders in the sector has meant both that there is a high level of donor co-ordination on projects and that conditionalities are respected. Considerable attention has been paid, for example, to upgrading the capacity and ensuring the sustainability – through the imposition of affordable tariffs – of the sector's utility, the Waste Water Authority. Given that the absence of adequate waste water disposal systems for the majority of the population is socially unacceptable, as well as a threat to public health, to the natural environment and to the sustainability of one of Mauritius' most important areas of economic growth (tourism), it was proposed to allocate some 85% (€ 28m) of the 9th EDF programmable aid to the waste water sector in particular.

The actual investments in the environment for which EU funding is envisaged – which in principle include the West Coast Sewerage Project and components of the Plaines Wilhems project – have obvious merits in terms of social well-being, social equity, health, environmental protection and economic development. Inadequate waste water disposal systems are both a danger to public health and a manifestation of social inequality. They contribute to environmental degradation and can put at risk economic development (tourism and fisheries in particular). Both projects are in areas of high and growing population density levels and both include low-cost housing estates with low-income inhabitants. The provision of grant funds to the sector will make it possible for the waste water tariffs levied in order to guarantee sustainability of the investments to be set at more affordable levels. The specific objectives of the Community response are the improvement of living standards for the populations affected and the preservation of the natural resource base of the country, the general objective being that of sustainable and stable development.

B. Decentralised Co-operation Programme (15% of 'A' Envelope): It is foreseen that some 15% (€ 5m) of the 9th EDF "A" envelope be devoted to a demand-driven decentralised co-operation programme. In conformity with the provisions of the Cotonou Agreement and EC Development Policy, requests for such projects should meet with the general objective of poverty alleviation. Priority will be given to projects benefiting the most deprived areas of Mauritius, Rodrigues in particular, and the poorest segments of the population. Poverty alleviation is a high priority in both EC and Mauritian development policy, and participative programmes aimed specifically at poverty alleviation have been successfully undertaken under previous NIPs.

9th EDF Financial Data

Focal areas	Allocation	% of overall A allocation
Environment	28	85%
Decentralised co-operation programme	5	15%
Total	33	100%

The amounts shown above, account solely for EDF (European Development Fund) allocations – programmable aid.

7.10 Namibia

Relations with the EU: Politically, EU relations with Namibia can be generally considered as good.

The EC and EU Member States are, by far, Namibia's most important co-operation partners, with total planned aid disbursements for 2003 of more than € 70 m (of which € 20 m from the EC).

Under the European Development Funds (EDF) 7, 8 and 9, total aid resources made available to Namibia amounted to € 193 m.

Namibia also benefited and will most likely continue to benefit substantially from a number of other main co-operation instruments (e.g. SYSMIN, EIB managed resources, EC Budget Lines, Beef Protocol).

The new (9th EDF) Country Strategy Paper and National Indicative Programme was signed on 7th June 2002, with a global allocation of € 91 m from the 9th EDF. Preparations to commit these funds are well under way. EC's primary focus under the 9th EDF shall be Rural Development (including land reform) and Human Resources Development. (EC support of € 21 m to the

"Namibia Education Sector Programme" [2003-2007] was already approved in July 2003).

Country Strategy: The strategy for co-operation has been jointly defined on the basis of the following criteria:

- Response to the medium term challenges
- Clear complementarity with other donors and with EU Member States in particular
- Relevance to poverty reduction and employment creation
- Convergence with key priorities under NDP2
- Existence of a structured sector policy dialogue and sufficient capacity within the relevant line
- Ministries
- Lessons derived from past experience as reflected in mid-term reviews and evaluations
- Potential spill-over of support to the regional level in particular in the context of the EPA.
- EC and NAO capacity to manage and monitor programmes.
- Potential capacity of NSAs to participate in the areas of cooperation.

Taking into account these aspects, the fundamental priority of EU-Namibia co-operation will be support to rural development. The rural development clearly extends well beyond agriculture and takes into account relevant economic and social sectors which have a bearing on rural areas. Directly linked to this approach, the Community's second focal area will be sustaining Human Resources Development.

HIV-AIDS will be addressed through both focal sectors as the main cross cutting issue. These sectors of support have also been identified in the Country Strategy Evaluation (CSE) as areas in which EC assistance has performed better and where there is a strong case for continued support. Together with interested EU Member States, the EC and GRN have launched two ongoing studies for a Rural Development Strategic Framework (RDSF) and for a SWAP (Sector Wide Approach) in education and training.

Crosscutting and complementary issues to the focal sectors are related to trade and regional integration and the enhancement of institutional capacities of GRN. 9th EDF resources for the 2001-7 horizon are in line with 7th and 8th EDF support, though there has been an attempt to enhance the focus of EC aid by limiting core support to two sectors and limited support to complementary issues.

Priorities for Co-operation

Rural Development Strategy

In order to contribute to poverty reduction, the EC's primary focus under the 9th EDF shall be rural development. The key considerations for this choice are that:

- Poverty in Namibia is primarily a rural phenomenon with 85% of consumption-poor households located in rural areas.
- Decentralisation and land reform are central challenges for rural development and Government requires donor assistance to implement the necessary reforms.
- Previous successful EC support has been focused on the rural areas and there are opportunities to extend and build on this support. Since Namibia 's independence the EC has been the largest donor providing support to the Ministry of Agriculture, Water and Rural Development and in the context of the rural development strategic framework is the lead donor in the policy dialogue.
- The Namibia-EC Rural Development Strategic Framework focuses on rural livelihoods and while the development of agriculture is emphasised, the wider range of rural income opportunities will be addressed, streamlining the national policies of NDP2 and catalysing donor support in an integrated framework. This includes supporting economic diversification, new income generating capacities and SME development.
- There is complementarity with the priorities of the NPRAP for the development and diversification of the agricultural sector towards other areas. It takes into account of the need to

treat the land issue in the context of the wider rural development constraints.

- The rural development response strategy will be complementary to the activities identified by other donors including support to the land issue. The EC will associate relevant donors in the design of its support programme and its implementation.

The key requirements to foster rural livelihoods include improvement of productive and rural social services, economic diversification of poor rural households, the land issue and support to the decentralisation process in rural areas.

Land will be a central issue to social-economic development because of the rural base of the majority of households. The issue will be addressed as a critical determinant for the ability of the poor to accumulate assets, sustainable resource use, land agricultural productivity, financing of local government and the development of financial markets.

Non-state actors such as the private sector, trade unions, NGOs and CBOs may provide value added in the rural development focal sector, especially where governmental structures are not represented or only weakly present.

It will be essential to mitigate the impact of HIV/AIDS on rural livelihoods since death and migration will reduce the total population in rural areas. The knock-on effects in terms of a reduced labour force, increased household expenditure on health and a consequent higher dependency ratio will have to be taken into account.

Human Resource Development Response Strategy

The choice of support to Human Resources Development is based on the following considerations: Since the Transitional National Development Plan and in subsequent development plans (NDP 1 and 2) education has been stressed as central to Namibia 's economic development. Poverty reduction, employability, the strengthening of the democratic process and greater equity in income distribution remain a major rationale for investment in education.

- The movement towards a Sector Wide Approach is motivated by the conviction that it would provide greater and more sustainable benefits. The SWAP should support the development of services, which are responsive to the need of the poor.
- This sector offers the best opportunities for sector support. A strategic plan 2001-2006 is in place for basic education and a MTEF has been established during 2001. The EC can benefit from lessons learnt from the ongoing sector programme of Sida , UK and the Netherlands .
- The EC is the main donor working with both Ministries of education and is playing a key role in emphasising the need to move towards a SWAP. With GRN and other interested donors (Sida, DFID, Netherlands) the EC is launching a study which should provide an overall framework for donors to jointly support the sector. The leverage of EC aid could catalyse support from other EU donors who were planning to phase out.
- The EC is the lead donor regarding the Ministry of Higher Education, Employment Creation and Technology and one of the main donors with regard to basic education. The expected withdrawal of three significant donors from basic education (the Netherlands , the United Kingdom and USAID) increases the relative importance of EC sector assistance and reinforces the justification for continued assistance. EC and Sida shall be the lead donors in the SWAP.
- The Ministry's Basic Education's Strategic Planning Advisory Group (SPAG) where the key donors and relevant Ministries ensure sector co-ordination is the most effective Government led co-ordination process in Namibia .
- There has been positive experience with previous EC assistance in education and training as evidenced by the 2001 Mid-term review of the ongoing programme. The challenge will be to move from a 'project approach' to a SWAP.

The SWAP will consider the entire sector (pre-primary, primary/basic, secondary, tertiary, technical and vocational training) and its necessary interaction with the private sector. It should take into account the issues of accessibility (access, enrolment and equality of opportunity, especially gender issues), effectiveness (quality plus relevance), efficiency (results in relation to inputs), financial and institutional sustainability. The Community will support priorities within an overall sector framework as set out in such Government policy intentions as the Strategic Plan 2001-6 and the future Namibian Training Authority. Targeted budgetary support under the conditions of Article 61.3 of the Cotonou Agreement will be considered wherever possible.

SWAP will take into account key crosscutting issues such as the impact of HIV-AIDS on learner and teachers, the role and linkages with the private sector and other NSAs (University, Vocational Training Centres, Community Skills Development Centres etc.), girls education (access, retention and enrolment) and the decentralisation of the education system. In the perspective of a growing convergence of education and training, vocational training and skills development are a central part of core cross-sectoral strategies for pro-poor growth rather than a sub-sectoral activity, particularly in the light of broader economic trends. The SWAP process should involve all social partners at all levels of the system.

Response Strategy in non focal sectors

The EC will be led to consider further support activities mainly for the following purpose:

- Capacity building for development planning ;
- Institutional capacity building support for non-state actors;
- Contributions to trade and regional integration;
- A reserve for insurance against possible claims and to cover cost increases and contingencies.
- Funds available under the "Sysmin" allocation (pending request under the 8th EDF and included in "B envelope" – 25 M€) will be also used in support of rural development.

9th EDF Financial Data

	Allocation (A-envelope)*	% of overall allocation
• Focal area : Rural Development and land reform	34 M€ *	60 %
• Focal area : Human Resources Development (HRD)	21 M€	30 %
• Non focal areas		10 %
Total	73 M€ *	100 %

The amounts shown above, account solely for EDF (European Development Fund) allocations programmable aid.

Main Development Projects

- Support to rural development and land reform initiatives,
- Support to the Education sector programmes in Namibia
- Trade and regional integration programme
- Rural towns sewerage scheme (RTSS), Luderitz
- Capacity building for development planning
- Technical assistance to NAO
- Namibia Integrated Health Programmes
- Support Programmes to the Mining Sector (SYSMIN)
- Tourism Development Programmes
- Lifestock Marketing Project
- Fisheries Training Institute
- HIV/AIDS Programmes
- Micro-projects Programmes
- National Agricultural Services Programmes

7.11 Rwanda

Relations with the European Union: The European Union and its member states were among the first international actors to acknowledge the post-genocide regime. During the period after the genocide, EC co-operation was focused on humanitarian aid and rehabilitation. Two programmes for the total of €114 million have been the backbone of the rehabilitation effort in Rwanda. Once the primary commitments were made, Article 301 of the Lome Convention gave substantial delegation of power and responsibility to the local representation of the European Commission in Kigali. An EU Special Envoy for the Great Lakes Region was designated in 1996.

The third phase of co-operation between Rwanda and the EC began in 2000 with the signature of the 8th EDF, with a transitional approach between the rehabilitation phase and long-term development. On the total amount of this NIP (EUR 110 million), projects for an amount of €100 million are already decided and in operation. Three projects focus on institutional support with technical/logistical support for the Ministry of Finances, general population consensus carried out in 2002 and support for good governance and justice sector. The total contribution of these projects amount to €21.2 million. A large part of the infrastructure component of the NIP 8th EDF (55% of the total allocation) was committed in December 2002 to Bugasera/Karenge water supply systems (€19.5 million) and to the rehabilitation of the Kigali/Kayonza road and technical support for road sector management (€33.125 million). NIP 8th EDF contributed to the structural adjustment programme with €20 million and €6.15 million is funding the continuation of rural micro-projects and urban labour intensive works.

The 9th EDF *National Indicative Programme* has been signed in March 2003 with an emphasis is on poverty reduction. The focal sector is rural development, including rural economy, as well as transports and water supply in rural areas. The support to economic reform program will continue. The importance of institutional capacity building, transition to democracy and justice and the reinforcement of decentralised structures were also underlined. The respective amounts are €124 million for the A envelop and €62 million for the B envelop.

Belgium, France, Germany, United Kingdom, Luxembourg and Sweden are amongst the most important donors in Rwanda.

The Government of Rwanda has made great progress in the co-ordination of development aid both in budgetary programming and at the institutional level. However, co-ordination between various donors needs to be improved. Within the European Union, regular co-ordination meetings are held between the member states and the European Commission.

Country Strategy: Based on the following criteria and principles, a structured package of interventions under the 9th EDF in Rwanda at macro, sector and micro level has been identified.

- Poverty reduction is the overarching goal of the Response Strategy.
- Bearing in mind that poverty is largely a rural phenomenon in Rwanda, the natural focus of the Response Strategy will be at the local level in the rural sector.
- The importance of institutional capacity building, transition to democracy and justice and the reinforcement of decentralised structures will continue to remain amongst the priorities of the Response Strategy.

In accordance with the Cotonou Agreement, the emphasis is on the complementary roles and contributions of the State and Non-State actors and ensuring the widest possible participation of the civil society organisations. Particular attention will be given to increasing women's participation in all aspects of programming this response strategy.

Priorities for Co-operation

9th EDF - A Envelope (€124m)

Focal Areas

- Rural development (€62m - 50% of overall envelope)
- Macro-economic support (€50m - 40% of overall envelope)

Non-focal Areas (€12m- 10% of overall envelope)

- Governance (25% of the overall envelope)
- Civil society
- Integration and regional stability

Focal Areas

A. Rural Development (€62m - 50% of overall envelope) wanda is a rural country, with 90% of the population engaged in agricultural activities. All economic development must thus be channelled through the rural productive sector. The modernisation of the rural sector will be done through an increase of agricultural production, aiming to improve food security and thus contribute to poverty eradication. The emphasis is on export promotion, diversification of productive activities and the development of the private sector.

Rural development also requires an improved transport infrastructure. An adequate transport network that reduces travel costs and time is one of the key factors to ensure economic growth, trade investment, population integration and inter and intra-co-operation in Rwanda and the Great Lakes Region.

The improvement of the living conditions of the rural populations also entails the rehabilitation of health and education structures, as well as increased access to drinking water and sanitation.

An essential element of the Strategy Response is also support given to the decentralised structures. The development and reinforcement of local structures is essential for community development and increasing community participation.

B. Macro-economic Support (€50m - 40% of overall envelope): Budgetary support will continue to be given in the context of structural adjustment framework.

Non-focal areas (€12m- 10% of overall envelope)

C. Good Governance and Institutional Support: Good governance will be addressed at all levels and in all sectors of the Response Strategy. Good governance, institutional capacity building and support to local reconciliation initiatives are necessary preconditions for the follow-up of the genocide and the transition towards democracy.

D. Civil Society: Funds managed by the EC Delegation in Rwanda will be used, in accordance to the Cotonnou Agreement:

1. to support institutional development in order to improve the structure of the civil society
2. to reinforce the management, negotiation and intervention skills of the Civil Society Organisations (CSOs) in order to help them gain influence in decision-making and access to development opportunities.
3. to identify areas of concentration and dialogue at the local, regional and national level. iv) to reinforce the dialogue between the state and non-state actors.

E. Integration and Regional Stability: The Government of Rwanda has reconfirmed its wish to increase its economic integration through organisations, such as the *Common Market of Eastern and Southern Africa* (COMESA) and the *East African Community* (EAC). Rwanda has also been active in the Regional Integration Facilitation Forum and belongs to "Nile Basin Initiative". The demobilisation and reintegration of ex-fighters will receive particular attention. This has already been taken into account in the form of budgetary support and in the context of "Multi-Country Program for Demobilisation and Reintegration of ex-Combatants (MDRP) in the Greater Great Lakes Region".

9th EDF; B Envelope (€62m): Designed to cover unexpected expenses, such as emergency aid when such aid cannot be financed under the A Envelope.

Major Development Projects

Sector/project

I. Institutional support

- Technical/logistic support for the Ministry of Finance
- General population census
- Support for good governance and justice sector

II. Structural adjustment programme

III. Infrastructure component

- Bugesera/Karenge water supply systems
- Rehabilitation of the Kigali/Kayonza road and technical support for road sector management

IV. Rural micro-projects and urban labour intensive works

Rwanda	% NIP	Amounts M€	Financing decision
A Envelope		**124**	
I. Rural development	50%	62	
Community development		25	2003/2
Sensibilisation of farmers on issues related to land reform		1	2004/1
Agricultural information system		1	2004/2
Interventions on classified road network		25	2004/1
Drinking water Programme in rural milieu- phase 2		10	2004/1
II. Macro-economic support	40%	50	
Structural adjustment (SAP)		50	2003/1
III. Non-focal sectors	10%	12	
Institutional support programme		6	2003/1
Regional integration		1	2003/1
Support to civil society		2	2004/1
Reintegration of demobilised and vulnerable groups in the urban districts		3	2003/2
B Envelope		**62**	
Total	**100%**	**186**	

7.12 Seychelles

Relations with the EU: Political relations with the EU and its Member States have improved since the return to multi-partyism, the lessening of links with states such as Libya and Iraq and a commitment to a more liberal political system. Three Member States (UK, France and Germany) also constitute Seychelles' main trading partners.

Apart from EDF funding (€ 6 m under Lomé IVbis), Seychelles benefits from a substantial Fisheries Agreement (€ 6.9 m). A new Agreement – the largest tuna protocol signed by the EC with a third country – entered into force in January 2002. It provides for € 3.46 m in financial compensation annually (2002-2005) and for € 3.48 m for fisheries development activities.

Foreign currency shortages have had a some negative impact on some EU-funded projects (notably the Anse Royale Landfill).

Country Strategy: The guiding principles behind EC development policy are ownership by developing countries of their own development process and increased attention to the social dimension of growth and development. Emphasis is given to poverty reduction, with a view to its eventual eradication, and to the smooth integration of developing countries into the world economy. Particular attention is given to human rights, to the environmental dimension, to equality between men and women and to good governance.

In accordance with the provisions of the ACP-EC Partnership Agreement, Seychelles and the EC accept the key role of new actors in addressing all issues of mutual concern and of ensuring consistency and increased impact of development co-operation. In this respect, the integration of the private sector and of civil society has been duly encouraged and consultations with them have been held during the drawing up of the Country Strategy Paper and 9th EDF Indicative Programme.

Priorities for Co-operation

Focal Sector: Environment (85% of overall A allocation)

Non-focal Sector: Capacity Building (15% of overall A allocation)

Focal Area: Environment – solid waste sector

The environment is an area in which not only a clear and stable policy framework exists, which receives high government priority, but which impacts clearly and directly on the wellbeing or otherwise of important economic sectors, tourism and fisheries in particular. It is also an area with which the EC is familiar, and in which it has recent co-operation experience. The environment sector was therefore chosen as the sole focal sector for Seychelles' 9th EDF Indicative Programme (€ 3.9m). The activities which it is proposed to fund under the Programme, which relate more specifically to environmental health (solid waste disposal), will have a direct and positive impact on the population as a whole, in the form of improved public health and general living standards. They will also help to sustain Seychelles' reputation as one of the greatest areas of natural beauty in the world, and will preserve the logic of activities carried out in the context of other EC policy areas (e.g. development support, through the Fisheries Agreements, to coastal and lagoon fishing). The production of landfill gas, as an energy source, may also be considered.

The activity which it is funded through programme aid consists of a Solid Waste Management Programme – a much-needed programme, the desired impact of which will be earlier by virtue of the proposed EC grant funding. Specifically, it is envisaged to allocate 85% of 9th EDF funds (approx. € 3.3m) to building appropriate landfilling facilities.

Non-focal area: Capacity building

The non-focal area will focus on capacity building, in both the state and the non-state sectors. State capacity building will centre on training for the Ministries of Administration and Manpower Development and Education and Youth. Capacity building for non-state actors will aim at empowering NGOs and delivering quality services through, in particular, strengthening NGO information and co-ordination capacity and, inter alia, developing a culture of volunteering popular participation.

Activities in the NGO sector will aim at empowering the NGOs and delivering quality services, in principle through the NGO association LUNGOS (Liaison Unit of NGOs of Seychelles). Such activities would include strengthening co-ordinating capacity and providing backstopping and secretariat facilities for NGOs.

Some 15 % (€0.6m) of the 9th EDF "A" envelope is allocated to this area, 50 % of which for state capacity building, 50 % in support of NGO capacity building (funds for Non-State actors will be directly accessible and will be attributed, in principle, to member organisations of LUNGOS).

9th EDF Financial Data

Focal areas	Allocation	% of overall A allocation
Environment	3.3 M€	85 %
Capacity building	0.6 M€	15 %
Total	3.9 M€	100 %

The amounts shown above account solely for EDF (European Development Fund) allocations – programmable aid.

Main Development Projects funded

- Melon fruit fly evaluation
- Tourism capacity building project
- Le Niol Water Treatment Works
- Anse Royale Landfill
- Consolidation of handicraft development Handicraft Development Programme
- Rural Development Programme
- Old Tuna Quay : Rehab. Works and Supervision
- T.A to Seychelles Fisheries
- Agricultural Development Projects

- La Digue Environment & Transport project
- Victoria market rehabilitation works
- Integrated biodiversity project
- Biodiversity conservation
- Credit Line to small enterprises
- T.A. to small industry

7.13 Somalia

Relations with the EU: The EC is the largest donor in Somalia. As it is not part of the Lomé IV Convention, the Commission has, in the past (1994-2001), used a very large number of financial instruments in order to ensure a certain aid level. This includes 6th EDF Balances, Rehabilitation Budget lines, ECHO, Human rights, Bananas, Mines, Food security, NGO co-financing and other budget lines. The Commission is also managing Italian (and some Danish) co-financing. With the Cotonou Agreement, the ACP-EU Council was able to grant (December 2001) a special aid to Somalia under Article 93.6. An amount of 50 M€ from the 8th EDF and a further 149 M€ from the 9th EDF have been allocated to the country while ECHO Commitments for 2003 will be 6 M€. Annual average disbursements are presently 15 M€ and estimated to increase to 24 M€ in 2003 and some 40 M€ in 2004.

EC co-operation in Somalia is defined by the "Strategy for special aid to Somalia" (April 2002). Given the Somali context, flexibility, strict neutrality and contacts at local level have been key elements for the ongoing EC interventions, which are based on the "peace dividend approach" and imply multi-sectoral capacity delivery, covering the whole spectrum from humanitarian aid to relief through rehabilitation to development.

The EU has declared since the beginning its support to the IGAD's peace initiative to which the Commission has provided a substantial financial contribution (1.5 M€ already granted, in addition to other contributions from the international community). Following the declaration on cessation of hostilities the 26 October 2002 in Eldoret (Kenya), the EU launched a timely statement reiterating its full support to the IGAD peace process and stressing its readiness to lend its political, financial and technical support to the proceedings of the peace conference. On 22nd July 2002, the General Affairs Council had already adopted a set of conclusions on Somalia aimed at providing a detailed political contribution to the whole process. In particular, the EU encourages a negotiated replacement of the Arta TG by a broad base, all inclusive government and, in parallel, a "bottom-up approach" which would provide direct support to emerging regional administrations. Moreover, the EU conclusions state that, as peace advances, a more "proactive" peace building support leading to direct support to administrations could complement the ongoing strictly neutral "peace dividend" approach, the guiding principle for EU co-operation since 1994. The Commission and EU Member states are key members of the IGAD Partners Forum (IPF), a group of governments and international organisations, which support IGAD activities, and also have a place on the IGAD Standing Committee on Somalia.

Country Strategy: EC co-operation in Somalia in the past years was already set up in accordance with the orientation expressed later in Article 93.6 of the Cotonou agreement which defines a certain number of specified priorities: institution building and economic and social development, taking into particular account the needs of the most vulnerable sections of the population. The fundaments for future EC Co-operation will keep along the same basic lines. Nevertheless, a certain number of adjustments are necessary to deal with specific evolutions in the social economic and political scenarios. In this context, a more gradual reorientation should encourage and support the Somali political forces and in particular the to pursue peaceful national reconciliation and the restoration of basic administrative and social services.

The overall long-term objective is to contribute to the alleviation of poverty and to the promotion of a more peaceful, equitable and democratic society in Somalia. In order to realize this, a multisectoral, flexible approach incorporating the full range of humanitarian, relief, rehabilitation and development assistance following a 'local area approach' is required. EC assistance to Somalia is administered through the SACB (Somalia Aid Coordination Body) and thereafter essentially distributed through a network of NGO's and UN agencies.

Priorities for Co-operation

The Commission advocates pursuing its multi-sectoral approach with a series of complementary and mutually reinforcing interventions in the following areas:

- Enhancement of good governance.
- Reduction of widespread vulnerability;
- Access to social services;
- Economic growth and diversification;
- A limited number of clusters of activities and interventions have been identified with particular relevance to the achievement of results in the above-mentioned:
- Good governance is enhanced; reconciliation and sustainable peace-building is supported:

Broadly speaking, three entities will be addressed: administrative structures, including at the decentralised level, in particular major municipalities in Somaliland and Puntland; parliament(s) as the basis of democratic practice; and civil society. The envisaged Commission interventions are:

- Support administrative structures in applying principles of good governance;
- Support the contribution of civil society to the enhancement of good governance;
- Contribute to reconciliation and sustainable peace building.

The widespread vulnerability, to which the majority of the population is exposed, is reduced: Years of continuous conflict combined with extreme climatic conditions have eroded the coping mechanism of the population, while the absence of any support service, formerly provided by state agencies, has further weakened the population in terms of vulnerability. The following cluster of interventions aiming to enable the population to develop their own strategies to cope better with the hostile situation, has been identified:

- Improve skills and knowledge for sustainable and effective management of natural resources;
- Improve access to agricultural and pastoral infrastructure, inputs and services;
- Improve adequate prevention, monitoring and control of emergencies.
- Access of the population to affordable social services is improved:

The limited access to health services contributes significantly to the vulnerability of the population; likewise, the decade-long absence of formal education has deprived a whole generation of its right to education. In past years the EC has been very active in health and education; further support in these areas is indispensable and will focus on the following issues:

- Support integrated public health programmes;
- Improve health programmes to fight against contagious diseases;
- Improve access to quality education.
- Sustainable economic growth and diversification is enhanced:

Most infrastructures have been to a large extent destroyed or have become dysfunctional due to a lack of maintenance. Private sector development be it in service delivery, trade or investment, is also considerably hampered by the absence of regulatory legal frameworks and the existence of non-physical trade barriers. Economic growth and diversification are also suffering from an almost complete absence of supportive services. The following priorities for intervention have been identified:

- Sustainable rehabilitation of transport infrastructure;
- Establishment of regulatory frameworks and support services for private sector development.

Main Development Projects Funded

- Support to Local Human Rights and Peace Organisations in Somalia
- Journalist Training for Somalia

9th EDF Financial Data

Focal area	Allocation
Enhancement of good governance; Reduction of widespread vulnerability; Access to social services; Economic growth and diversification;	9th EDF 149 M€ 8th EDF 50 M€

- Community Based Building of Peace & Democracy in Somalia - Civic Education.
- Demobilisation in North West Somalia
- Rehabilitation of the Road Network in North West Somalia
- Berbera Corridor - Urgent rehabilitation & technical assistance to the Somaliland Road Authority
- Mine Action Operations in Burao district, Northwest Somalia
- Demining, Kalabayd-Tog Wajale Road and Hargeisa-Burao Road, NW Somalia – Somaliland
- Community-Based Soil Conservation on Watershed Basis in Awdal Region – North West Somalia
- Rehabilitation of irrigation infrastructures and support to rural activities in Sahil region, Phase II
- Irrigation System Rehabilitation in Lower Shabelle region
- Agricultural Support project, Belet Weyne District, Hiran Region
- Sustainable improvement of Camel Milk Production and Trade, Gardo District, Northeast Somalia
- Improved Agricultural Production in Oases in Bari region, Northeast Somalia
- Rural Water Supply And Community Management in Hargeisa District

- Access to Water and Institutional Capacity Building In Mudug & Galgadud Regions
- Development of Chambers of Commerce in Somalia
- Somalia Micro-finance development Programme
- Itinerant Training Programme for Somali Veterinary Professionals
- Livestock Export Related Veterinary Project in Northeast Somalia
- Establishment of Technical Veterinary Training School, Sheikh, Somaliland

7.14 Sudan

Relations with the EU: Formal EC-Sudan development co-operation was suspended in March 1990 and ongoing development assistance was phased out due to concerns about lack of respect for human rights and democracy, and because of the civil war.

In November 1999, the EU and Sudan started a political dialogue aimed at addressing concerns about human rights, good governance and rule of law and democratisation. Parallel discussions were held in 2002 and 2003 with the SPLM/A. In June 2002, after acknowledging improvements in several areas of the dialogue, the EU pledged to fully normalise relations and to resume co-operation as soon as a peace agreement is signed between the GoS and the SPLM/A. Preparations for the resumption of cooperation were launched, including an 18 M€ 'Humanitarian Plus' assistance programme.

Full cooperation can start as soon as a political settlement of the conflict in southern Sudan is reached. Funds amounting to 243 M€ from the 6th EDF have been programmed in order to provide assistance in the areas of food security and education/capacity building, and 135M€ (envelope A) plus 20M€ (envelope B) have been allocated to Sudan under the 9th EDF.

In December 2003 the EU send a Troika mission to Sudan and reconfirmed its continuation of the political dialogue. During this mission, particular attention was given to the crisis in Darfur

The EIB can not restart operations before a solution is found for the approximately 60 M€ debts and arrears owed by Sudan to the European Community. The reimbursement or rescheduling of this debt shall be negotiated in the larger framework of a possible Highly Indebted Poor Countries Initiative (HPIC), for which Sudan could become a beneficiary.

Although formal development assistance to the Sudan could not be implemented since 1990, the EU has provided substantial humanitarian assistance to the victims of the civil war and natural disasters, according to basic humanitarian principles. Since 1994, over 300M€ have been made available to the population of Sudan in the form of direct relief assistance. This amount includes 199 million € of ECHO funding.

Country Strategy: Formal assistance to Sudan has been suspended since 1990. In June 2002 the EU agreed that a gradual normalisation of relations and decided that a resumption of co-operation shall be contingent upon a completion of the peace negotiations between the GoS and the SPLM/A. The EU offers its full support and assistance for the consolidation of a comprehensive peace agreement. Technical preparations for programmes to be financed once an agreement is signed, and co-operation resumed, have been ongoing since 2002. A Country Strategy Paper has been prepared jointly with the GoS and is ready for signature.

Formal development assistance (EDF) to the Sudan has not been implemented since in 1990 Earlier programmes were phased out during 1990 and 1991.

7.15 Swaziland

Relations with the EU: Swaziland has signed the Cotonou Partnership Agreement on 23 June 2000 and is a signatory of the Lome Conventions. The EU is worried by the pertaining crisis of the judiciary system which has resulting in the resignation, as a sign of protest, of the entire court of appeal and by the fact that Swaziland has still not ratified the Convention on the Elimination of All From of Discrimination against Woman (CEDAW).

Therefore, at the request from the EU made in 2002 a political dialogue has been initiated within the framework of the Cotonou Agreement. However, the political dialogue is progressing slowly. The overall objective that has been pursued through the Swaziland-EU co-operation has been to assist the Government of Swaziland in its efforts to alleviate poverty in the context of helping the economy of Swaziland on a more sustainable footing and of promoting its further integration into the world economy.

As regards bilateral trade, in 2002 the total Swazi exports to the EU amounted to € 129 million and the imports to € 19 million, showing a positive trade balance with the EU of € 110 million. Agricultural products are the predominant products exported by Swaziland to the EU, as they represent more than 85% of total exports and are concentrated on three main products: cane or beet sugar, citrus fruit and other fruit and nuts. Swaziland has taken full advantage of its quota under the Lomé Sugar Protocol in 2002. The main Swaziland imports from the EU are manufactured goods and machinery and agricultural products.

. **Country Strategy:** Within the framework of the EU-ACP Cotonou Agreement, the European Commission signed with the Government of Swaziland on 23 September 2002 a framework programme outlining its cooperation strategy (Country Strategy Paper (CSP) and National Indicative Programme (NIP)) over the next six years In the 9th EDF human resources development is identified as focal sector.

Priorities for Co-operation

The overall indicative allocation for the 9th EDF amounts to € 43 million from which € 31 million under the envelope A and € 12 million under envelope B.

Focal Area:

- Education and Training Sector up to 65%

Non-focal Areas:

- Smallholder Irrigation- Lower Usuthu up to 13%
- Decentralised Poverty Reduction Programme up to 13%
- Complementary actions for Trade and Regional Integration: up to 5%

- Complementary actions for Institutional capacity building
- for development planning and non-state actors: up to 4%

Within the focal and non-focal areas of support, gender equality, HIV/AIDS, decentralisation, community participation, capacity building and, where appropriate, environmental management, will form important cross-cutting thematic issues.

Apart from the above-mentioned financial instruments of which the A-envelope is the main programmable basis for the Indicative Programme, the 9th EDF includes also the Investment Facility as a financing instrument managed by the European Investment Bank. The Investment Facility does not as such form part of the Indicative Programme. EC budget lines could be used to finance specific operations, in particular for HIV/AIDS related operations, environmental and natural resources conservation and support to democracy and human rights initiatives. Financing is decided in accordance with the Commission's procedures for the budget line concerned and depends on the availability of funds.

Focal Areas

Under the focal area, the following specific objective shall be pursued: By 2006 to contribute to consolidating the achievements of Education For All through equitable access to education at pre-primary and primary levels, and to introduce a quality post-secondary Vocational Education and Training (VET) system.

The major interventions will include support to education infrastructure facilities and equipment, and TA-led capacity building in the areas of Primary and Pre-primary Education; Vocational Education and Training; and Program Management and Coordination

The major policy measures to be taken by Government to ensure a successful implementation of the response strategy in this sector are: the increase in the share of education budget resources going to non-salary related expenditure; enactment of appropriate legislation or amendments to statutory instruments; the adoption of an improved national curriculum, of a national qualification framework, and of a quality assurance policy framework; the reduction of class sizes.

Non-focal Areas

A. Lower Usuthu Smallholder Irrigation Project: The specific objectives of this project are to reduce the level of poverty and to improve the standard of living of the population in the Lower Usuthu Basin in a sustainable way. This will be achieved through increased household income, enhanced food security and improved access to social and health infrastructure by creating the conditions for the transformation of subsistence level smallholder farmers into small-scale commercial farmers. Approximately 2,600 households will be directly integrated into the commercial economy through the provision of irrigation infrastructure, development of the policy and legal framework for smallholder irrigation, as well as the establishment of farmer-managed and self-financing irrigation schemes.

B. Decentralised Poverty Reduction Programme: The specific objective of this programme is to reduce poverty through a process of sustainable social and economic development in favour of the core poor living in rural and peri-urban areas, especially women. The programme will contribute to the improvement of education, health, water supply and sanitation facilities, transport communications, the provision of community facilities including rural electrification, and enable access to business training and micro-lending facilities for income generating projects. The programme will be demand-led in that individual projects will be undertaken at the initiative of and with the active participation of the local community concerned. The decentralised approach of the micro-projects programme will give added value through the provision of networking and training facilities for communities, local and regional government development officers and NSA, who will be involved at all levels of the programme.

C. Complementary Actions for Trade and Regional Integration: Support under the 9th EDF to trade and regional integration will complement and be coherent with other initiatives in this area. These are the Trade Capacity Building Project and the Private Sector Support Programme, and regional programmes such as the BLNS Economic Integration Support Package and the Intra-ACP project for Capacity building in support of Economic Partnerships. The following areas will be considered for assistance:

- The formulation and implementation of further private sector friendly reforms with respect to market supervision, trade, investment and competition policies.
- Export diversification through the promotion of non-traditional export products by both large companies and SMEs.
- Improvement and maintenance of trade statistics and statistical analysis and applied research capacities..
- Support to customs and standardisation mechanisms to facilitate the implementation of future trade agreements.

D. Complementary Actions for Institutional Capacity Building: The following areas are considered for assistance.

- Support to the Ministry of Economic Planning for co-ordination and monitoring of external aid and for the effective management of EDF resources in the context of the 9th EDF and for programming of the 10th EDF. Development of the Ministry of Economic Planning and Development's capacity in project planning, monitoring and evaluation will take account of the new rolling programming mechanism and the relationship with NSA introduced under the Cotonou Agreement.
- Support to reinforce the capacities of non-state actors as regards organisation and representation, particularly at the level of the apex bodies or federations of NSA, and for the establishment and operation of appropriate consultation mechanisms both among NSA and with the Government of Swaziland.
- Contribute to increased understanding and awareness of development issues, opportunities and areas of mutual interest as defined in the 9th EDF Country Strategy Paper through information activities.

9th EDF Financial Data

	Allocation (A envelope) M€	% of overall allocation
Focal area		
• Education and Training Sector	Up to 20.15	Up to 65%
Non-focal area		
• Smallholder Irrigation- Lower Usuthu	Up to 4.03	Up to 13%
• Poverty Reduction Programme	Up to 4.03	Up to 13%
• Complementary actions for Trade and Regional Integration	Up to 1.55	Up to 5%
• Complementary Actions for Institutional Capacity Building for Development Planning and Non-state actors	Up to 1.24	Up to 4%

Main Development Projects

- Lower Usuthu Smallholder Irrigation Development Project
- Fiscal Restructuring Programme
- HIV/AIDS Prevention and Care Programme
- Private Sector Support Programme
- Strengthening Capacity in Trade Promotion and International Trade Management.

7.16 Tanzania

Relations with the EU: The EU maintains a generally good and close relationship with Tanzania. It is Tanzania's main trading partner and one of its most important providers of external aid. Around 31% of all imports come from the EU, while around 37% of all Tanzanian exports are destined for the EU. Exports are mainly coffee, cashew nuts, tobacco and cotton. Imports are mainly machinery, consumer goods and transport equipment.

Foreign investment of significant size is envisaged only in the mining sector and possibly tourism.

The EC and the 15 Member States disburse some €400 million annually to Tanzania, accounting for about 50% of all aid inflows. Sweden, Denmark and United Kingdom are amongst the most important donors. Donor co-ordination is particularly active in Tanzania.

As donors have been shifting towards sector approaches over the last years, this coordination has also become more effective and open. The EC has a lead co-ordinating role in the roads sector whereas the IMF/WB institutions have taken a lead when it comes to structural adjustment and macro-economic reforms.

Tanzania has since 1975 been one of the biggest recipients of EC aid, be it from NIP resources, Stabex, structural adjustment support, NGO co-operation, food aid or EIB support. Since the outbreak of the conflicts in the Great Lakes region and following large influx of refugees, Tanzania also benefits from substantial amounts of humanitarian aid managed by ECHO. Under ECHO's Global Plan for 2003, Tanzania will receive € 24 million. The focal areas for support in the past have included transport infrastructure, agriculture, communications infrastructure and human resource development.

The 9th EDF Country Strategy Paper/NIP was signed on 14th March 2002 (€ 355 million). Its preparation has been marked by a highly consultative process including the national administration, non-state stakeholders and the donor community. Focal sectors will remain the same as for earlier EDFs, namely transport (roads) and basic education combined with the provision of general untied budget aid for the country's poverty reduction strategy. Support to build institutional capacity at local levels and further decentralisation of decision-making to local entities will be provided under the non-focal sectors.

Country Strategy: Based on the following criteria and principles, a structured package of interventions under the 9th EDF in Tanzania at macro, sector and micro level has been identified.

- Poverty Reduction is the overarching goal of the Response Strategy.
- Good governance will be addressed at all levels and in all sectors of the Response Strategy both as a prerequisite for support and as an area of support in itself.
- Bearing in mind that poverty is largely a rural phenomenon in Tanzania, the natural focus of the Response Strategy would be at the local level. The Strategy would therefore ultimately aim at making a difference in rural Tanzania, by improving living conditions for the rural population, regardless of the sectors to which resources are allocated and the channels through which the funds flow.
- The Cotonou Agreement has emphasised the complementary roles and contributions of the State and non-state actors in the development process and the importance of ensuring the widest possible participation of all sectors of society. The purpose of extending partnership to non-state actors in the implementation of this CSP will hence be to contribute to the consolidation of a stable and democratic environment, to increase ownership of the development processes and to ensure greater sustainability of cooperation programmes.
- Close co-operation with the donor community, particularly EU member states, to ensure coherence, impact and efficiency of EC's aid form parts and parcel of this Strategy. Coordination will be active both in sector policy dialogue and around specific support actions.
- Gender equality should be mainstreamed in all aspects of programming this response strategy with the ultimate aim of reaching equality between women and men. Likewise, sustainable management of the environment and natural resources is a crosscutting issue to be incorporated into all areas of co-operation. Possibilities to involve the private sector as a partner should be explored throughout.

Priorities for Co-operation

Focal Areas

- Transport Infrastructure (Roads) (40% of overall envelope)

- Basic Education (15% of the overall envelope)
- Macro Support (34% of the overall envelope)

Non-focal Areas

- Governance (10% of the overall envelope)
- Percentage indications are based on a resource envelope of 290 M€ (A-envelope allocation) and would also remain valid, should more funds be added to this base case envelope

Focal Areas

A. Transport Infrastructure (Roads) (40% of overall envelope)

An improved road network is important for Tanzania's economic and social development. Moreover because of the country's population dispersal and geographic distribution, an adequate road network that reduces travel costs and time is one of the key factors to ensure economic growth, trade, investment, population integration and inter and intra-co-operation in Tanzania and the East Africa region.

The road sector component of this CSP will support the Government's National Transport Policy to improve access to local, regional and international markets and services. Four strategic areas that would contribute to the reduction of transport costs and travel time are proposed:

- Support the road sector policy reform programme and strategy implementation - stressing accountability, transparency and efficiency - and provide support to build up the capacities of all road sector institutions, in particular TANROADS;
- Finance backlog, periodic and routine maintenance to bring the network to a maintainable condition, with a focus on reducing existing backlog of maintenance as well as emergency repairs;
- Continue to support the development of the main road network defined by the Government with a focus on high priority corridors having benefited from earlier EC support;
- Active donor co-ordination has played a key role in pursuing sector reforms. The history of co-operation in the road sector has revealed the importance of sound sector policies and

institutional reforms as the base for long-term sustainability of all other proposed actions.

B. Basic Education (15% of the overall envelope): Broad-based basic education plays a key role in strengthening human capabilities and reducing poverty in Tanzania. Correlatively, lack of education and a low-skilled workforce are identified as two of the structural factors causing constraints to growth. All national development plans including the PRSP therefore give prominence to investment in human capital and to the creation of a well-educated nation.

Tanzania's education sector is in urgent need of reform and financial support to reverse the negative trend of deteriorating indicators. Lately, the Government has shown firm commitment towards sector reform with the preparation of an Education Sector Development Programme and by re-launching policy dialogue with donors. EC has actively contributed towards reforming and improving the country's education sector both financially and in its role as lead donor co-ordinating international support.

The education sector component of this CSP will support the Government's Education Sector Development Programme to attain increased gender-balanced and equitable access to higher quality basic education in line with the overall objectives identified for this sector. The ESDP should seek to integrate the universal Education For All goals. A better-educated population is then expected to result in higher standards of living and higher levels of social and economic development. It would further promote gender equality and advance the position of women and the girl child.

The Local Government Reform Programme (LGRP) has a direct impact on the ESDP as it envisages the devolution of school and teacher management to local levels and a more active participation by the local population in the management of facilities and control of funds. It is therefore imperative to link the two reform programmes and ensure consistency in the design and implementation of these processes.

C. Macro Support (34% of the overall envelope): Government will allocate significant funds to priority sectors identified in its Poverty Reduction Strategy, with the objectives to reduce income poverty, to improve quality of life and the social well-being of the poor whilst maintaining macro-economic stability. EC will support the Government in its efforts to combat Tanzanian poverty by contributing to the general budget, together with a number of other donors. Donor support to the budget will then permit substantially higher levels of allocations to priority sectors than without such support: It is expected that donors will finance about 55% of the priority recurrent expenditure or 30% of the overall budget, as in the past for the coming years.

The instrument for channelling funds would be the newly established Poverty Reduction Budget Support Facility (PRBS) put in place in 2000 to accommodate external budget aid (other than from World Bank and IMF) to the general budget. PRBS will be co-financed by nine donors, including the EC and six Member States. This will considerably reduce aid transaction costs.

The Cotonou Agreement allows for general budgetary aid as long as public expenditure management is transparent, accountable and effective. Tanzania must therefore ascertain the necessary standards in the management of these funds. The expected strong increase of untied financial flows through the public sector system will raise major issues in terms of "buying value for money" as well as of transparent financial management and accountability.

Non-focal Sectors of Co-operation

D. Governance (10% of the overall envelope): Based on the emerging democratic culture in Tanzania together with the enhanced emphasis at EU-ACP policy level of good governance, it is recommended to provide support to this area within the framework of this CSP. Good governance will be promoted in all areas of co-operation, both as a central element for the success of the country's development efforts but also to improve the efficiency and the effectiveness of 9th EDF programme funds. A three-pronged approach is proposed.

- the governance component would be embedded within the identified areas of cooperation at both macro and sector-specific levels so that issues of proper management of public funds, financial accountability and dissemination of information would be brought to the fore.
- component targeted at promoting good governance at the local level, close to the majority of the population and the highest incidences of poverty. The objective would be to improve service delivery at local level and to encourage a culture of participatory management where local societies can gain influence in decision-making and access to development opportunities. Such support could best be conceived within the framework of Government's current decentralisation efforts via its Local Government Reform Programme. It would focus on capacity building.
- The EC would also consider supporting other reform efforts pursued by the Government related to promoting good governance in Tanzania, in particular in relation to the implementation of the national anti-corruption strategy.

Major Development Projects

- S. Highlands Telecommunications
- Rehabilitation Wazo Hill-Bagamoyo Road
- Road Maintenance South Iringa & Ruvuma Regions
- Mwanza Regional Transport Programme
- Backlog Maintenance Project Central Corridor
- Mwanza-Tinde & Nzega - Isaka Roads
- Institutional Support Roads Sector
- Institutional Strengthening Water Supply in 4 Towns
- Mwanza Sewerage Rehabilitation
- Support for Tanzanian STD and AID
- Mwanza Water Supply
- Iringa Water Supply
- Support for Education Sector Development Programme (SESDP)
- Support for Introduction of Value Added Tax (VAT)

9th Financial Data

	Allocation (A enveloppe)	% of overall allocation
Focal area		
• Transport infrastructure	116 M€	40%
• Macro-economic support	98.6 M€	34%
• Education	43.5 M€	15%
Non focal area		
• Governance	31.9 M€	10%
Total	**290 M€**	**100%**

The amount shown above accounts solely for EDF (European Development Fund) allocations – programmable aid.

- Structurall Adjustment Programme (SAF IV
- Poverty Reduction Budget Support (PRBS)
- Stabex Coffee/Tea/Cotton
- Serengeti Conservation Programme.
- Institutional Strengthening Tourism Sector
- SADC Wildlife Management Training
- SADC Monitoring/Surveillance of Fishing Activities
- Support for S & E African Minerals Dev. Centre
- Inst. Support for East African Statistical Tr. Centre
- Special Progr. Refugee Affected Areas (SPRAA)
- Support to Prevention of Corruption Bureau (PCB)

7.17 Uganda

Relations with the EU: The EU is Uganda's major trading partner and absorbs about 50% of its exports. Ugandan exports include coffee, tea, tobacco, cotton, and fish. Fish has become the most dynamic export product.

Uganda is a major recipient of EU aid and is considered to be at the forefront of improving budget management structures, such as allowing the use of modern aid instruments (medium term financial planning, sector policies, sector budget support). The EU is a major donor in Uganda, and is mainly active in transport, health and education, rural development, and decentralised co-operation.

For the 9th EDF the country has been allocated € 246 M (envelope A) and € 117 (envelope B). The CSP/NIP was signed in Kampala on 30 May 2002A programme for Poverty Alleviation Budgetary Support is under execution (PABS).

Uganda also receives funding from the stabex funds, the European Investment Bank and the Commission's budget lines for humanitarian aid, NGO co-financing, demining and human rights and good governance operations.

The EC response to the development and poverty reduction challenges in Uganda – notably concerning the identification of the focal sectors of support - is designed to assist in sectors that are considered key for the future development of the country. The EC support through the 9th EDF will be integrated into the PRSP process and limit direct project funding to a strict minimum. The response reflects in particular the following elements and criteria:

- the development priorities of the government, as laid down in the PEAP(Poverty Eradication A, PMA (Plan for Modernisation of Agriculture), RDSP and MTCS;
- the financial requirements and implementation capacities in the sectors concerned;
- the historic development relationship between the EC and Uganda, its strengths and weaknesses;
- complementarity with other donors, in particular EU Member States.

The indicative financial allocation of the 9th EDF is divided between an allocation under the A-envelope of 246 million € and a B-envelope of 117 million €. The A-envelope, is programmed in the 9th NIP whereas the B-allocation covers unforeseen needs such as emergency assistance, contributions to internationally agreed debt relief initiatives and support to mitigate adverse effects of instability in export earnings.

Priorities for co-operation

Focal Areas

- Macro economic support (38% of A envelope)
- Transport (38% of A envelope)
- Rural Development (15% of A envelope)

Non-focal Areas

- Improving public service delivery (9% of 'A' Enveloppe)

Focal Areas

A. Macro economic support (38% of A envelope)

- **Budgetary discipline**

In the framework of the PRSC, GoU is committed to further strengthening the MTEF (Medium term Expenditure Framework) process and improving public services efficiency. Effectiveness will be measured in terms of outcomes and by progress in the reform implementation. Given GoU's strategy to improve its poverty eradication objectives through focused policies, continued EC macroeconomic support can be programmed. Such support will further facilitate GoU's process towards integrating its development priorities with the PAF (Poverty Action Fund) and the MTEF, including for social sectors. In order to successfully report on its undertakings, GoU will have to demonstrate its ability to actually implement good governance.

The budget process in on track and the current macroeconomic stability and growth allows the Government to provide substantial public resources to activities aimed at poverty alleviation. Global EC support to the budget will allow GoU to directly fund the poverty eradication priorities identified in the PEAP(Poverty Eradication Action Plan). It will also encourage GoU to speed up the application of improved co-ordinated evaluation and monitoring mechanisms for all sectors, including good governance and social sectors.

Social Sectors: Social sectors play a key role in the poverty eradication strategy of the Government encompassed in goal 3 of the PEAP. In order to increase ownership in the process, macroeconomic support does not earmark the use of funds provided. Instead the achievement of results in these sectors, as measured by performance indicators, will condition continued budget support. Evaluation and monitoring in education and health are already well co-ordinated through bi-annual sector reviews that monitor targets, set new targets and judges whether progress against agreed undertakings is satisfactory. During these reviews, the Commission will ensure that the EU development priorities for social sectors are fully reflected in the targets retained.

Performance Indicators: Release of EC funds for macroeconomic support will be triggered by agreed performance indicators. In line with the targets adopted by GoU for the PRSC, EC support will be linked to satisfactory reviews of the PRSC: efficient and equitable use of public funds; improved service delivery through cross-cutting reforms; improved quality of education; improved quality of health care; improved access and quality in water and sanitation.

Economic Reforms

EU assistance to economic reform in Uganda will have three key focuses:

- Support to private sector development
- Support to regional integration
- Support capacity building in finance and planning

B. Transport (38% of A envelope): Improvements of the rural transport infrastructure are crucial for economic growth and reduction of poverty in Uganda's rural areas. An improved main road network alone will not bring adequate transport infrastructure within reach of most rural producers, hence further development of the district road network will be necessary. Institutional development at both central and district levels will be required to achieve the announced goals. Finally, an improvement in maintenance is required to consolidate investments in transport infrastructure.

Interventions funded from the resources of the 9th EDF are foreseen in the following areas:

- Institutional support
- Support to maintenance
- Integration of the agricultural high potential areas of South West Uganda into the national road network at national level and at district level
- Performance indicators

C. Rural Development - (15% of the A-envelope)

- Support to the PMA (Plan for Modernisation of Agriculture)
- Given the dominant role of agriculture in Uganda's economy, with 85% of Ugandans living in rural areas, sustainable development cannot take place without support to rural areas. GoU's objective of poverty eradication through a sustainable and dynamic rural sector forms the basis of the PMA, an integrated multi-sectoral framework to develop the ability of the poor to raise their incomes. Therefore, rural development and more precisely support to the PMA have been identified as the second focal sector for co-operation. The support to the PMA will be channelled through budget sector support.

Performance Indicators

The PMA framework responds to goal 3 of the PEAP: increase the ability of the poor to raise their incomes. Although the expected results have been clearly identified, the way their achievement will be measured is still an issue to be agreed upon by the stakeholders, including member states and the Commission. The process will also be subject to regular reviews on the basis of GoU's evaluation and monitoring mechanisms.

Non-focal Sectors of Co-operation (9% of the A-envelope)

GoU has undertaken actions that focus on improving public service delivery in the context of decentralisation by reducing corruption and ensuring law and order. Commission support will target:

- Decentralisation
- Rule of Law and governance
- Human Rights / Democracy
- Institutional support to non-state actors.

9th Financial Data

	Allocation (A enveloppe)	% of overall allocation
Focal area		
• Macro-economic support & economic reform • Transport • Rural development	101 M€ 101 M€ 40 M€	38% 38% 15%
Non focal area		
• Capacity building in good governance • Institutional support to non-state actors	17 M€ 8 M€	6% 3%
Total	**246 M€**	**100%**

Major Development Projects

- Acholi Programme and the Karamoja Programme

- Kagamba-Rukungiri Road in Southwestern Uganda
- National Forest Management & Conservation Project
- Protected Area Assessment Plan
- Rehabilitation of roads in Queen Elisabeth National Park and Lake Mburo National Park
- Smallholder Tea Development Programme
- Agro-forestry programme
- Rural health programme in the south-west; West Nile health programme
- support to the Uganda Blood Transfusion Service (UBTS)
- Air Cargo Handling Facilities at the Entebbe International Airport
- Gaba I Rehabilitation Project
- Mid Western Towns Water Supply Project
- Support to Feasible Financial Institutions and Capacity building Efforts
- Uganda Programme for Trade Opportunities and Policy
- South West Uganda Road Maintenance Project
- Support to Civil Society Programme

7.18 Zambia

Relations with the EU: The Commission, with a presence in Zambia since 1975, is considered as a major partner and the Cotonou Partnership Agreement a significant instrument. Commissioner P. Nielson visited Zambia on 23 rd and 24th January 2003. Commissioner Nielson had fruitful bilateral meetings with President Mwanawasa and the main Ministers involved in the Zambia/EU partnership.

In line with Cotonou, good governance, human rights, democracy and corruption have remained important issues in the dialogue between EU and Zambia.

The EU is not the major origin of imports to Zambia nor the major destination of exports from Zambia either. Main imports from EU have been machinery or parts for machinery, vehicles and equipment (66% of total from EU – 2000). Major exports to EU have been cobalt, copper, cut flowers and cotton yarn (68% of total to EU – 2000). Zambia can benefit from the Everything but Arms initiative.

The bilateral co-operation between the Government of the Republic of Zambia and the European Commission progressed satisfactorily during the last years. Zambia is a good performing country in the utilisation of the EDF resources.

Country Strategy: The Zambia/EU Country Strategy Paper and National Indicative Programme was prepared taking in account the PRSP dialogue and discussions with the most important stakeholders (Government, civil society and Member States). The country strategy proposed as focal sectors Transport and Institutional Development and Capacity Building together with Macroeconomic support and capacity building for economic governance. The EU support assist the Government to redefine its role and purpose as the country move towards a better functioning market economy. The shift from the centrally planned economy in a one-party state to a private sector driven economy in a multi-party democracy involves profound cultural and attitude changes.

The strategy document obtained the positive opinion of the EDF Committee in November 2001, and was formally approved by the Commission in December 2001. It was signed on 11 July 2002 on the occasion of the Consultative Group Meeting in Lusaka.

Priorities for Co-operation

9th EDF Focal Areas

An allocation of 240 M€ and a B-allocation of 111M€ has been made available. Focal sectors are *capacity building* aimed at creating a more conducive environment for private sector development and *transport.* In addition *macro-economic* support is foreseen linked to the PRSP and social sectors/poverty alleviation.

In the Transport Sector the following specific objectives shall be pursued:

- reduction of backlog in road maintenance,
- increased national funding of road maintenance,
- decrease of vehicle over-loading,

- improved capacity for management of road maintenance,
- improved access to rural areas with high productive potential, and
- facilitate improved decision making concerning future railway development in relation to development of other transport modes.
- For indicative purposes, approximately € 90 M shall be reserved for this sector.

The major interventions foreseen are:

- Preventive maintenance of trunk, main and district roads;
- Maintenance and rehabilitation of feeder roads;
- Transport mode study (rail/road) and studies for track upgrading.

The major policy measures to be taken by the Government as a contribution to the implementation of the response strategy in this sector are:

- improved financing of road maintenance and enhanced axle load controls;
- reform of the institutional framework for the management of feeder roads and
- an improvement of the financing mechanism of maintenance for same.

In the Institutional Development and Capacity Building focal sector the following specific objectives shall be pursued:

- strengthen the financial and economic management capacities of the Zambian public service;
- build capacities for public-private dialogue as a basis for improving the policy and institutional environment for private sector development;
- build capacities of non-state actors; and
- increase access of private and public actors to distance learning courses.

For indicative purposes, approximately € 40 M shall be reserved for this sector.

The Community will support the macroeconomic reform programme of the Government. Special attention shall be given to the objective of poverty reduction, particularly with a view to ensuring equitable access to the social services. Macro-economic support shall be delivered under a three-year programme. Funds shall be disbursed on an annual basis. If an annual disbursement is not realised within the time limits foreseen, the corresponding amount can be transferred to one of the other sectors of co-operation in the Indicative Programme. Such a decision can be taken in the context of the annual review.

For indicative purposes approximately € 90 M shall be reserved for this type of support.

Non-focal Areas

An indicative amount of € 20 M is envisaged for the following purposes:

health, HIV/AIDS and education.

9th EDF Financial Data

	Allocation (A envelope) €	**% of overall allocation**
Focal Area		
• Transport	90	37.5
• Institutional reform and capacity building	40	16.8
• Macro-economic support	90	37.5
Non focal areas		
• Education	10	4.1
• Health	10	4.1
Total	**€ 240**	**100%**

Main Development Projects

- Micro projects programme

- Rehabilitation Kabwe-Kapiri Mposhi Chisamba Roads
- Rehabilitation and Privatisation of Mpulungu Harbour
- Private Sector Development programme
- Rehabilitation Monze-Zimba Road
- Export Development Programme II
- Mining Sector Diversification Programme
- Strengthening the Zambia Safe Blood Transfusion Programme
- Zambia Education Capacity Building programme
- Public Welfare Assistance Scheme
- Support to the Cultural Sector
- Support to the NAO's Office

7.19 Zimbabwe

Relations with the EU: On 18 February 2002 , the Council decided to take "appropriate measures" following the conclusions of the consultations held under Art. 96 of the ACP-EC Partnership Agreement and restrictive measures (CFSP) against Zimbabwe (visa ban and freeze of assets against the Government and ZANU-PF ruling elite). EDF development assistance to Zimbabwe has been suspended except for those projects in direct support of the population (health, education, micro-projects and decentralised co-operation, democratisation, respect for human rights and the rule of law). A "Restructuring exercise of the EC Aid Portfolio" has been carried out in co-operation with the NAO and is currently under implementation. As a result € 38.7 million are available at this stage. This figure excludes all 9th EDF funding of € 127 million, As these resources were automatically frozen by the Council February 2002 decision (the Country Strategy Paper and the 9th EDF programming exercise are blocked).

The EU position is kept under constant review and the Council has already decided twice (in 18 February 2003 and 19 February 2004) to extend these measures which now apply until 20 February 2005. Any lifting or easing of the measures against Zimbabwe would be difficult to justify unless the Government of Zimbabwe takes actions to remedy the situation and achieve positive progress as regards the respect for human rights, democratic principles and the rule of law.

The EU has taken every opportunity to convey to the Government of Zimbabwe its concern at increasing political violence and ill-treatment of the opposition and civil society and, in the last months, has issued Declarations related to these matters: A declaration of 3 June on the Zimbabwe stay-away, which was widely published in the local press; a declaration on Freedom of Press in Zimbabwe issued on 18 September 2003, a declaration issued on 28 November 2003 expressing concern at the current situation in Zimbabwe and finally, a declaration on 10 February 2004 on recent event in Zimbabwe. These declarations call the Government of Zimbabwe to respect fundamental rights urging it to engage in active and meaningful dialogue with internal stakeholders for a way forward to solve the current crisis.

The European Parliament has passed strong resolutions on Zimbabwe on 5 June and 15 December 2003 , in which it calls for the urgent opening of formal talks between the Government of Zimbabwe and the opposition with a view to establishing an interim national unity coalition government to organise free and fair elections.

Country Strategy: Zimbabwe remains one of the few ACP countries which have not yet signed the 9th EDF Country Strategy Paper (CSP) and National Indicative Program (NIP). Signature was suspended o n 18 February 2002 , by the Council Decision under Art. 96 of the ACP-EC Partnership Agreement, concluding consultations with Zimbabwe and establishing appropriate measures.

The Country Strategy programming process in Zimbabwe started in September 2000 and was completed and agreed upon by both the European Commission and the Government of Zimbabwe in July 2001. It was characterised by intensive dialogue between the European Commission and the National Authorising Officer (NAO) and with the EU Member States and other major donors in Harare . The participation of non-state actors in the process was a new feature of the Cotonou Agreement and this was successfully introduced in the Zimbabwean process.

The CSP strategy was built on the basis of two scenarios: a 'probable' scenario based on the assumption of a further deterioration of the situation in Zimbabwe and an 'alternative' scenario based on an improvement of the situation in terms of governance and economic stabilisation. The strategy focuses on two social sectors of health and education.

However, due to the rapidly deteriorating relations between the EU and Zimbabwe, culminating in the suspension of cooperation with Zimbabwe on 18 February 2002, the CSP was never discussed by the EU Member States in the framework of the European Development Committee, which has to approve it before adoption. It therefore remains a draft document and no further progress in implementing the 9th EDF Programme has been possible in the current circumstances.

Priorities for Co-operation

Despite the 18 February 2002 Council Decision and the freezing of the signature and implementation of 9th EDF CSP/NIP, the European Commission assistance to Zimbabwe since the beginning of the crisis continues to be very important.

Following this Council Decision the Commission has suspended financial support for all projects except those in direct support of the population. The key clauses of the Council's Decision state that:

"Financial support for all projects is suspended except those in direct support of the population, particularly those in the social sectors. Financing shall be re-oriented in direct support of the population, in particular in the social sectors, democratisation, respect for human rights and the rule of law".

The treatment of projects therefore depended upon the degree to which they provide direct support to the population and three groups of programs/projects were identified:

(a) The bulk of the EDF portfolio already aims to provide direct support to the population. These projects are therefore unaffected by the Council decision:

Project title	Project value (million €)	Spent to 12/03 (million €)	Available for spending in 2004/2005 (million €)
Small-Scale Irrigation Programme	14	13,2	0.8
Veterinary Faculty, University of Zimbabwe (to close in 12/2003)	8	6,8	1.2
11th Micro-Projects Programme (to close in 06/2003)	7,2	6,3	0,9
12th Micro-Projects Programme	22,8	10,0	12,8
Decentralised Co-operation Programme	7,2	4,1	3,1
Health Sector Support Programme II	33	10,8	22,2
Total	**92,2**	**51,2**	**41,0**

(b) A second group of projects designed in the late 1990s, combined direct support to the population with support for capacity-building and policy reform in Government ministries, or multi-donor basket funds that are no longer operational. In these cases, the approach was to suspend the capacity-building and policy reform activities and to re-allocate their budgetary allocations to direct support for the population.

Project title	Project value (million €)	Spent to 12/03 (million €)	Already available for direct support to population (million €)	To be reallocated from support to Ministries to direct support to the population (million €)
Health Sector Support Programme I	24,5	4,2	20,3	
Education Transition and Reform Programme	11,4	1,5	6,9	3 (Rider expected in late 2003)
STABEX 1994	4,9	2,2 (plus interest)	1,2	1,5
Total	**40,8**	**7,9**	**28,4**	**4,5**

Under Health Sector Support Programme I (HSSP I) funds are reallocated from the Health Services Fund and technical assistance for public-private partnerships to purchases of essential drugs.

Under the Education Transition and Reform Programme (ETRP) funds are reallocated from policy support and vouchers and scholarships to School Improvement Grants (school fee exemptions for children in 4 poor districts) and other recommended areas.

STABEX 1994 supports research, input credit and smallholder training for the cotton and coffee sectors. The coffee and cotton trusts allocate a budget to each activity at the beginning of each year. The European Commission has ensured that no further allocations are made to the (Government-owned) coffee and cotton research stations. The remaining funds from both sectors are allocated to complete an existing Stabex funded project supporting small-scale irrigation projects in the Honde Valley in Eastern Zimbabwe , which have experienced cost overruns, and to other projects in the cotton and coffee sectors that provide direct support to small-scale producers.

(c) The third group of projects refers to those not providing direct support to the population. They have been suspended and funds earmarked are partly already reallocated to direct support for the population:

Project title	Project value (million €)	Spent to 12/01 (million €)	Already released for new projects (million €)	To be released for new projects (million €)
Agricultural Services and Management Programme	12,7	1,9	6,7	4,1
Support Services Framework Contract (to close in 12/02)	1,2	0,3		0,9
Total	**13,9**	**2,2**	**6,7**	**5**

The main project involved was the Agriculture Services and Management Programme, which has been closed.

Disbursements in € for the implementation of EDF programs/projects in recent year has been as follows:

2000	2001	2002	2003
8,000,613	15,534,378	14,562,726	11.724.425

Apart from EDF support, the European Commission has financed other actions from EC budget lines:

- Under the European Initiative for Democracy and Human Rights, for which Zimbabwe is a focal country, € 5.1 million are provided for the period 2002-2005.
- Under the food and humanitarian budget lines: At this stage, for the season 2003-2004, and due to evidences of continuous important needs and the absence of other donors for the critical period up to May 2004, the European Commission has also pledged aid for a total amount of € 85 million (60 million for food aid -52 via WFP and 8 via Euronaid-NGO's) and around € 25 million for humanitarian aid (ECHO). I n order to avoid that food aid efforts are hampered by politicisation, the European Commission is applying concrete and internationally agreed EU guidelines for food distribution in Zimbabwe building up reinforced monitoring capacities in this field.

The European Commission is fully committed to continue to provide the Zimbabwean population with food and other humanitarian aid exclusively through international and non-governmental structures.

Main Development Projects

Health:

Health Sector Support Programme 1 (8/ACP/ZIM/10)

The overall objective of this Programme is to promote social justice through improved quality of life amongst the most vulnerable by developing a sustainable and efficient health system. Programme implementation began in 2000 and will continue for 5 years.

Health Sector Support Programme II (8/ACP/ZIM/19)

The overall objective of this programme, decided in July 2001, is to reduce the incidence and alleviate the impact of HIV/AIDS and other priority diseases in Zimbabwe .

The programme is supporting the procurement of essential drugs and supplies, and the recapitalisation of the National Blood Transfusion Service through purchase of supplies and equipment necessary to continue to deliver on its core business. It is also supporting the enhancement of the management capacity of both the National Pharmaceutical Company of Zimbabwe (NatPharm) and the Zimbabwe National Blood Transfusion Service (NBTS).

Education

Education Transition and Reform Programme (ETRP) (8/ACP/ZIM/13)

The overall objective of the ETRP is to contribute to a more efficient, equitable and sustainable education system in Zimbabwe. The purpose is to improve access and learning outcomes of poor children, particularly girls, in primary and secondary education in eight districts through the following project components: (i) Institutional Capacity Building (ii) School Improvement Grants (SIG) in four very poor districts and (iii) Support to disadvantaged children through scholarships and vouchers in four less poor districts.

Rural Development

Agricultural Services and Management Project (ASMP) (8/ACP/ZIM/7)

The objective of the Agricultural Services and Management Project (ASMP) was to enhance the performance and sustainability of the agricultural sector and smallholder sub-sector in particular.

Following the decision of the General Affairs Council of February 2002, the project was suspended and it was agreed to de-commit ASMP funds to finance new projects that directly benefited the people of Zimbabwe .

Small Scale Irrigation Programme (6/ACP/ZIM.031 & 32)

The overall objective of the project was to improve communal farmers living conditions through increased incomes and food security. The project purpose was to construct a 900 ha. irrigation scheme in Musikavanhu and Nyanyadzi South and settle 860 families, each with an average irrigation plot size of 1.0ha.

Faculty of Veterinary Science (7/ACP/ZIM/039)

The overall objective of the project was to improve animal health and to increase livestock productivity and farm incomes. This is being achieved mainly through support for training of future vets.

Macro-economic Support

Structural Adjustment Support Programme (2nd 'tranche'): €21 Million

The second 'tranche' of the Structural Adjustment Support Programme (SASP II) allocation to Zimbabwe was disbursed in February 1998. A total of Z$ 392,5 million Counterpart funds (CPF) was generated and deposited into the Reserve Bank of Zimbabwe in March 1998. The CPF were used to support the Government expenditures in the health and education sectors, as well as technical assistance to the Ministry of Finance and Economic Development.

Projects and Programmes Outside the Focal Sectors

Micro Projects

Zimbabwe/EU Micro project Programme (8 ACP/ZIM/016, 7/ACP/ZIM 96 & 97)

The purpose of the Micro-project Programme (MPP) is to assist local communities with financial and technical support to plan, implement and control sustainable projects in the focal sectors of Rural Development, Health and Education.

Implementation of these projects suffered due to the hyper-inflationary environment, foreign currency, and fuel shortages, unemployment, food insecurity and reduced stakeholder participation and in some cases had to be scaled down. Technical ministries and Rural District Councils were also constrained by the shortage of human and material resources.

Decentralised Co-operation

Zimbabwe Decentralised Co-operation Programme (ZDCP) (8 ACP ZIM 11)

The overall objective of the programme is to alleviate poverty through enhancement of self-reliance of selected rural and urban communities. The purpose of the programme is to improve demand driven service delivery to five disadvantaged communities by Local Communities, NSAs and private sector taking into consideration gender and environmental issues.

The ZDCP website was launched and three issues of the "ZDCP Today" newsletter were produced. The project also increased its advocacy work by participating in radio talk shows

Other Projects

Support Services Framework Contract (8/ACP/ZIM/006)

This contract was intended to be used to assist implementation of the National Indicative Programme by providing ad-hoc technical expertise in areas such as project preparation, monitoring and evaluation.

Minefield Clearance (7 ACP ZIM 51 & 68)

The purpose of the project was to increase agricultural production and to improve animal disease control in the area of intervention. The project, for which the field activities were concluded in December 2000, has been said to be one of the most successful projects of its type anywhere in the world. At its completion a total of 6,500,000 m^2 of ground were cleared and the total number of mines destroyed was 162,419.

The project was finally closed in 2001 after all claims had been settled with the contractor following the extension of the financial allocation of the project by 20%.

Other Instruments

European Investment Bank (EIB)

The European Investment Bank did not make any new lending to Zimbabwe during 2001 and 2002. This was principally because of Zimbabwe 's default on its debt-service obligations to the EIB since September 2000, but also because the adverse economic situation made the investment climate extremely unattractive.

By October 31st 2002 the arrears amounted to € 57.2 million.

Regional Projects

SADC Scholarship Programme for Bachelor of Veterinary Science Students (7/ACP/RPR/306)

The financing agreement was signed in 1994 and the project provides scholarships to nationals of other SADC countries to train for the Bachelor of Veterinary Science degree at the University of Zimbabwe .

SADC Regional Food Security Training Programme (8/ACP/RAU/003)

The purpose of this project is to improve the quality of service, advice and analysis provided by organizations in SADC concerned with food, agriculture and natural resources.
The mid-term evaluation was done in 2002 and the project also developed its Strategic Business Plan for the years 2003 – 2009.

STABEX 1994

The STABEX 1994 transfer granted € 3,121,146 for cotton and € 2,907,877 for coffee. Its objective was to partially compensate economic operators for losses incurred and to assist the productive capability of the cotton and coffee sectors through the improvement of research and training. As part of the programme, the Government of Zimbabwe committed itself to continue the liberalisation of agricultural markets as well as facilitating exports and investments and liberalising trade.

Following the suspension of cooperation with Zimbabwe , support under STABEX 1994 was reoriented away from direct support to the Coffee and Cotton research centres and focused on direct support to small coffee producers in the Honde valley.

STABEX 1995

Discussions are under way on a possible humanitarian use of these funds following the suspension of cooperation in February 2002.

Humanitarian Aid (ECHO)

Emergency relief programme program for flood victims in Chimanimani district in Zimbabwe in 2001

The European Commission granted the German NGO HELP €500,000 to support the population's recovery from Cyclone Eline in February 2001 by providing foodstuffs and agricultural inputs and implements.

Humanitarian Aid in 2002-2004

The European Commission adopted in June 2002 a € 2 million Financing Decision in support of nutritional surveillance and supplementary feeding. Under the regional Southern African Financing Decision of September 2002, about half of the € 30 million for the region benefits operations in Zimbabwe, covering among other things, supplementary feeding, home based care programmes for HIV/AIDS patients, procurement of agricultural inputs, water and sanitation improvements and a significant programme of support to the World Food Programme transparently distribute food aid and to monitor effectively its non-partisan distribution.

A further € 13 million Financing Decision was adopted on 12 May 2003, supporting continued humanitarian aid efforts addressing the same sectors as in 2002 and adding support to HIV/AIDS orphans.

An appeal to the Emergency Reserve for an additional € 25 million has been launched and ECHO hopes to be able to present a further regional Financing Decision for Southern Africa during July of 2003, to finance operations in the third and fourth quarters of 2003. About half of this amount benefited operations in Zimbabwe .

Food Aid Operations

The food shortage situation for the period 2002 to 2004 has been critical.

The European Commission has continued to be fully committed to provide the Zimbabwean population with food and other humanitarian aid exclusively through international and non-governmental structures.

The mobilization of the significant quantities required to feed the people of Zimbabwe has been achieved despite a number of logistical as well as bureaucratic difficulties. Not least has been the considerable delay in acquiring the relevant import certifications from the Zimbabwe authorities and the registration of international NGOs. Once in country secondary transport to distribution centres has been affected by the on-going fuel supply crisis.

A total amount of € 123,3 million has been pledged to finance food aid operations (€ 63,3 million for the season 2002-2003 and € 60 million for the season 2003-2004. Most of the funding has been done via the UN World Food Program (WFP).

In order to avoid that food aid efforts are hampered by politicisation, the Commission is applying concrete and internationally agreed EU guidelines for food distribution in Zimbabwe building up reinforced monitoring capacities in this field.

Other Budget Lines

NGO Co-financing (B7-6000)

Seven projects approved in previous years are currently ongoing.

Environment (B7-6200)

There is one ongoing project.

European Initiative for Democracy and Human Rights (EIDHR) (B7-7020)

Zimbabwe is one of 31 focus countries chosen for activities to be funded under the European Initiative on Democracy and Human Rights for the period 2002-2004. A total of € 2 million has been made available from the budget line over the period 2002-2004.

Zimbabwe was chosen as a focus country due to the EU's concern for the political and human rights situation. Human rights issues were also the subject of discussion with the Zimbabwean government throughout 2001 in the context of the Article 8 dialogue and Article 96 consultations under the Cotonou Agreement. The EU also considers that EIDHR activities can be effective in Zimbabwe due to the presence of robust, independent actors in the Parliament, the judiciary, the press and a local civil society committed to the promotion and protection of human rights. The strong interest of the international human rights NGOs' community in the situation in Zimbabwe is also an important factor.

8

Regional Cooperation and Integration in South Asia: Experience of SAARC

The ideas, attempts and formation of co-operation organizations, associations and alliances have been a systematic and regular pattern in contemporary international relations. Human history is as old as man and like men, such arrangements and organizations, international and regional, are living organisms. They live, transform and renew themselves to serve changing needs. In this context, South Asian Association for Regional Cooperation (SAARC) and Common Market for Eastern and Southern Africa (COMESA) are no exception. Occupying two important and strategic locations and regions in both African and Asian continents, they have evolved historically and adapted themselves to current challenges facing the economies of their member-states. An in-depth study of their history, present and future horizons have proved them as a vehicle for regional co-operation and integration towards the ultimate goal of socio-economic development of their societies.

Regional and sub-regional bodies have been generally motivated by the desire to attain some common development objectives as well as to reap the economic benefits that would accrue from better utilization of complementarities and economies of scale from an enhanced market across a wider geographical area. With globalization in full swing, issues of regional co-operation and integration ceased to be a luxury. It has become not only a vital development vehicle and choice but also strategic option.

A study of SAARC and COMESA and their roles in regional cooperation and integration is thus significant because with the changing world scenarios, regional arrangements have become genuine tool for the socio-economic survival of their respective peoples. Despite the fact that globalization, which is technology-based phenomenon, brings enormous opportunities, the fact remains that there are also serious pitfalls. As a technology and market-driven process, globalization is indifferent to human, cultural and environmental values. Equity and fairness are also beyond the caring of markets and technologies. Regional arrangements are thus important to collectively withstand negative manifestations of globalization and averting threats to the cultural and environmental values of regions concerned. With their glorious civilization and special peculiarities in the regions that have seen oldest civilizations of mankind, both SAARC and COMESA have the potential of contributing to the development of their peoples in the political, economic and cultural fields.

The two regional organizations although different in geography and history are united by daunting challenges in their respective regions. Together they have to find their way amidst prevailing international environment and geo-political realities that face the two regions of the world. It is incumbent upon developing countries in Africa and Asia to formulate and co-ordinate policy priorities with a view to enhance stability, economic development and regional economic cooperation. A package that addresses these needs is urgently needed to harness the new opportunities and meet the current challenges in a more collective and structured manner. This would enable the countries of SAARC and COMESA regions to transcend the size of their individual markets and utilize the benefits of economies of scale in production. This can further lead to economic and industrial diversification and rationalization of complementarities and their positive exploitation.

People of Asia and Africa share a common destiny i.e. to improve their lives and determine their place within the global community of nations through joint action, based on reliance on their resources and collective strength. Time has come for Africa and Asia to recognize and realize the importance of economic integration. This has the potential to open up the markets and establish free trade areas among its member states which could act as a pre-requisite for attaining successful economic development in the years to come. In a world witnessing an increasing liberalization of trade, booming investment, rapid movement of capital, consolidation of the role of the private sector, regional cooperation and integration is becoming a vital necessity.

The issue of regional cooperation and integration has been generally referred to as a rhetoric that has not been matched by actions on the ground. With the unfolding global developments, the need to speed up cooperation and integration processes in both Asia and Africa has become even more compelling. Recent developments in the rapidly evolving global trading system, especially the formation and consolidation of formidable trading blocs leave Africa and Asia with little choice but to commit themselves more firmly to regional co-operation and integration.

This chapter focuses on the regional cooperation and integration process in South Asia with an overview of SAARC. COMESA has been separately dealt with in the third chapter of this book.

On the whole, majority of the attempts made in the developing world have been plagued with serious difficulties. Some of these have stemmed from the unequal level of development of the member states, others from inequalities in resources and labour forces and economic and political ideals and still others from the insufficiently developed linkages between the nascent regional units and the rest of the world economy. Unequal distribution of the costs and benefits of the regional cooperation has often led to resentment and resistance, which sacrificed long term benefits to be achieved through more equitable cooperation to the short-term advantages of a return to bilateral economic relationships. Success among the attempts at regional cooperation have been achieved mainly in the regions with a relatively developed economic, educational, technological and scientific infrastructure, and with the capability and the will to provide a significant and dependable level of investment in programmes of economic cooperation.

Compared to the rest of the world, the South Asian countries remain in unacceptable levels of poverty, human deprivations, population pressure and environmental degradation. Although there is an immense prospect for growth in the region, the South Asian countries have yet to seriously exploit the potentials inherent in the regional cooperation for mitigating these evils.

The increased pace of economic globalization has presented to the South Asian countries new opportunities and exposed them to new challenges. The weak economic structure of these countries has left them ill-equipped to cope with the complex nature of these challenges. As countries across the Third World are trying to safeguard their interest by imparting new vigour and depth to their existing framework of regional cooperation by instituting and joining new regional formations and adopting schemes for the deeper integration, South Asia is seriously being jeopardized.

There is compelling logic underlying the process of constructive regionalism. It enhances the member countries capacity to cope with the common challenges of globalization. In the context of the segmentation of the world trading system, regionalism has emerged as the last resort to escape marginalization and develop collective leverages in global negotiations.

South Asian countries have a number of inherent advantages in regional cooperation. They command a huge potential market with their combined population of more than 1.5 billion people. What is needed is to enlarge, integrate and unify this market by removing barriers to trade and take other measures for regional cooperation. By working together, the countries of South Asia may propel their ongoing trade reforms in a coordinated fashion. Using the lowest tariffs among the agreeing countries as the basis for coordination, they could create more trade and systematically attract FDI to the region.

The first ever attempt at regionalism in Asia was made at the 'Asian Relations Conference' in March 1947, but it largely focused on the de-colonization movements taking place in Asia. The region witnessed a few efforts by mid 1950s. However, these efforts were either promoted by anti-colonial ethos or by the prodding of ex-colonial masters. Their scope and membership even included extra regional powers and invariably remained too diffused to have any lasting and visible impact.

During the Cold War period, regional politics in South Asia emerged primarily to support and sustain military alliances and to rebuild, coordinate and integrate markets and economies of allies. The South Asian nations could not do more than preoccupy themselves with quarrels and conflicts. In fact, the divisions and conflicts in South Asia were seen to serve the greater and better purpose in Cold War politics.

The first regional grouping in Asia emerged in East Asian region. It was the SEATO (South East Asian Treaty Organization), a military alliance supported by the United States. From South Asia, Pakistan became a member of SEATO, as well as CENTO (Central Treaty Organization), a military and economic alliance of Britain, Iran, Pakistan and Turkey. After the Bandung Conference of 1955, Non-Alignment as an international group emerged at the Belgrade Conference of 1961. Except Pakistan, all other South Asian countries became its member. India, due to its dominant position was a leading player in the region.

Tensions between India and its neighbours were exploited to serve extra-regional interests. The dominant strategic interests associated with the Cold War did not allow any attempt to create regional groupings outside the Cold War context to succeed. South Asia was eventually divided in the Cold War rivalries. Thus, regionalism could neither be imposed from the global hegemonic forces, nor could it be evolved through autonomous initiatives from within the South Asian regions. Despite this situation, each South Asian country had bilateral relations with various regional economic groupings. These countries also remained members of international groupings such as UNCTAD and the Group of 77.

In the mid 1980s, regionalism eventually came into being in South Asia with the formation of SAARC. It sought to achieve the integrated package of greater cooperation in the following phases:

- the establishment SAARC Preferential Trading Arrangement (SAPTA). The agreement to this effect was signed in April 1993 and entered into force in December 1995;
- the establishment of a South Asian Free Trade Area (SAFTA) by the year 2010 by the least developed Member States and by 2008 by other Member States;
- the establishment of a South Asian Customs Union (SACU) by the year 2015; and
- the commencement of the process of implementing the remaining measures for moving towards a South Asian Economic Union by the year 2020.

8.1 Overview of SAARC

The South Asian Association for Regional Cooperation (SAARC) was established when its Charter was formally adopted on December 8, 1985 by the Heads of State of Bangladesh, Bhutan, India, Maldives, Nepal, Pakistan and Sri Lanka. It is an Association based on the consciousness that in an increasingly interdependent world, the objectives of peace, freedom, social justice and economic prosperity are best achieved in the South Asian region by fostering mutual understanding, good neighbourly relations and meaningful cooperation among the Member States which are bound by ties of history and culture.

The spirit of the SAARC is reflected in its objectives and the principles, which provides a platform for the people of South Asia to work together in a spirit of friendship, trust and understanding. It aims to accelerate the process of economic and social development in the Member States. Cooperation in SAARC is based on the respect for the principles of sovereign equality; territorial integrity; political independence; non-interference in the internal affairs of Member States; and mutual benefits. Regional cooperation is, in fact, seen as a complement to the bilateral and multilateral relations of its Member States.

Decisions at all levels in SAARC are to be taken on the basis of unanimity; and bilateral and contentious issues are to be excluded from the deliberations of the Association. The Charter of the Association provides for the following:

The Summit is the highest authority of the Association consists of the Heads of State or Government, who meet annually at the Summit level. To date, eleven Summits have been held: Dhaka (1985), Bangalore (1986), Kathmandu (1987), Islamabad (1988), Malé (1990), Colombo (1991), Dhaka (1993), New Delhi (1995), Malé (1997), Colombo (1998) and Kathmandu (2002).
The Twelfth SAARC Summit was held recently in Islamabad (2004). Thirteenth Summit is scheduled to be held in Dhaka, Bangladesh.

The Council of Ministers comprises of the Foreign Ministers of Member States. The Council is responsible for formulating policies; reviewing progress; deciding on new areas of cooperation; establishing additional mechanisms as deemed necessary; and deciding on other matters of general interest to the Association.

8.1.1 Standing Committee: The Standing Committee comprising the Foreign Secretaries of Member States is entrusted with the task of overall monitoring and coordination of programmes; approving of projects and programmes, and modalities of financing; determining inter-sectoral priorities; mobilising regional and external resources; and identifying new areas of cooperation. The Standing Committee is assisted by a Programming Committee (which is not a SAARC Charter body) comprising senior officials to scrutinize the Secretariat Budget, finalize the Calendar of Activities and take up any other matter assigned to it by the Standing Committee. The Programming Committee has also been entrusted to consider and submit to the Standing Committee recommendations for action on the Reports of the Technical Committees, SAARC Regional Centres and the SAARC Audio Visual Exchange (SAVE) Committee.

8.1.2 Technical Committees: At present, there are seven Technical Committees functioning in various fields under the agreed areas of cooperation. The Technical Committees formulate specialized programmes and projects in their respective fields under the SAARC Integrated Programme of Action (SIPA). They are also responsible for monitoring the implementation of such activities and submit their reports to the Standing Committee through the Programming Committee. These committees initiate cooperation in important areas such as trade, manufactures and services; basic needs; human resources development; database on socio-economic indicators; energy modeling techniques; plan modeling techniques; and poverty alleviation strategies.

8.1.3 Specialised Ministerial Meetings: Since the establishment of the Association, a number of SAARC ministerial meetings have been held to focus attention on specific areas of common concern, such as international economic issues, environment, housing, tourism, women, youth, health etc. and these have now become an integral part of the consultative structure.

SAARC Secretariat is based in Kathmandu. It coordinates and monitors implementation of SAARC activities, prepares for SAARC meetings and serves as a channel of communication between the association and other regional organizations and inter-governmental institutions.

A SAARC Preferential Trading Arrangement (SAPTA) has been established and negotiations are continuing on the reduction of tariffs and other impediments to a more free flow of trade within the region. The agreement on SAPTA was signed on 11 April 1993. It entered into force on 7 December 1995. The basic principles underlying SAPTA are:

- overall reciprocity and mutuality of advantages so as to benefit equitably all contracting States, taking into account their respective level of economic and industrial development, the pattern of their external trade, and trade and tariff policies and systems;

- negotiation of tariff reform step by step, improved and extended in successive stages through periodic reviews;
- recognition of the special needs of the Least Developed Contracting States and agreement on concrete preferential measures in their favour; and
- inclusion of all products, manufactures and commodities in their raw, semi-processed and processed forms.

8.1.4 South Asian Free Trade Area (SAFTA): The Tenth SAARC Summit in Colombo decided to set up a Committee of Experts to draft a comprehensive treaty framework for creating a free trade area within the region, taking into consideration the asymmetries in development within the region and bearing in mind the need to fix realistic and achievable targets. Four Meetings of the Committee of Experts have since been held. Till such time as the SAFTA is given effect to, the process of trade negotiations under SAPTA may be continued for further trade liberalisation in the region.

The South Asian States have adopted Conventions on the Suppression of Terrorism, Narcotic Drugs and Psychotropic Substances; Preventing and Combating Trafficking in Women and Children; and Promotion of Child Welfare in South Asia. SAARC has undertaken high level Regional Studies on trade manufacturers and services, environment as well as on the alleviation of poverty.

A dialogue with Regional Organizations such as ASEAN and EU has been developed by SAARC and interaction takes place annually. It discusses multilateral issues which are of common concern to its members and has identified areas on which collective positions could be projected and promoted in the international forums. These include the world trade and financial issues, environmental issue, disarmament and development issues. Beyond official linkages, SAARC has also encouraged and facilitated cooperation among Chambers of Commerce and Industry through SAARC Chambers of Commerce and Industries and the private sector and among legal communities of SAARC through SAARC laws.

At the 12th SAARC summit, the Heads of State /Governments adopted the Islamabad Declaration which contained the roadmap for South Asian co-operation and the establishment of a South Asian Economic Union and the common currency goal based on the lines of European Union. The summit also adopted the SAFTA Agreement as well as an Additional Protocol to the existing Convention on the Suppression of Terrorism.

As per the Agreement, SAFTA will come into force from January 1, 2006, and the developing countries of the region will reduce their tariffs to between zero to five percent for least developing countries. The SAFTA accord also allows any contracting States to pull out of the treaty at any time, after it comes into force from January 1, 2006. Such withdrawal shall be effective on the expiry of the six months from the date on which a written notice thereof is received by the Secretary General of the SAARC. A SAFTA Ministerial Council comprising Commerce/Trade Ministers and a Committee of Experts have been envisaged in SAFTA for the administration and implementation of the Agreement. SAFTA Agreement also suggests a number of measures that a member may adopt, including the removal of barriers to the intra-SAARC investment, harmonization of customs facilities, transit facilities for efficient intra-SAARC trade and simplification of procedures for business visas. Any dispute that may arise among the contracting States regarding the interpretation and the application of the provisions of this (SAFTA) Agreement or any instrument adopted within its framework concerning the rights and obligations of the States will be amicably settled through a process initiated by a request for bilateral consultations. The Agreement has been described as a major 'milestone' towards further broadening of economic cooperation and to ensure equitable distribution of benefits of trade.

The Additional Protocol of the Convention on Suppression of Terrorism is described as a 'landmark' agreement. It deals with tackling the problem of financing of terrorism. It reaffirmed commitment of SAARC to condemnation of terrorism in all its forms and manifestations as it affected the security, stability and the development of the region. The Protocol reiterates the commitment to implement all the relevant international Conventions to which they are a party.

The seven-page 43-point Islamabad Declaration envisioned South Asia to be a peaceful and stable region where each nation was at peace with itself and its neighbours and where conflicts, differences and disputes were addressed through peaceful means and dialogues.

8.2 Assessment

The emergence of the SAARC in 1985 coincided with the winds of economic liberalization blowing over the Indian sub-continent. Sri Lanka liberalized its economy in 1977, partial liberalization of the Indian economy began in 1985, and the late 1980s saw the initiation of economic liberalization both in Bangladesh (1987) and Pakistan (1988). With open economies in the four major SAARC countries, there was a need to explore the benefits of economic cooperation. The early 1990s also witnessed the end of the Cold War, and globalization of trade and investment began taking place. This was further strengthened by the information revolution when Netscape was introduced to the Internet in 1994.

The importance of some of the old bilateral links gradually diminished with the global lowering of the tariff barriers. Military related links, too, became less relevant. Cooperation in the spheres of economies became more important. The initiation of SAPTA and the move towards establishment of SAFTA are the steps to avail itself of the vast opportunities for deeper regional integration that lies ahead.

After initially focusing on the non economic issues, SAARC embraced economic cooperation in the mid 1990s. However, SAARC's economic cooperation have not yielded any impressive results in the global context. There are a plethora of impediments to economic cooperation in the SAARC and external stimuli from mega regional blocs or powerful nations to strengthen economic cooperation between the member countries have not been very forthcoming. Although SAARC is today involved in multifarious areas of activities, its approach towards regional cooperation has been compartmental rather than holistic, and lacks a long term architecture. As a result despite significant success registered by the SAARC over the years –particularly in serving as a confidence building measure for the countries of the region—it has yet to meet the rising expectations of the peoples of the region.

Despite the slow progress of regional cooperation in South Asia, the actual working of the SAARC since its establishment has raised high hopes of peace in this region be-devilled by conflicts of all kinds. It is true that at present South Asian regional cooperation is far from the stage where EU and ASEAN have reached, yet it cannot be denied that a small beginning has been made in this direction, which would produce far reaching results in the future. The inception of the SAARC represents unity in diversity. The seven Member States are of different sizes, having diverse political system & varied security perception yet, despite the disparities, these neighbouring countries have made significant progress towards, finding common grounds for economic, social & cultural cooperation. The SAARC members have fully realized that a solution to every nation's problems is possible by a collective approach. Thus, SAARC has become a living reality today, because the inspiration for regional cooperation emanated from common aspiration.

8.3 Prospects

The fact that the SAARC is at the threshold of its third decade has raised hopes that it has an abiding place in the modern era of regional groupings and that it has enough capability to go forward. A study of the working of the SAARC since its inception, reveals that the concept of regional cooperation in South Asia has made considerable headway. It has gained meaningful acceptance on account of its vigorous efforts for effecting economic cooperation and cementing neighbourly relations among the member countries.

It has been fully realized by now, that if the SAARC is to forge its way ahead, it will have to comprehend the relevance of the political logic of economic cooperation and also the trade liberalization for effecting economic integration. Evidently, inter-regional or intra-regional trade can add to the viability of the SAARC. Moreover, Himalayan resources, transport and communication linkages and industrial cooperation are some of the most patent avenues which have great potential for SAARC. The SAARC may also take unified position through its negotiations and arrangements with outside regional groupings, such as WTO, Group 77 etc. SAARC may also further accelerate its progress by establishing its linkages with other regional organizations like ASEAN, IOR-ARC etc. and other world powers like Japan or China for mutual benefits.

The success of SAARC largely depends upon the synchronization of the interests of both, big and small nations. In this context, it may be suggested that bilateral problems may not result in its malfunctioning eventually. Unless the key political issue (the Indo-Pakistan conflict over Kashmir) is sorted out, economic cooperation is not likely to cross the critical threshold at which solely quantitative increases of volume in trade and investment can help bring about qualitative improvements in political relationship. SAARC has to find a way of sorting out bilateral political problems outside the SAARC framework at an informal level, because meaningful regional cooperation is not possible given the existing bilateral problems.

Although, there have been serious and strong differences amongst the member countries on various issues, it should not cause disappointment. To avoid and checkmate the political constraints for its bright prospects, the role of India in the wider context, may be more vital. It may have more accommodating spirit so as to keep the morale of SAARC community high.

It is hoped that the recent Indo-Pakistan peace initiative will achieve positive results and that it will create a favourable climate to operationalise SAFTA at the earliest and to achieve the ultimate objective of a South Asian Union on the lines of the European Union.

South Asia will never achieve its full potential unless disputes and tensions are resolved peacefully. The leaders of SAARC should move towards solving the disputes boldly with the objective of seeking honourable solutions with mutual respect and in the spirit of accommodation. If we fail, cynicism will take over and the SAARC will lose its creditability and momentum.

In order to give the dream of an Economic Union and common currency goal a touch of reality, it is necessary to transform the entire approach and policies of Member States towards SAARC. The biggest challenge is to make the mainstream SAARC process a dynamic exercise with a multiplicity of stakeholders and institutions.

At this stage, we must all strive towards sustainable consensus and Governments apart, the civil society must emphatically promote awareness about the need and advantage of regional cooperation. There ought to be much greater interaction between the civil society and the political class across the different countries of South Asia. This is anticipated to contribute significantly towards a greater South Asian solidarity which is essential for the progress and prosperity of all our peoples.

References

A.D.V. de S. (ed), *Globalization and South Asia: Retrospect and Prospect*, Sri Lanka Association for the Advancement of Science, 1999, Colombo.

Another Attempt at SAFTA, *The Hindu,* January 8, 2004.

Baru, S., "Regional Economic Cooperation: Threat or Opportunity?" in Gunewardena, V. (ed), *Regional Cooperation and integration: Perspective from Europe and South Asia,* European Commission to Sri Lanka, 1998, Colombo.

De Melo and Arvind Panagria (eds), *New Dimensions of Regional Integration*, Cambridge University Press, 1994.

De Silva, K. M., "SAARC and the Future of South Asia: a view from the Periphery", *South Asian Survey,* Vol. 6. No. 2, 1999.

Dubey, M., *New Regionalism and the Countries of the South,* South Centre, 1997, Geneva.

Eduardo Faleiro, "South Asian Economic Cooperation", *South Asia Politics,* August, 2003.

Ghose, S. and Mukherjee, S. (eds), *Emerging South Asian Order: Hopes and Concerns,* Media South Asia,1996, Calcutta.

Kalegama, S., "SAARC: from Association to a Community—A small country Perspective", *South Asian Survey,* Vol. 6, No. 2, 1999.

Lama, M.P., "Add Spark to SAARC", *The Times of India,* January 6, 2004.

Mistry, P.S., "Regional Integration and Development: Panacea or Pitfalls?", RIS Occasional Paper, No. 47, New Delhi, 1995.

Muni, S.D., "Regionalism Beyond the Regions: South Asia Outside SAARC", in Gonsalves, E. and Jetly, N. (eds), *The Dynamics of South Asia: Regional Cooperation and SAARC,* Sage, 1999, New Delhi.

Panagariya, A. "Trade Policy in South Asia: Recent Liberalization and Future Agenda", *World Economy,* June, 1999.

Pigato, M. etal., *South Asia's Integration into the World Economy,* The World Bank, 1997, Washington D.C.

Rao, Bhaskar N., "SAARC or no SAARC, We are Neighbours", *South Asia Politics,* February, 2003.

Text of the Joint Press Statement issued by the India and Pakistan on the meeting between Prime Minister Vajpayee and General Musharraf.

Text of the Prime Minister Atal Bihari Vajpayee's speech at the 12th SAARC Summit, in Islamabad, January 4, 2004.

Text of the Prime Minister Atal Bihari Vajpayee's speech at the fist Hindustan Times Leadership Initiative on the Peace Dividend—Progress for India and South Asia, in New Delhi on December 12, 2003.

The Islamabad Declaration adopted by the 12th SAARC Summit.

Treaty of South Asian Association for Regional Cooperation.

Website of SAARC, http/: www.saarc-sec.org

9

India-Africa: Partners for All Seasons

India has been recognised as an attractive investment destination for investment and a large and growing market for business. The fundamentals of the Indian economy have become strong and stable. There has been consistent high growth in recent years and there are definite indications of continuation of this trend in the future. India is emerging as a global player in Information Technology and is in the forefront of the unfolding new era of Knowledge Economy, with its large pool of scientific and creative human resources and Research and Development (R&D) facilities. There is a change in the mindset of Indians who have become more confident and outward looking. The Indian market is being driven by a powerful new force of entrepreneurship unleashed by the economic reforms and liberalization of recent years.

Of the twelve fastest emerging markets in the world, six are in Africa, so India is very keen to engage in sustainable projects with Africa. In 1991, bilateral trade between India and Africa was estimated at 890 million dollars. By March 2003 it had reached six billion dollars on the back of strong annual trade with South Africa, which stands at 2.4 billion dollars. South Africa and four of its neighbours are keen to seal a preferential trade agreement with India in hopes of spurring trade and turning historical ties into economic opportunities. The Southern African Customs Union trade bloc, comprising Botswana, Lesotho, Swaziland, Namibia and South Africa, are hoping tariff barriers can be removed to boost trade.

9.1 India–Africa: A Comparative Perspective

As countries of the South, both India and countries of Africa share similar histories of colonialism and struggle for independence. Indeed the great Mahatma Gandhi whetted his appetite for freedom in South Africa. In more recent times both have stood together in the battle to gain a more equal share of the world's trade and a voice in its fora. African countries are undertaking similar economic reforms and both the continents are engaged in the search for more open, responsive and accountable government.

While Africans were being shipped to the Americas as slaves, Indians were being shipped to east and southern Africa as indentured labour. And so there are also strong blood ties between the two continents. All in all, there is a strong basis for cooperation between the two continents that goes far beyond the edifying rhetoric of South-South cooperation.

After what came to be known as the "lost decade" of the eighties induced by falling commodity prices, debt, war and mismanagement, Africa is now in its fifth year of economic recovery with growth in GDP outstripping population growth for the first time in many years. But growth is not so strong as to assure the commonly agreed goal of reducing absolute poverty by half by the year 2015.

Africa's population continues to grow and is soon expected to exceed that of India. India has one billion people, compared to Africa's population of 700 million. But according to United Nations estimates, by the year 2050 India' s population will maintain itself at about 1.5 billion people while Africa's population is expected to increase in size well into the next century when it is projected to plateau at over 2.5 billion. In other words, India's population will stabilize after 50 per cent growth in population; while, if current trends continue, Africa's population will stabilize after a growth of 350 per cent.

This makes for very different per capita income projections. The World Bank expects that the absolute poor will decline in India over the next generation but increase significantly in Africa. Income inequality in Africa is the highest of any region in the world. In Africa, those in the top 20 per cent receive nearly 10 times the income of those in the bottom 20 per cent. The comparative multiple for South Asia is 4.5 times. Forty four per cent of Africans live below locally defined poverty lines. Excluding North Africa, the figure is 51 per cent. In Sub-Saharan Africa the poverty line, on average, is defined as about 30 rupees per person per day.

In India, contraception has reduced population growth rate to 1.6 per cent annually and this could fall down to 1 per cent by 2010. In 1991 literacy in India was only 52 per cent, well below the level of many African countries. In less than a decade, literacy has shot up to 64 per cent, accompanied by a shrink in the urban-rural gap and male- female literacy gap.

Another challenge, cutting across all the other challenges is to properly assure equal opportunities and outcomes of development for girls and women. This is another area where the experience of India, particularly in attempting to ensure gender equality at the local levels, is of great interest to Africa.

With regard to growth, Africa is struggling to obtain the necessary supply side response to the numerous macro-economic initiatives it has taken to propel to the higher heights if we are to break out of the vicious poverty circle.

The most visible measure of long-term political and economic viability is often investment rates. To achieve the 8 per cent per annum growth rate needed if Africa is to halve poverty by 2015, investment rates would need to be about 45 per cent of GDP. Given that the average savings rate is about 15 per cent of GDP and with development assistance at 12 per cent of GDP, this leaves a financing gap of 18 per cent of GDP that needs to be covered on an annual basis.

It is shocking that fifteen years after economic structural adjustment began, Africa should be looking solely to foreign aid to plug this gap rather than to internally generated domestic savings or indigenous private entrepreneurs. This is not just because of the debt overhang, though that is a contributory factor. Nor is it because Africa's incomes are so low as to preclude increases in domestic savings. Incomes in India are even lower. But domestic savings here have averaged 26 per cent of GDP between 1990 and 1999 – 11 per cent of GDP higher than Africa, where per capita incomes are 20 per cent higher! The accumulated loss of faith by Africans in the regimes that govern them is so profoundly and deeply rooted that Africans either prefer immediate consumption to savings; or are exporting their savings through capital flight. Africa has the highest rate of capital flight of any region in the world.

This links with the second indicator of long-term viability- the direction of talent, which is still outward-bound from Africa. According to the Association of African Universities, over 1000 African universities have watched their learning resources evaporate in recent years. As reported by the World Bank for the period 1990 to 1995, about 23,000 lecturers emigrated each year from African universities to countries where conditions were more congenial. The vacancy rates in the academic units of African universities range from 34 to 50 per cent. Of the nearly 2,000 African PhD degree awardees in USA and Canadian universities between 1986 and 1996, less than 40 per cent returned to Africa.

Foreign Direct Investment (FDI) is another measure of confidence. The rate of return on FDI to Africa is 29 per cent, higher than in any other region of the world. Yet only 4 per cent of the total investment pouring into developing countries is going to Africa. By contrast India has been experiencing a boom in investment including repatriation of capital by Indians living abroad.

There is much Africa could learn from India on improving the African business environment for private sector investment, public-private partnership as well as strengthening capital markets. India has been especially successful at developing its small- and medium-scale enterprises; an area where we lag behind terribly in Africa; condemning would-be entrepreneurs to the fringes and so-called informal sector. Fundamentally, we need Africans to believe in Africa; like Indians are starting to believe in India.

Critical to this confidence in future is the issue of governance. India is the world's largest democracy and has a proud record of regular elections. Many African countries have recently reverted from one party or military to multiparty systems of governments. African continent, is grappling more severely with strengthening the rule of law and the divisions of power between the legislative, executive and judiciary arms of governance; as well relations between citizens and state institutions.

Driven by the belief that a capable state is a pre-requisite for a capable economy, Africans are interested in best cases and lessons learned in promoting improvements in governance. Several aspects of India's governance, including systems of accountability for impact found in the Planning Commission, policies of fostering civil society, and others, have attraction for study.

Perhaps nowhere has the rebirth of India been more profound than in the area of information technology - one that is believed to be as a key to jump starting Africa into the new millennium. Vikram Seravai spoke of satellite delivery of national education in 1969. Sabeer Bhatia, another son of India, went on to invent Hotmail, the most popular form of Internet based e-mail, and sold it for US$400 million to Microsoft! Over 700 ICT firms in Silicon Valley are owned by Indians – mostly graduates of Indian institutes of technology. India has one of the most vibrant, government-led national information and communication strategies. India has had considerable success in pulling back or making use of the diaspora. Indian ICT experts are a source of information on business opportunities for start-ups back home. Software production is a mantra to Indian excellence. India has also been aggressive in the development of language infrastructure through IT - an area of considerable interest to Africa, given its multiplicity of languages.

The Africans wants to ensure that they are drivers and not passengers on the information highway. They have played a central role in launching a continent-wide effort to accelerate the adoption of information systems, the African Information Society Initiative (AISI), and house its secretariat. Since then they are active in promoting information and communications as one of the most hopeful ways of accelerating Africa's development.

Software production is a potential entry point for Africa into ICT production. Compared to hardware, it is less capital intensive, more labour intensive, and has a longer shelf life. While there is a limited pool of expertise in this area in Africa, Indian software houses face a large-scale migration of human resources. Nonetheless, there are opportunities for African IT companies to work with Indian counterparts in gaining skills, resources and new software development culture and quality. ECA, which now has a network of ICT experts within the African diaspora, would be especially interested in studying how India went about tapping this valuable human resource and fund of goodwill in India's case. A final challenge, which in some ways encompasses and certainly impacts, upon several of the other challenges just mentioned, is globalisation. While Sub-Saharan Africa has a GDP comparable to that of India, it is a much smaller player in international trade and investment. African capital markets are newer and do not cover a full range of functions. They are smaller and are not yet well integrated.

The World Bank estimates that high tariffs, anti dumping regulations and technical barriers to trade in industrialized countries cost Sub-Saharan African countries US$ 20 billion annually in lost exports. In other words, they lose more because of trade barriers than we gain because of aid.

Despite different standing in the international economic system, both India and Africa face challenges from the largest players. The World Trade Organization is alone among the economic blocks in allowing one vote per country, but de facto both find it hard to have the issues taken seriously by the great trading powers. If countries of the south fail to take a joint stance, they would find themselves ruled by the law of the jungle in which the only the fittest - those who have the unfair advantages of history - will survive.

India is urging that the transparency and supervision demanded from the financial institutions of the south be equally demanded from the financial institutions of the north. Calling for restoration of confidence in the multilateral trading system, India is pressing for developed countries to fulfill their commitments regarding special and differential treatment for countries of the south; for strengthening the system of preferences extended to these countries; as well as preventing the spread of excessive liberalization to the exclusive benefit of the north.

As we contemplate collaboration between India and Africa to nurture and foster the common interests between the two countries, a number of relationships such as joint policy research; the exchange of personnel; holding policy dialogues on developing information technology and software industries; joint studies of common governance challenges; and collaboration on common positions in the international arena can be further strengthened.

9.2 India's Economic Diplomacy

India's contact with Africa goes back to 2500 B.C. or earlier. The eastern coast of Africa was a natural trading destination for Indian merchants, as the force and direction of the monsoon winds automatically ferried their trading ships between India and Africa. More recently, since the middle of the nineteenth century, Indians have settled down in large numbers in Africa, both as indentured labourers and as traders. The presence of a large Indian diaspora in Mauritius, South Africa and other countries in the eastern coast of Africa is a legacy of this history.

The two regions have gone similar kind of socio-political and economic transition, including the liberalization of their economies. As members of the Non-Aligned Movement, the Commonwealth, G-15 and the newly formed Indian Ocean Rim Initiative, India and Africa share common views on most international issues. The two regions have a close understanding in the United Nations and the other international fora and are committed to strengthening South-South solidarity and cooperation.

Africa has always figured prominently in India's external relations, before and after independence. Development cooperation has always been the principal component of India's Africa policy. This has taken different forms – trade, technical assistance, joint ventures and consultancy services.

International trade plays a vital role in getting together countries geographically apart and creating in them a sense of belonging. The dimension of commercial exchanges between India and Africa is steadily widening, although it started in a modest way. India started as an exporter of old traditional items; but, in later years, Africa had been importing from India sophisticated manufactured goods also.

Table 9.1 gives an insight into India-Africa bilateral trade relations.

Although India has enjoyed historically closer economic and political relations with Africa, but its present bilateral trade is not encouraging. It accounts for hardly five per cent of India's trade with the entire world. The exports stood at 5.74 percent and 5.99 per cent in 2003 and 2004 respectively, while the imports were 5.58 per cent and 4.14 per cent in 2003 and 2004 respectively. The trade turnover (i.e. exports plus imports) has increased from US $ 6453.06 million in 2003 to US $ 6988.55 million in 2004. India's trade deficit (i.e. imports minus exports) with the region has reduced from US $ 396.44 million in 2003 to US $ -616.79 million in 2004. This shows a healthy growth rate of 25.57 per cent in exports in the year 2003-04 and a decline in the imports to -6.97 per cent for the same year.

Main items which India exports to Africa are as follows: Drugs, pharmaceuticals and fine chemicals; Engineering goods; Transport equipments and vehicles; Project goods; Machinery and equipments; Small and medium scale machinery; Plastic and linoleum products; Wheat; Consultancy services; Cotton manufacturers; Chemicals and allied products; Iron and steel manufacturers; tobacco, spices and tea; Non- basmati rice; Cotton yarn, fabrics; Rubber manufactured products and Jute manufactures.

Table 9.1: India's Bilateral Trade with Africa (US$ mn)

	2002-2003			2003-2004			
	WORLD	AFRICA	%share	WORLD	AFRICA	%share	%growth
EXPORTS	52719.43	3028.31	5.74	63842.97	3802.67	5.99	25.57
IMPORTS	61412.13	3424.75	5.58	78149.61	3185.88	4.14	-6.97
Trade Turnover	114131.56	6453.06	--	141992.58	6988.55	--	--
Trade Balance	-8692.70	396.44	--	-14306.65	-616.79	--	--

Source: *Directorate General of Commercial Intelligence and Statistics* (DGCIS), Ministry of Commerce and Industry.

India's imports from Africa consist mainly of: Hides and skins; Leather; Petroleum crude; Crude oil; Pearls, precious and semi precious stones; Dyeing, tanning and colouring materials; Wood and wood products; Metalliferous ores and metal scrap; Non-ferrous metals; Raw cotton; Primary steel, pig- iron based items; Organic/inorganic minerals; and other crude minerals.

India's trade with African countries suffers owing to certain handicaps of general nature, which with marginal variations, are equally applicable to almost all the countries in Africa. These include: Unfavourable economic conditions in Africa; Traditional and continuing trade concentration with the former colonial powers; Unfavourable terms of trade; High debt service ratios; Lower inflow of external capital; Inadequate infrastructural facilities like irregular shipping services and inadequacies on the part of India, particularly lack of knowledge and information on opportunities in Africa and poorly organized commercial wings in the Indian diplomatic missions in African countries. Other factors are: language barriers – languages like Portuguese, French and Arabic being the official and business language in a number of countries hamper the process of information dissemination; Stiff competition from European countries; Lack of awareness among the Indian Business Community of the vast potential in Africa.

9.3 Suggestions for Trade Promotion

A special strategy needs to be evolved for trade promotion. The strategy could include steps such as:

- Sending teams to potential markets;
- Organizing meetings for exporters in India for special attention to these markets;
- Asking our diplomatic missions to carry out surveys special reports, and
- Giving extra incentive for exports.

In the face of new challenges and the process of globalization, the private sector has a significant role to play in the countries of Africa and India. Since the African private sector is composed chiefly of small and medium scale enterprises these need to be focused on. They are key factor in the creation of new jobs, and their existence is fundamental to making the most of policies of modernization and privatization.

Countries like Eritrea, Ethiopia, Zaire, Rwanda, Somalia, Burundi, and Madagascar, which have been devastated by prolonged civil wars, need to be rehabilitated. Major western donors and multilateral agencies have promised assistance for which India could get project for supply of technology experts. Mauritius has emerged as a major economy with modern facilities. Indian industries should be encouraged in this direction.

Francophone Africa has not been properly tapped. Special attention needs to be given to this region. It is necessary to overcome language barrier and putting in special promotional efforts for non-explored regions.

9.3.1 Technical Assistance: Another area of cooperation is technical assistance to African countries by providing training in India, deploying Indian experts for short and long terms, underwriting feasibility and techno economic studies, organizing technical workshops and supplying of equipments. This field of cooperation under the Indian Technical and Economic Cooperation (ITEC) Programme and the Special Commonwealth African Assistance Plan (SCAAP) launched in 1964 has been the principal instruments of India's efforts to assist the newly independent countries of Africa in the development of their manpower resources. It covered extension of technical cooperation, aid and credit; establishment of mutually beneficial trade relations and provision of capital aid ant technical expertise to help build medium and small scale industries.

The scope of ITEC programme is rather extensive and multi-dimensional and covers at least 40 countries of Africa. Training facilities have been provided in such diverse fields as development of water resources, foreign trade promotion, rural development, small-scale industries, standardization, journalism, railways etc. Equipment supplied has been mainly in areas of scientific laboratories, agriculture and engineering. Assistance in setting up industrial estates and technical training institutes is rater significant.

9.3.2 Joint Ventures: India also recognizes the need for cooperation with the friendly countries of Africa in the matter of setting up of joint ventures and sponsoring programmes of joint collaboration. Indian participation in joint ventures covers a wide and exciting spectrum, including paper and pulp, machine tools, electric fans, steel furnitures, bicycles, razor blades, chemicals, textiles, soft drinks and auto parts. Important African countries that are beneficiaries of such projects are Botswana, Egypt, Kenya, Mauritius, Nigeria, Senegal, Tanzania and Zambia. Indian contribution to these joint ventures is in terms of supply of capital equipment and know-how.

Joint ventures have played a major role in stepping up the theme of two-way cooperation, thus paving the way for the much desired self-reliant industrial development. Africans are now beginning to realize and accept that economic and technical cooperation among developing countries (ECDC and TCDC) is an extremely beneficial way of boosting the process of economic development. Table 9.2 gives a general picture of Indian investments in Africa.

9.3.3 Consultancy Services: Another programme of economic cooperation that has earned India many laurels relates to consultancy services. The Metallurgical and Engineering Consultants (India) Limited (MECON) has provided consultancy for two steel mills in Nigeria. Other important Indian Firms such as Water and Power Consultancy Services (WAPCOS), the Steel Authority of India (SAIL), Bharat Heavy Electricals (BHEL), Telecommunications Consultants India, Hindustan Machine Tools (HMT) have been active in Nigeria, Ethiopia, Tanzania, Mauritius, Kenya, Egypt, Algeria, Libya, Zambia, Zimbabwe and Namibia.

In the matter of consultancy and technical assistance special mention may be made of the work of the Indian railway-men in Africa. Rail India Technical and Economic Services (RITES) and Indian Railway Construction Company (IRCON) have helped railways in a number of African countries, such as Algeria, Ghana, Mozambique, Nigeria, Zaire, Zambia and Zimbabwe in the last two decades. While RITES specializes in feasibility studies, staff training, manpower planning, systems design etc, the IRCON helps in the construction of new railway lines, railway electrification and telecommunication installations. Special mention may also be made of the work of the National Small Industries Corporation (NSIC). Devoted to the small industries in India, the NSIC shares its experience with the small-scale sector in Africa. It offers turnkey projects in all kinds of industries such as engineering, chemicals, electrical, food, textiles and leather.

Table 9.2 Summary of Indian Joint Ventures in African Countries

Country	In operation No.	Equity	Under Implementation No.	Equity	Total No.	Equity
Botswana			1	6.3	1	6.3
Egypt	1	1.7	8	216.1	9	217.8
Kenya	9	418.0	4	311.2	13	729.2
Liberia			1	9.9	1	9.9
Mauritius	2	26.4	24	252.2	26	278.6
Morocco			1	1169.5	1	1169.5
Nigeria	13	57.8	6	76.3	19	134.1
Senegal	1	142.2	2	822.8	3	965.0
Seychelles	1	30.8	1	30.8	2	61.6
S. Africa			4	530.1	4	530.1
Tanzania			6	54.6	6	54.6
Uganda	1	7.0	4	80.8	5	87.8
Zimbabwe			1	3.5	1	3.5
Zambia			2	75.3	2	75.3
Total	28	683.9	65	3639.4	93	4323.3

Source: India Investment Centre, New Delhi.

In many international fora it has been emphasized that cooperation, coordination and mutual support among South-South countries, especially Africa and India, would be highly beneficial to global trade issues. Collectively these countries can make significant impact on the activities of World Trade Organization (WTO). It is essential that the countries of the South pool their resources and collaborate effectively in order to safeguard and advance their vital and common interests.

India and many African countries have been engaged in a wide variety of mutually beneficial programmes in the past and, with the growing liberalization of the economic, are poised for a significant enhancement of bilateral interaction. India could share with the African countries the five decades of its experience and expertise in various areas, ranging from agriculture and small-scale rural industries to infrastructural projects such as roads, railways, telecommunications, energy, cost effective housing and entrepreneurial development. The potential is limitless. India has, through considerable research, developed low-cost and effective technologies appropriate to the resource base of Africa. India and many African countries have developed a strong tradition of cooperation in the area of human resource development through ITEC programme.

From the above analysis it can be seen that Africa and India are important potential trading partners, in spite of the nominal share in each other's total trade. Over a period of time, the quantum of commercial exchanges and the volume of trade between India and Africa have grown. Both regions have been engaged in a wide variety of mutually beneficial programmes in the past. But the actual levels of bilateral trade and economic cooperation between India and Africa do not reflect the real potential. This needs to be explored further.

Traditionally, relations between India and countries of Africa continent have remained close and cordial. However, commercial relations have not grown commensurately. The main reasons that affected our trade with the region were: distance, language barriers, inadequacy of information about business opportunities, incidence of civil strife, macro-economic instability and the modest progress made in liberalization and privatisation.

Commerce and Industry Minister, Government of India announced the Focus Africa Programme with a focus on seven countries of Sub-Saharan Region viz. South Africa, Nigeria, Mauritius, Tanzania, Kenya, Ghana and Ethiopia on 31st March 2002 along with the announcement of the EXIM Policy for the years 2002-07. With a view to further enhance India's trade with Africa the scope of this Programme was further extended with effect from 1st April 2003 to all the other countries of the Sub-Saharan African region, where India has Diplomatic Missions i.e. Angola, Botswana, Ivory-Coast, Madagascar, Mozambique, Senegal, Seychelles, Uganda, Zambia, Namibia and Zimbabwe, along-with the six countries of North Africa viz. Egypt, Libya, Tunisia, Sudan, Morocco and Algeria. As many Missions in Sub Saharan Africa are concurrently accredited to other countries in the region, the Programme in effect, therefore covers the entire African continent.

Under this Programme, the Government of India extends assistance to exporters, Export Promotion Councils, etc. to visit these countries, organise trade fairs and invite African trade delegations to visit India. The initiatives taken under this Programme have received an encouraging response from the Indian exporting community. It is likely to further boost bilateral trade in the coming years.

India-Africa economic and commercial cooperation, if implemented in the right perspective, will enable these regions to emerge as strategic partners in this millennium.

10

India-COMESA Relations: Exploring South-South Cooperation

South-South Cooperation has come to assume an important role in third world diplomacy in recent years. Having realized that structural linkages with industrially advanced nations of the West remain the chief obstacle to their own economic development, the countries of the Third World have come to increasingly recognise the need for closer cooperation among them. It is now well recognised that the responsibility for the development of the South lies in the South and in the hands of the people of the South. Starting with the Non–Aligned Movement in 1961, the UNCTAD-I and the formation of the 'Group of 77' in 1964, and the creation of the 'Group of 15' in 1989, the least developed countries (LDCs) have moved a long way to devise ways and means to contribute to each other's economic and social progress by effective utilization of complementarities between their respective resources and requirements. The trend towards South-South cooperation, as also the failure to negotiate through the meaningful 'North-South' dialogue for reallocation of international resources and skills on the basis of mutual benefit of all parties concerned, has provided a strategic dimension to the concept of economic cooperation among the LDCs. This would also increase their bargaining strength and countervailing power in the negotiations with the developed countries and would at the same time serve as a valuable complement to international economic cooperation.

The non-aligned nations have adopted economic cooperation among themselves as an alternative means to reduce their dependence on the industrially advanced countries. The concept of South-South cooperation emerge as a universal principle during the 1970s, both as a strategy in support of the development efforts of the developing countries and as an instrument for promoting collective self reliance in order to ensure their effective participation in the international economic system. It is realised that strengthening of South-South cooperation was necessary to create a more truly interdependent global economic order. It is to be noted that South-South cooperation is not to be seen as a substitute for North-South cooperation but as a complementary dimension of such cooperation.

It may also be noted that for cooperation, if it is to be meaningful, can only take place in the form of regular exchange of knowledge and resources among developing countries on the basis of their respective areas of specialization. Such exchange cannot take place among LDCs that are placed at more or less similar levels of underdevelopment. It can become substantive only when it takes place between countries that are placed at different levels of their informal hierarchy. It is in this context that the role of industrially more advanced countries like India, South Africa, Egypt, Brazil etc. may become crucial. In particular, with its acknowledged industrial and technological progress, India may come to play a dominant role in this regard, India today ranks eighth among the industrial nations and possesses the third reservoir of technical and scientific manpower in the world. India's GDP is the largest in the Indian Ocean region. India's GDP is also growing fast at an average rate of 6 to 7 per-cent in the mid-1990s. India is also well endowed in terms of human and natural resources. All these factors contribute to India playing a possible leadership role in South-South cooperation. It is in this background that an attempt is made in this chapter to understand and analyze India's relation with COMESA countries.

It is important for India and the African countries to work out adequate policy packages, institutional structures, technologies, inter-regional development schemes etc. to develop mutually beneficial and more effective linkages in a genuine spirit of South-South cooperation as an alternative to existing exploitative North-South tie-ups. India has been geared towards strengthening horizontal South-South linkages and towards promoting self reliance through transfer of technologies appropriate to the needs of her partners.

Regional trade bloc like COMESA has a lot to learn from India as an ideal source of technology and expertise suitable for the region. COMESA countries have historical ties, which dates back to the days of liberation struggle.

India's exports to COMESA countries in 2003- 2004 amounted to more than 1.47 billion US dollars, representing more than 30 per cent over the previous year. India is cooperating with COMESA in the Area of irrigation and Indian Experts from Water and Power Consultancy Services (WAPCOS) have carried out a study and made presentations and eleven COMESA countries have expressed interests in this cooperation. Apart from setting up joint ventures, there exists considerable demand in the region for Indian technology plant and machinery in the sectors like power generation and transmission, sugar, cement, textiles, chemicals, pharmaceuticals and agro-processing.

The Export-Import (EXIM) Bank of India has published an occasional paper on COMESA countries titled "*Select COMESA Countries: A Study of India's Trade and Investment Potential*". According to this study there is high potential for increasing bilateral trade and investment between India and the countries under the COMESA.

To promote bilateral and regional commercial relations with the COMESA region, EXIM Bank has extended lines of credit (LoCs) to support export of eligible goods on deferred payment terms. The operative LoCs covering this region include million each to the Eastern and Southern African Trade and Development Bank, the Industrial Development Bank Ltd, Kenya and the East African Development Bank.

India's potential exports to these countries include machinery and transport equipment, petroleum products, paper and wood products, textiles, iron and steel, plastic and linoleum products, rubber manufactured products, agro products, chemicals and pharmaceutical products.

The EXIM Bank study indicated that these countries could be good sources for importing of petroleum, metallurgical goods, raw cotton, fruits, chemicals, non-metallic mineral manufactures, precious stones, textile yarn, gold, nickel and ferro-alloys.

Export-Import Bank of India and Eastern and Southern African Trade and Development Bank (PTA Bank) signed an Agreement in March 2005 for a Line of Credit (LOC) of US$ 5 million from EXIM Bank to PTA Bank, to promote India's exports to 16 (sixteen) Eastern and Southern African member countries of PTA Bank. This LOC marks yet another initiative on the part of EXIM Bank to promote exports from India to Africa, in line with the "Focus Africa" initiative of Government of India.

This is the sixth LOC extended by EXIM Bank to PTA Bank. While the previous five LOCs are on medium term basis, this LOC is on short term basis and is expected to give a boost to export of raw materials and commodities to the African market, for which tremendous demand exists. Under the earlier LOCs aggregating US$ 45 million, exports of items like sugar plant, cement plant, sanitary machinery, tissue paper plant, medical equipment and pharmaceutical products, were catalyzed.

PTA Bank is a Regional Development Bank, established in 1985, pursuant to the Treaty for the Common Market for Eastern and Southern African States (COMESA). PTA Bank's regional member countries are Burundi, Comoros, Djibouti, Egypt, Eritrea, Ethiopia, Kenya, Malawi, Mauritius, Rwanda, Somalia, Sudan, Tanzania, Uganda, Zambia and Zimbabwe. China became the only non-regional member of PTA Bank recently. Besides these 17 member countries, African Development Bank is also member of PTA Bank. PTA Bank provides financial and technical assistance to promote economic and social development in member countries.

India's exports to African member countries of PTA Bank amounted to US$ 1.47 billion, in 2003-04, representing an increase of 26 per cent over the previous year. Indian companies have set up a number of joint ventures/wholly owned subsidiaries in the region, in various areas of operations, including software development services, broadcasting and telecasting, plastics, chemicals, textiles, electricity generation and transmission and investment management services. Tourism, pharmaceuticals, electronics, computer software and accessories, information technology related products, financial services and textiles are some of the common sectors across most COMESA countries that hold potential for Indian investors.

In February 2003, the government of India and COMESA signed a Memorandum of Understanding (MoU) which among other things identified different possible areas of cooperation including: pharmaceuticals, information technology, agriculture, biotechnology, low cost housing material, tourism, non conventional energy, infrastructure etc.

Visit by the Secretary of External Affairs in February 2005 has further reinforced the already existing good relations between COMESA and INDIA that the two have developed over the last two years.

The following table shows the trend in bilateral trade relations of India with COMESA member countries. The figures are not satisfactory. The total export of India to the world was US$ 52,719.43 million and US$ 63842.97 million in 2003 and 2004 respectively, but the share of COMESA was only US$ 1092.03 million in 2003 which amounted to 2.07 per cent of its share with the world. This, however, increased to US$ 1384.12 million which was 2.16 per cent of its share with the world in 2004. This low degree of bilateral trade is attributed to the non membership of a major Southern African country to COMESA i.e. South Africa. It alone accounted for0.92 per cent and 0.84 per cent of India's exports in 2003 and 2004 respectively. Among all the COMESA countries, Egypt accounts for the highest percentage with 0.57 per cent and 0.58 per cent in 2003 and 2004 respectively. Other countries sharing significant portion of India's exports include Kenya (0.39 per cent and 0.36 per cent); Mauritius (0.31 per cent and 0.32 per cent); Sudan (0.20 per cent and 0.17 per cent); Uganda (0.12 per cent and 0.14 per cènt); and Ethiopia (0.12 per cent and 0.13 per cent).

As India's imports from the world has increased from US$ 61,412.13 million to US$ 78,14961 million in 2003 and 2004, its percentage share of imports to COMESA have declined from 0.57 per cent in 2003 to 0.29 per cent in 2004. India's total imports from COMESA in 2003 were US$ 351.83 million and US$ 232.26 million in 2004. Among the COMESA countries, Egypt accounted for maximum imports with 0.37 per cent and 0.13 per cent in 2003 and 2004 respectively. The other countries in hierarchy are Kenya (0.05 per cent); Sudan (0.04 per cent); Mauritius (0.03 per cent); Zambia (0.02 per cent); and Zimbabwe (0.02 per cent). (See Table 10.1).

10.1 Major Items of Export to COMESA

- Cotton Yarn fabrics
- Machinery and Instruments
- Man made yarn fabrics
- Plastic and Linolium Prod
- Transport Equipments
- Manufactures of Metals
- Drugs, pharmaceuticals and fine Metals
- Inorganic/Organic/Agro Chemicals
- Rubber manufactured products
- Electronic Goods
- Paper
- Wood Products
- Paints/Enamel/Varnishes
- RMG of Cotton including accessories
- Non-Ferrous Metals
- Jute Yarns
- Tobacco unmanufactured
- Dyes, intermediates etc
- Man made staple fibre
- Glassware
- Ceramics
- Cement

Table 10.1: India's Bilateral Trade with COMESA

Countries	EXPORTS				IMPORTS			
	2002-2003		2003-2004		2002-2003		2003-2004	
	US$mn	% share	US$mn	% share	US$mn	% share	US$mn	% share
WORLD	52719.43	--	63842.97	--	61412.13	--	78149.61	--
Angola	37.31	0.07	70.55	0.01	7.20	0.01	0.00	
Burundi	4.53	0.01	5.49	0.01	0.00	--	0.30	0.00
Comoros	6.39	0.01	1.95	0.00	0.32	0.00	0.48	0.00
DRC	4.31	0.01	11.15	0.02	0.00	--	0.09	0.00
Djibouti	37.42	0.07	73.67	0.12	0.82	0.00	1.19	0.00
Egypt	298.24	0.50	367.49	0.58	226.57	0.37	98.21	0.13
Ethiopia	61.97	0.12	80.43	0.13	10.55	0.02	7.54	0.01
Kenya	203.59	0.39	229.48	0.36	33.55	0.05	41.93	0.05
Madagascar	--	--	--	--	--	--	--	--
Malawi	30.81	0.06	38.21	0.06	1.70	0.00	4.98	0.01
Mauritius	164.36	0.31	203.02	0.32	16.13	0.03	7.54	0.01
Rwanda	6.16	0.01	5.05	0.01	0.00	--	0.00	--
Seychelles	1.18	0.01	10.08	0.02	0.05	0.00	0.07	0.00

Contd...

Sudan	105.18	0.20	107.38	0.17	24.49	0.04	31.22	0.04
Swaziland	12.93	0.02	29.07	0.05	0.04	0.00	1.69	0.00
Uganda	65.87	0.12	87.73	0.14	1.97	0.00	2.05	0.00
Zambia	30.95	0.06	39.86	0.06	14.40	0.02	18.55	0.02
Zimbabwe	15.83	0.03	23.51	0.04	14.04	0.02	16.42	0.02
TOTAL	**1092.03**	**2.07**	**1384.12**	**2.16**	**351.83**	**0.57**	**232.26**	**0.29**

Source: *Directorate General of Commercial Intelligence and Statistics* (DGCIS), Ministry of Commerce and Industry.

10.2 Major Items of Imports from COMESA

- Cotton raw and waste
- Leather
- Pulp and waste paper
- Crude fertilizer
- Electronic goods
- Metaliferrous ores
- Non Metallic
- Non ferrous metals
- Other textile
- Non-electrical machinery
- Artificial resins, plastic materials etc
- Wool Raw
- Raw hides and skins
- Other crude minerals
- Inorganic Chemicals
- Primary steel Pig Iron based items
- Organic Chemicals
- Transport Equipments
- Cotton Yarn and fabrics

10.3 Trade Potential

For enhancing India's trade relations with the COMESA countries focus should be on identifying such potential areas where India and COMESA member countries can promote trade in future. Thus, COMESA's requirements needs to be complemented with India's export capabilities/comparative advantage.

10.3.1 Identifying Commodities with High Export Potential [1]: For identifying the commodities where India has a high potential for exports to COMESA, the following criteria has been examined by the Exim Bank in its study of the Select COMESA countries:

1. Demand existing in the COMESA market, based on commodity composition of COMESA's imports;

2. Commodities where India has a comparative advantage in global exports, based on India's share in global trade;
3. Commodities whose exports to COMESA have registered High growth rate in recent years, based on commodity composition of India's exports to COMESA; and
4. Commodities where India has been doing well in others markets.

Commodities that satisfy the first criterion and at least one of the three criteria have been defined as commodities with high export potential in the COMESA market. Based on such analysis the commodities that have been identified are: machinery and transport equipments;. petroleum products; paper and wood products; textiles; plastic and linoleum products; rubber manufactured products; and chemicals and related products.

10.3.2 Commodities Having Import Potential [2]: For enhancing trade relations with COMESA countries, India has focused on the following items that can be imported from COMESA member countries: petroleum; metallurgical goods; raw cotton; fruit; vegetables and preparations; chemicals and non-metallic minerals manufactures. India can also import precious stones, optical goods and textile yarn from Mauritius; gold from Uganda and gold, nickel and ferro-alloys from Zimbabwe.

10.3.3 Market Access: The greatest benefit that can be derived for the Indian exporter/investor is in terms of market access. [3] Along with preferential access to the whole COMESA region, with a market of more than 350 million consumers, and specific bilateral agreements, most of these countries are also members of other trading blocs. For example Angola; D.R. Congo; Malawi; Mauritius; Namibia; Seychelles; Swaziland; Zambia and Zimbabwe are also members of Southern African Development Community (SADC). Namibia and Swaziland are members of Southern African Customs Union (SACU). Kenya and Uganda are members of East African Community (EAC).

10.3.4 Strategy for Boosting Trade and Investment: The strategy for enhancing bilateral trade and investment relations between India and the COMESA countries would include among others:

- The speedy formation of the PTA between Indian and the COMESA countries, with liberalisation of the investment regime and other facilitating measures would be an important step towards realising potential bilateral trade and investment between India and the COMESA region.
- Dissemination of information relating to trade/investment opportunities to potential exporters and investors in India, as also prospective partners in Africa would prove to be a critical element of the strategy to enhance India's presence in the COMESA region. This can be achieved by means of trade/economic missions to and from the COMESA countries, which would be the suitable fora for active marketing of Exim's LOCs; an interactive portal for identification of project profiles, partner search, match making.
- Specialised e-learning courses for providing technology assistance, manufacturing process know-how, trouble shooting and other technical services; training facilities for African entrepreneurs and technical personnel under Government of India's International Technical and Economic Programme (ITEC) programme would also add to the entrepreneurship development of the human resources in the COMESA countries.
- Indian companies can develop a regional hub for the entire COMESA region, for enhancing bilateral trade and commercial relations. The creation of such a hub would encourage and lend support to prospective companies who are interested in developing commercial relations and establishing presence in the COMESA region.
- Encouraging the Indian Entertainment Industry as well as the Indian Tourist Operators to use the virgin locales in the COMESA region would also facilitate the increased presence of India in the region.

Notes

1. Exim Bank, *Occasional Paper No. 91*, "Select COMESA Countries: A Study of India's Trade and Investment Potential", March 2002, p 86.

2. *Ibid*, p. 88.

3. *Ibid*, p. 89.

11

Conclusions

11.1 Strengthening African Capacities

Any survey of inter-regional co-operation for the twenty century would need to be structured around the following:

- Assessment of co-operation among countries of the region;
- Potential for collective gain through co-operation;
- Bilateral collaboration as the primary basis for moving regional co-operation using the mutually beneficial bilateral co-operation between the countries of the region;
- Inter-regional co-operation and integration in the twenty-first century with a focus on economic co-operation. [1]

Regional co-operation is and must be the first step to raise the capacity of any region to integrate into the global village in a way that is gainful and beneficial for the population of the concerned region. It presents boundless opportunities for mutual growth and prosperity. Regional co-operation would make the strong nation stronger and more credible while weak and vulnerable, in an increasingly indiscriminate globalizing world, could lean on collective strength. One of the pre-requisites to regional co-operation is bilateral co-operation. However, we must also encourage sub-regional co-operation as a move towards fostering regional co-operation in the longer run.

In this context, the first section of the book has focused on the Africa's experience of regional co-operation and integration. Its experience of regional economic integration has been dealt in the second chapter while the third chapter deals with the specific case of COMESA—the largest regional organisation working at the sub-regional level in eastern and southern Africa.

Africa's adoption of a policy of regional co-operation and integration has been more conducive to African realities and could perhaps result in Africa's capacity to better co-exist within the world of regionalism and globalisation. African leaders have long envisaged regionalism as a viable strategy to pursue with a view to uniting the continent both politically and economically. While regionalism in Africa has taken different forms to accommodate the changing national, regional and international environment, all organizations that aim to integrate regional economies in Africa have adopted market integration as a component of their strategy, with a view to increasing intra-regional trade. Although this strategy is not going to solve Africa's economic problems in "totality", it will certainly not be counter productive to the African agenda.

The model for such integration is the European Union, it continues to be highly regarded by most African leaders as a solution to Africa's growing marginalization with the world economy. The creation of North-American Free Trade Agreement (NAFTA) and the successful EU monetary integration has only served to reinforce the commitment of the African leaders.

In response to these events, the member states of the OAU in 1991 signed the Abuja Treaty creating African Economic Community (AEC), which calls for the total integration of the African economies by 2025. Due to the persistent adverse political and economic conditions, the actualization of the AEC treaty never took place and dissatisfaction with the ineffective working of the OAU led African leaders to search for an alternative organization resulting in the establishment of African Union in 2002.

There are a host of obstacles that could hamper the effective realisation of the objectives of the African regionalisation. These have been studied at three levels—among African countries; African and other developing countries; and African and industrialized countries.

Among African Countries

- Lack of political will;
- Lack of adequate financial arrangements;
- Absence of key sub-regional/regional promoters;
- Weak inter-country infrastructural facilities;
- Emergence of economic crisis in the 1980s;

- Political instability;
- Inter-state border disputes and wars.

South-South Relations (African and other developing Countries)

- Lack of inter-regional payments arrangements;
- Lack of sufficient information on projects for cooperative ventures;
- Traditional preference to promote trade with, and seek investments from industrialized countries;
- Myriad problems relating to existing institutional frameworks for multilateral collaboration.

North-South Relations (African and Industrialized Countries)

- Hostile international environment (debt crisis, falling commodity prices, declining foreign investments, etc.);
- New preoccupations by industrialized nations (EU is inclined to assist Eastern Europe; USA is keen on growing the North America Free Trade Area and Japan is preoccupied with the Pacific Rim of Asia);
- Perplexing perception of Africa as an unstable polity;
- Continuing use of SAPs as a discriminating factor for financial assistance, investments and debt relief on the continent;
- So-called international fatigue in helping the "basket case" of Africa remains although left more or less unspoken.

With a view to establish solid institutional framework characterized by growth and development capabilities, partnership between Africa and group of developed countries (EU) and with a group of developing economies (SAARC), particularly India has been envisaged. The gaps between aspirations and achievements have been difficult to bridge. Many of the obstacles that have been cited for the failures of Africa's economic integration needs to be sorted out. In this context the following section provides an agenda for developing strong partnership between the continent of Africa; EU and India.

11.2 European Union and Africa

EU is the world's biggest aid donors - responsible for 55 per cent of all overseas development aid. It is the biggest trading partner for developing countries. Half of Africa's exports go to the EU. EU's 'Everything Arms Initiative' gives the poorest countries duty and quota free access to our market of over 450 million people for all their exports except arms. Europe is the major driver of the WTO's Doha Development Agenda. The EU took the lead in proposing the abolition of export subsidies for agricultural products in 2004. The EU is trying to help developing countries integrate into the world economy; it is the world's biggest provider of trade-related assistance, at around 500 million Pounds per year. It is negotiating the Economic Partnership Agreements. These are not traditional liberalisation agreements, but development tools. They are intended to put trade at the service of development by marrying together "aid for trade" with progressive market opening, at a gradual and appropriate pace. Europe is increasing its spending on aid. The EU set in 2002 an intermediate target for increasing development aid by 2006. This target now looks almost certain to be exceeded. The EU Commission adopted a package of proposals in April 2005 aimed at speeding up progress towards the Millennium Development Goals. In this background, we have to focus on European response towards Africa.

11.3 Importance and Urgency of the European Response

Both as a part of European values and interest, EU is actively being involved in African Affairs. A number of reasons are attributed to it.

- Firstly, because Africa is on her doorstep; less than 10 miles from mainland Europe.
- Secondly, because a resurgent Africa means potentially a huge geo-strategic partner for Europe, given its wealth in natural resources, and huge markets for European goods and services.

- Thirdly, a more stable and secure Africa would be a key contribution to destroying safe havens for terrorists. And stability and security would help to reduce large refugee flows both within the continent and to Europe.
- Fourthly, and crucially, there is a moral, historical and cultural element to the need for a European response. Europe has unique ties to Africa. The histories of the two continents have long been connected. The present day borders of African countries, and the week infrastructure between countries, are in part colonial legacies.

11.4 EU's Role in Strengthening African Capacities

- Africa could benefit enormously by developing closer economic and political ties with a developed region like EU.
- Efforts must be made to explore new mutually profitable opportunities for economic partnership between them in the present context.
- Africa can learn a lot from the rich experience of EU's efforts in regional economic integration carried out since half a century.
- EU can also benefit from closer economic co-operation with Africa. Some factors and potential opportunities based on principles of comparative advantage, which could render Africa a more attractive economic partner for EU are as follows:

Geographical Location and Geo-strategic Position of the African Continent. Since historical times, this was the prime attraction for Europe and the sole reason for the colonization of Africa.

Relatively Cheap Labour. Africa has abundance of cheap labour as compared to other partners of EU.

Natural Resources. Africa is rich in natural resources; particularly, its oil has been a major attraction for the developed nations since centuries.

Political Climate. Africa is, now since last decade, moving on the path of democratization. We see the end of the authoritarian regimes in a number of countries.

Regional Market. Africa has currently opened up to the rest of the world. It has adopted several important measures for trade liberalization both within Africa and with outside world. This is another opportunity that could be attractive for foreign partners including investors from Europe.

Hence, efforts must be made for improving the investment climate in Africa. Political instability and institutional weaknesses which restrict Foreign Direct Investments (FDI) should be warded off.

Institutional Linkages

- Active linkages with selected institutions of higher learning in Africa and Europe should be established. Institutional mechanism designed especially to support "sustained research" on co-operation and economic integration in Africa should be established and the existing one should be strengthened.
- Short and long term programmes and activities should be designed with the primary objective of contributing to the success of regional economic integration in Africa, and enhancing at the same time, the prospects for EU-Africa trade and investments.
- Construction of models and developing alternative solutions for Africa-EU business and application in the ongoing problems to facilitate better implementation of strategies is another area where both the regions can collaborate,
- Appropriate training and African capacity building in academic institutes of Europe is a necessity for strengthening the bilateral co-operation between the two regions. This may increase the competitive capacities of African economies in the global market-place.
- Dissemination of information on African integration and economic co-operation and the potential benefits to African and European social and financial communities is an

important necessity that merits higher education and investigation

- The initiation of "track II" level policy dialogues and collaborations between think-tanks of the two regions with focus on topics of relevance to regionalism and economic co-operation in Africa may serve as a significant measure. Project analysis and evaluation are services that these think-tanks may provide to benefit African and European industries as well as international organizations, potential investors and business development in general.

European policy towards Africa should not be driven by guilt. But it should be underpinned by shared responsibility between African and European. The Commission proposes, therefore, that a greater share of the rise in overall aid should go to sub-Saharan Africa. It proposes to apply all its other ideas on policy coherence and quality of aid to Africa first, as a matter of priority. And it proposes a number of concrete actions in areas identified by Africans themselves as crucial to their development. These include financial support to develop the African Union's capacity, including the €250 million support for African peacekeeping missions, for example in Darfur; reconnecting Africa's infrastructure to tackle transport costs – twice as high as in Asia; and measures to support the social sectors such as health and education.

No real development without security and that security depends on political stability. Assistance in these fields is of the utmost importance and the European Union will keep providing it. Often carried on through the good offices of the African Union and other regional organisations, conflict prevention, crisis management, peacekeeping, and post-conflict reconstruction are necessary tasks in many parts of sub-Saharan Africa. So are the efforts to stimulate and support good governance - the civilian components of conflict prevention, ranging from women's education to judicial expertise. There again the European Union is well placed to make a difference.

Beginning from this point, Europe can and must, go further. Africa must be responsible for its own development, with rich nations playing a supporting role. Action is not and should not be confined to governments. Grassroots movements should also help in building momentum.

11.5 India and Africa

India is the largest, richest and the most well endowed member of South Asia. It is the only country which borders by land or sea all other countries of South Asia. Regional co-operation in South Asia, therefore, hinges upon good relations and cooperation with India. While co-operation among all south Asian countries is desirable, practical difficulties such as natural barriers like the ocean or sheer distances, limit the scope of equal interaction among all members. Therefore, for Africa, the greatest opportunity for cooperation lies with India.

India's Role in Strengthening African Capacities

- Although trade volume between the two regions is not high, yet both countries have variety of products. This indicates future scope for expansion. A major economic partnership could be developed with Africa. To strengthen the relationship a major bilateral arrangement could also be worked out.
- Excellent political relations between the two countries could be converted into economic partnership by declaring either bilateral preferential trading or free trade arrangement. This could give a new direction to future economic relations.
- Both the regions should increase the volume of bilateral trade and investment by jointly identifying priority areas and sectors for specific attention.
- India and Africa should accord priority to an enhanced policy dialogues and strengthened bilateral co-operation in science and technology; research and development; and the environment.

- Indian and African companies need to explore setting up of global trading Joint Ventures for tapping dynamic markets in the world.
- There is insufficient knowledge in India about the diversity of Africa's economic capabilities. For example, many Indian business people are not aware of opportunities in Francophone Africa, especially the West African countries. There is a need for greater education in India about the different regions of Africa and the economic potential of these regions.
- Africa and India can also regularly share their respective experience of regional economic co-operation and integration.
- Africans of Indian descent can be a major facilitator for promoting African investments in India, especially in research and development and in sectors like environment sustainability; bio-technology; pharmaceuticals; information technology; and infra-structure sector.
- India has many excellent institutes for research and development in agriculture; pharmacy; electrical and nuclear engineering. India and Africa can therefore, cooperate in appropriate transfer of technology.
- India's impressive growth in software development and export can be another area where Africa can learn from Indian experience.
- Strengthening two-way investment relations between India and Africa holds a key to forging a sustained dynamic economic partnership for mutual benefit in the global economy in the 21st century.
- Co-operation at international fora such as United Nations, NAM, WTO, G-77 could further strengthen co-operation between the two developing regions of the world as they share common problems and challenges in the 'post Cold War' global order. Being the founders of Non-Aligned Movement (NAM), both India and Africa can play an important role in re-orienting NAM to post cold war realities.

- India and Africa could co-operate more closely on various international issues such as international terrorism; HIV/AIDS/; violation of human rights; disaster mitigation; environmental degradation; and sustainable development.
- Importance of tourism and culture as agents of free movement and exchange of people should also be emphasized.
- Educational institutions and think-tanks in both regions can play a vital supportive role for promoting public-private sector initiatives for strengthening economic partnership between India and Africa in the dynamic global market economy.
- Multiple level contacts between various segments of the civil society can be encouraged as there is a large number of Africans of Indian origin. Indian diaspora in Africa can be an important agent in promoting links between African NGOs and their counterparts in India.
- Recognising our shared community and common history as natural assets, enhanced people-to-people links through improved visa and consular services should be strengthened in between both the regions.

Africa and South Asia, particularly India, are the most well endowed regions with fertile land, rich natural resources and a highly intelligent and massive labour force. The untapped resources of this region will attract foreign investments and offer immense opportunities. In order to harness this potential the countries of these two regions must build trust and confidence in each other and cooperate on a regional as well as bilateral basis.

Note

1. Abstract from the text of the speech delivered by H. E. Lyonpo Yeshey Zimba, Foreign Minister, Royal Government of Nepal.

Appendices

Appendix 1

COMESA Treaty
(Text of Important Articles)

Preamble

The President of the Republic of Angola;
The President of the Republic of Burundi;
The President of the Federal Islamic Republic of the Comoros;
The President of the Democratic Republic of Congo;
The President of the Republic of Djibouti;
The President of the State of Eritrea;
The President of the Transitional Government of Ethiopia;
The President of the Republic of Kenya;
His Majesty the King of the Kingdom of Lesotho;
The President of the Republic of Madagascar;
The Life President of the Republic of Malawi;
The Prime Minister of the Republic of Mauritius;
The President of the Republic of Mozambique;
The President of the Republic of Namibia;
The President of the Republic of Rwanda;
The President of the Republic of Seychelles;
The President of the Somali Democratic Republic;
The President of the Republic of Sudan;
His Majesty the King of the Kingdom of Swaziland;
The President of the United Republic of Tanzania;
The President of the Republic of Uganda;
The President of the Republic of Zambia; and
The President of the Republic of Zimbabwe:

Conscious of the overriding need to establish a Common Market for Eastern and Southern Africa;

Bearing in mind the establishment among their respective States of the Preferential Trade Area for Eastern and Southern African States as a first step towards the creation of a Common

Market and eventually of an Economic Community for Eastern and Southern Africa;

Recalling the provisions of Article 29 of the Treaty for the Establishment of the Preferential Trade Area for Eastern and Southern African States to the effect that steps should be taken to develop the Preferential Trade Area established by that Treaty into a Common Market and eventually into an Economic Community;

Recalling further the decision of the Authority of the Preferential Trade Area for Eastern and Southern African States taken at its Tenth Meeting held in Lusaka, Zambia from 30 - 31 January, 1992 to transform the Preferential Trade Area for Eastern and Southern African States into a Common Market for Eastern and Southern Africa;

Inspired by the objectives of the Treaty for the Establishment of the African Economic Community and in compliance with the provisions of Article 28(1) of the said Treaty;

Determined to mark a new stage in the process of economic integration with the establishment of a Common Market for Eastern and Southern Africa and the consolidation of their economic co-operation through the implementation of common policies and programmes aimed at achieving sustainable growth and development;

Resolved to strengthen and achieve convergence of their economies through the attainment of a full market integration;

Having regard to the principles of international law governing relations between sovereign states, and the principles of liberty, fundamental freedoms and the rule of law; and

In view of further steps which have to be taken in order to advance the economic integration of Eastern and Southern Africa;

HEREBY AGREE AS FOLLOWS:

CHAPTER 1

THE COMMON MARKET FOR EASTERN AND SOUTHERN AFRICA

ARTICLE 1

Establishment and Membership

1. THE HIGH CONTRACTING PARTIES HEREBY establish among themselves a Common Market for Eastern and Southern Africa herein referred to as the Common Market.

2. Membership of the Common Market shall be open to the following Member States of the Preferential Trade Area for Eastern and Southern African States:

The Republic of Angola;
The Republic of Burundi;
The Federal Islamic Republic of the Comoros;
The Democratic Republic of Congo;
The Republic of Djibouti;
The Republic of Egypt;
The State of Eritrea;
The Government of Ethiopia;
The Republic of Kenya;
The Republic of Madagascar;
The Republic of Malawi;
The Republic of Mauritius;
The Republic of Namibia;
The Republic of Rwanda;
The Republic of Seychelles;
The Republic of Sudan;
The Kingdom of Swaziland;
The United Republic of Tanzania;
The Republic of Uganda;
The Republic of Zambia; and
The Republic of Zimbabwe.

3. The following States of Eastern and Southern Africa may become Member States of the Common Market upon fulfilling such conditions as may be determined by the Authority:

The Republic of Botswana; and The Republic of South Africa (Post-Apartheid).

CHAPTER 3

AIMS AND OBJECTIVES

ARTICLE 3

Aims and Objectives of the Common Market

The aims and objectives of the Common Market shall be:

(a) to attain sustainable growth and development of the Member States by promoting a more balanced and harmonious development of its production and marketing structures;

(b) to promote joint development in all fields of economic activity and the joint adoption of macro-economic policies and programmes to raise the standard of living of its peoples and to foster closer relations among its Member States;

(c) to co-operate in the creation of an enabling environment for foreign, cross border and domestic investment including the joint promotion of research and adaptation of science and technology for development;

(d) to co-operate in the promotion of peace, security and stability among the Member States in order to enhance economic development in the region;

(e) to co-operate in strengthening the relations between the Common Market and the rest of the world and the adoption of common positions in international fora; and

(f) to contribute towards the establishment, progress and the realisation of the objectives of the African Economic Community.

ARTICLE 4

Specific Undertakings

In order to promote the achievement of the aims and objectives of the Common Market as set out in Article 3 of this Treaty and in accordance with the relevant provisions of this Treaty, the Member States shall:

1. In the field of trade liberalisation and customs co-operation:

(a) establish a customs union, abolish all non-tariff barriers to trade among themselves; establish a common external tariff; co-operate in customs procedures and activities;

(b) adopt a common customs bond guarantee scheme;

(c) simplify and harmonize their trade documents and procedures;

(d) establish conditions regulating the re-export of goods from third countries within the Common Market;

(e) establish rules of origin with respect to products originating in the Member States; and

(f) recognise the unique situation of Lesotho, Namibia and Swaziland within the context of the Common Market and to grant temporary exemptions to Lesotho, Namibia and Swaziland from the full application of specified provisions of this Treaty.

2. In the field of transport and communications:

(a) foster such co-operation among themselves as would facilitate the production of goods and facilitate trade in goods and services and the movement of persons;

(b) make regulations for facilitating transit trade within the Common Market; and

(c) adopt a Third Party Motor Vehicle Insurance Scheme.

3. In the field of industry and energy:

(a) eliminate rigidities in the structures of production and manufacturing so as to provide goods and services that are of high quality and are competitive in the Common Market;

(b) provide an appropriate enabling environment for the participation of the private sector in economic development and co-operation within the Common Market;

(c) co-operate in the field of industrial development;

(d) adopt common standards, measurements systems and quality assurance practices in respect of goods produced and traded within the Common Market; and

(e) provide an enabling stable and secure investment climate.

4. In the field of monetary affairs and finance:

(a) co-operate in monetary and financial matters and gradually establish convertibility of their currencies and a payments union as a basis for the eventual establishment of a monetary union;

(b) harmonise their macro-economic policies;

(c) remove obstacles to the free movement of services and capital within the Common Market; and

(d) recognise the unique situation of Lesotho, Namibia and Swaziland within the context of the Common Market and to grant temporary exemptions to Lesotho, Namibia and Swaziland from the full application of specified provisions of this Treaty.

5. In the field of agriculture:

(a) co-operate in the agricultural development;

(b) adopt a common agricultural policy;

(c) enhance regional food sufficiency;

(d) co-operate in the export of agricultural commodities;

(e) co-ordinate their policies regarding the establishment of agro-industries;

(f) co-operate in agricultural research and extension; and

(g) enhance rural development.

6. In the field of economic and social development:

(a) harmonise the methodology of collection, processing and analysis of information required to meet the objectives of the Common Market;

(b) harmonise or approximate their laws to the extent required for the proper functioning of the Common Market;

(c) promote the accelerated development of the least developed countries and economically depressed areas through the implementation of special programmes and projects in various fields of economic development;

(d) adopt a regional policy that will look into all possible economic problems that Member States may face during the implementation of this Treaty and propose ways and means of redressing such problems in a manner that will satisfy the conditions of equitable and balanced development within the Common Market;

(e) remove obstacles to the free movement of persons, labour and services, right of establishment for investors and right of residence within the Common Market.

(f) promote co-operation in social and cultural affairs between themselves;

(g) co-operate in tourism and wildlife development and management;

(h) co-operate in the development and management of natural resources, energy and environment; and

(i) take, jointly, such other steps as are necessary to further the aims of the Common Market.

ARTICLE 5

General Undertakings

1. The Member States shall make every effort to plan and direct their development policies with a view to creating conditions favourable for the achievement of the aims of the Common Market and the implementation of the provisions of this Treaty and shall abstain from any measures likely to jeopardize the achievement of the aims of the Common Market or the implementation of the provisions of this Treaty.

2. Each Member State shall take steps to secure the enactment of and the continuation of such legislation to give effect to this Treaty and in particular:

(a) to confer upon the Common Market legal capacity and personality required for the performance of its functions; and

(b) to confer upon the regulations of the Council the force of law and the necessary legal effect within its territory.

3. Each Member State shall:

(a) designate a Ministry with whom the Secretary-General may communicate in connection with any matter arising out of the implementation and application of this Treaty, and notify such designation to the Secretary-General;

(b) transmit to the Secretariat copies of all relevant existing and future legislation and its official gazettes; and

(c) where it is required under this Treaty, supply or exchange information to or with another Member State and send copies of such information to the Secretariat.

4. The Member States undertake to accord the Common Market and its staff the privileges and immunities accorded to similar international organisations in their territories and in accordance with the Agreement on Privileges and Immunities.

ARTICLE 6

Fundamental Principles

The Member States, in pursuit of the aims and objectives stated in Article 3 of this Treaty, and in conformity with the

Treaty for the Establishment of the African Economic Community signed at Abuja, Nigeria on 3rd June, 1991, agree to adhere to the following principles:

(a) equality and inter-dependence of the Member States;

(b) solidarity and collective self-reliance among the Member States;

(c) inter-State co-operation, harmonisation of policies and integration of programmes among the Member States;

(d) non-aggression between the Member States;

(e) recognition, promotion and protection of human and peoples' rights in accordance with the provisions of the African Charter on Human and Peoples' Rights;

(f) accountability, economic justice and popular participation in development;

(g) the recognition and observance of the rule of law;

(h) the promotion and sustenance of a democratic system of governance in each Member State;

(i) the maintenance of regional peace and stability through the promotion and strengthening of good neighbourliness; and

(j) the peaceful settlement of disputes among the Member States, the active co-operation between neighbouring countries and the promotion of a peaceful environment as a pre-requisite for their economic development.

CHAPTER 4

ORGANS OF THE COMMON MARKET

ARTICLE 7

Organs of the Common Market

1. There shall be established as organs of the Common Market:

(a) the Authority;

(b) the Council;

(c) the Court of Justice;

(d) the Committee of Governors of Central Banks;

(e) the Intergovernmental Committee;

(f) the Technical Committees;

(g) the Secretariat; and

(h) the Consultative Committee.

2. The Secretary-General, in consultation with the Bureau of the Council may convene Sectoral Ministerial meetings to consider and take decisions on technical sectoral issues not having budgetary implications.

3. The decisions of the Sectoral Ministerial meetings taken in pursuance of the provisions of paragraph 2 of this Article shall take effect and shall be endorsed at the next meeting of the Council following the Sectoral Ministerial meeting.

4. The organs of the Common Market shall perform their functions and act within the limits of the powers conferred upon them by or under this Treaty.

ARTICLE 8

The Authority

Composition and Functions

1. The Authority shall consist of the Heads of State or Government of the Member States.

2. The Authority shall be the supreme Policy Organ of the Common Market and shall be responsible for the general policy and direction and control of the performance of the executive functions of the Common Market and the achievement of its aims and objectives and shall have such other powers as are vested in it under this Treaty.

3. Subject to the provisions of this Treaty, the directions and decisions of the Authority taken or given in pursuance of the provisions of this Treaty, shall as the case may be, be binding on the Member States and on all other organs of the Common Market other than the Court in the exercise of its jurisdiction, and on those to whom they may be addressed to under this Treaty.

4. The directions and decisions of the Authority shall be notified to those to whom they are addressed and shall take effect upon the receipt of such notification or on such date as may be specified in the direction or decision.

5. The Authority shall meet once every year and may hold extraordinary meetings at the request of any member of the

Authority, provided that such a request is supported by one-third of the members of the Authority.

6. Subject to the provisions of this Treaty, the Authority shall determine its own Rules of Procedure.

7. The decisions of the Authority shall be taken by consensus.

ARTICLE 9

The Council of Ministers

Composition and Functions

1. The Council of Ministers of the Common Market shall consist of such Ministers as may be designated by each Member State.

2. It shall be the responsibility of the Council to:

(a) monitor and keep under constant review and ensure the proper functioning and development of the Common Market in accordance with the provisions of this Treaty;

(b) make recommendations to the Authority on matters of policy aimed at the efficient and harmonious functioning and development of the Common Market;

(c) give directions to all other subordinate organs of the Common Market other than the Court in the exercise of its jurisdiction;

(d) make regulations, issue directives, take decisions, make recommendations and give opinions in accordance with the provisions of this Treaty;

(e) request advisory opinions from the Court in accordance with the provisions of this Treaty;

(f) consider and approve the budgets of the Secretariat and the Court;

(g) consider what measures should be taken by Member States in order to promote the attainment of the aims of the Common Market;

(h) make Staff Rules and Regulations and Financial Regulations of the Secretariat;

(i) make recommendations to the Authority on the designation of Least Developed Countries;

(j) designate economically depressed areas of the Common Market; and

(k) exercise such other powers and perform such other functions as are vested in or conferred on it by this Treaty.

3. Subject to the provisions of this Treaty, the regulations, directives and decisions of the Council taken or given in pursuance of the provisions of this Treaty shall be binding on the Member States, on all subordinate organs of the Common Market other than the Court in the exercise of its jurisdiction and on those to whom they may under this Treaty, be addressed.

4. The Council shall meet once a year immediately preceding a meeting of the Authority. Extraordinary meetings of the Council may be held at the request of a Member State provided that such a request is supported by at least one-third of the Member States.

5. Subject to any directions that the Authority may give and to the provisions of this Treaty, the Council shall determine its own Rules of Procedure.

6. The decisions of the Council shall be taken by consensus, failing which by two-thirds majority of the members of the Council.

7. Where an objection is recorded on behalf of a Member State to a proposal submitted for the decision of the Council, the proposal shall, unless such objection is withdrawn, be referred to the Authority for its decision.

ARTICLE 10

Regulations, Directives, Decisions, Recommendations and Opinions of Council

1. The Council may, in accordance with the provisions of this Treaty, make regulations, issue directives, take decisions, make recommendations or deliver opinions.

2. A regulation shall be binding on all the Member States in its entirety.

3. A directive shall be binding upon each Member State to which it is addressed as to the result to be achieved but not as to the means of achieving it.

4. A decision shall be binding upon those to whom it is addressed.

5. A recommendation and an opinion shall have no binding force.

ARTICLE 11

Reasons for Regulations, Decisions and Directives

Regulations, directives and decisions of the Council shall state the reasons on which they are based and shall refer to any proposals or opinions which were required to be obtained pursuant to this Treaty.

ARTICLE 12

Entry into Force of Regulations, Directives and Decisions of the Council

1. Regulations shall be published in the Official Gazette of the Common Market and shall enter into force on the date of their publication or such later date as may be specified in the Regulations.

2. Directives and decisions shall be notified to those to whom they are addressed and shall take effect upon the receipt of such notification or on such date as may be specified in the directives or decisions.

ARTICLE 13

The Committee of Governors of Central Banks

Composition and Functions

1. The Committee of Governors of Central Banks shall consist of the governors of the monetary authorities designated for that purpose by the Member States.

2. The Committee of Governors of Central Banks shall:

(a) be responsible for the development of programmes and action plans in the field of finance and monetary co-operation;

(b) monitor and keep under constant review and ensure the proper implementation of the programmes and plans adopted pursuant to the provisions of Chapter Ten of this Treaty on Monetary and Financial Co-operation;

(c) for the purposes of sub-paragraphs (a) and (b) of this paragraph, request the Secretary-General to undertake specific investigations;

(d) consider reports and recommendations from the Technical Committee on Finance and Monetary Affairs;

(e) submit from time to time, reports and recommendations to the Council concerning the implementation of the Finance and Monetary Co-operation programme; and

(f) have such other functions as are conferred upon it by or under this Treaty.

3. Subject to any directions which may be given by the Council, the Committee of Governors of Central Banks shall meet once a year and shall, subject to this Treaty, determine its own Rules of Procedure.

ARTICLE 14

Intergovernmental Committee

Composition and Functions

1. The Intergovernmental Committee shall consist of such Permanent or Principal Secretaries as may be designated by each Member State.

2. The Intergovernmental Committee shall:

(a) be responsible for the development of programmes and action plans in all the sectors of co-operation except in the finance and monetary sector;

(b) monitor and keep under constant review and ensure proper functioning and development of the Common Market in accordance with the provisions of this Treaty;

(c) oversee the implementation of the provisions of this Treaty and for that purpose may request a Technical Committee to investigate any particular matter;

(d) for the purposes of sub-paragraph (a) of this paragraph, request the Secretary-General to undertake specific investigations;

(e) submit from time to time either on its own initiative or upon the request of the Council reports and recommendations to the Council; and

(f) have such other functions as are conferred upon it by or under this Treaty.

3. Subject to any directions which may be given by the Council, the Intergovernmental Committee shall meet once a year and shall, subject to this Treaty, determine its own Rules of Procedure.

ARTICLE 15

Technical Committees

Composition and Functions

1. The Technical Committees of the Common Market shall be the following:

(a) the Committee on Administrative and Budgetary Matters;

(b) the Committee on Agriculture ;

(c) the Committee on Comprehensive Information Systems;

(d) the Committee on Energy;

(e) the Committee on Finance and Monetary Affairs;

(f) the Committee on Industry;

(g) the Committee on Labour, Human Resources and Social and Cultural Affairs;

(h) the Committee on Legal Affairs;

(i) the Committee on Natural Resources and Environment;

(j) the Committee on Tourism and Wildlife;

(k) the Committee on Trade and Customs; and

(l) the Committee on Transport and Communications.

2. The Technical Committees shall be composed of representatives of the Member States designated for that purpose.

3. The Council may establish such additional Technical Committees as may be necessary for the attainment of the objectives of this Treaty.

4. The Technical Committees shall meet as often as necessary for the proper discharge of their functions and shall determine their own Rules of Procedure.

ARTICLE 16

Functions of the Technical Committees

Each Technical Committee shall:

(a) be responsible for the preparation of a comprehensive implementation programme and a time-table prioritising the programmes with respect to its sector;

(b) monitor and keep under constant review the implementation of co-operation programmes with respect to its sector;

(c) for the purposes of paragraphs (a) and (b) of this Article request the Secretary-General to undertake specific investigations;

(d) except for the Committee on Finance and Monetary Affairs which shall submit its reports and recommendations to the Committee of Governors of Central Banks, submit from time to time reports and recommendations to the Intergovernmental Committee, either on its own initiative or upon the request of the Council, concerning the implementation of the provisions of this Treaty; and

(e) have such other functions as are assigned to it by or under this Treaty.

ARTICLE 17

The Secretariat and the Secretary-General

1. The Secretariat shall be headed by a Secretary-General of the Common Market who shall be appointed by the Authority to serve in such office for a term of five years and shall be eligible for reappointment for a further term of five years.

2. The Secretary-General shall be the chief executive officer of the Common Market and shall represent the Common Market in the exercise of its legal personality.

3. There shall be, in addition to the Secretary-General, two Assistant Secretaries-General who shall be appointed by the Authority, and such other staff of the Secretariat as the Council may determine.

4. The terms and conditions of service of the Secretary-General and the Assistant Secretaries-General shall be determined by the Authority. The terms and conditions of service of the other staff of the Secretariat shall be determined by the Council.

5. In appointing staff to offices in the Secretariat, regard shall be had, subject to the paramount importance of securing the

highest standards of integrity, efficiency and technical competence, to the desirability of maintaining the principle of equal opportunities and an equitable distribution of appointments to such offices among citizens of all the Member States.

6. In the performance of their duties, the Secretary-General and Assistant Secretaries-General and the staff of the Secretariat shall not seek or receive instructions from any Member State or from any other authority external to the Common Market. They shall refrain from any actions which may adversely reflect on their position as international officials and shall be responsible only to the Common Market.

7. Each Member State undertakes to respect the international character of the responsibilities of the Secretary-General, Assistant Secretaries-General and the other staff of the Secretariat and shall not seek to unduly influence them in the discharge of their responsibilities.

8. The Secretary-General shall:

(a) service and assist the organs of the Common Market in the performance of their functions;

(b) submit reports in consultation with the Intergovernmental Committee on the activities of the Common Market to the Council and the Authority;

(c) subject to the provisions of this Treaty, be responsible for the administration and finances of the Common Market;

(d) submit the budget of the Common Market to the Intergovernmental Committee;

(e) act as the secretary to the Authority and the Council;

(f) ensure that the objectives set out in this Treaty are attained and shall, either on his own initiative or on the basis of a complaint, investigate a presumed breach of the provisions of this Treaty and report to the Council in accordance with an investigative procedure to be determined by the Council;

(g) keep the functioning of the Common Market under continuous examination and may act in relation to any particular matter which appears to merit examination either on his own initiative or upon the request of a Member State where appropriate and report the results of his examination to the Member State or the organ of the Common Market concerned;

(h) subject to the provisions of this Treaty submit references to the Court concerning the alleged breach of any obligation under this Treaty in relation to the Common Market or as to any action or omission affecting the Common Market;

(i) promote the adoption of joint positions by the Member States in multilateral negotiations with third countries or international organisations;

(j) on his own initiative or as may be assigned to him by the Authority or the Council, undertake such work and studies and perform such services as relate to the aims of the Common Market and to the implementation of the provisions of this Treaty; and

(k) for the performance of the functions conferred upon him by this Article, collect information and verify matters of fact relating to the functioning of the Common Market and for that purpose may request a Member State to provide information relating thereto.

9. The Member States agree to co-operate with and assist the Secretary-General in the performance of his functions set out in paragraph 8 of this Article and agree in particular to provide any information which may be requested under sub-paragraph (k) of paragraph 8 of this Article.

10. There may be established, such sub-regional offices or branch offices of the Secretariat in the Member States as the Council may determine.

ARTICLE 18

Consultative Committee of the Business Community and Other Interest Groups - Composition and Functions

1. The Consultative Committee shall consist of such representatives, of the business community and other interest groups from the Member States as the Consultative Committee shall determine. The representatives may be accompanied by such experts and advisors as the Consultative Committee may deem necessary for its effective functioning.

2. For the purposes of paragraph 1 of this Article, the composition of the Consultative Committee shall be determined at a first meeting which shall be convened by the Secretary-General for that purpose.

3. The Consultative Committee shall provide a link and facilitate dialogue between the business community and other interest groups and other organs of the Common Market. The Consultative Committee shall:

(a) be responsible for ensuring that the interests of the business community and other interest groups in the Common Market are taken into consideration by the organs of the Common Market;

(b) be responsible for monitoring the implementation of the provisions of Chapters Twenty Three and Twenty Four of this Treaty and make recommendations to the Intergovernmental Committee;

(c) consult and receive reports from other interest groups; and

(d) take part in the meetings of the Technical Committees and may make recommendations to the Intergovernmental Committee.

4. The Consultative Committee shall meet as often as necessary for the proper discharge of its functions and shall determine its own Rules of Procedure.

CHAPTER 5

THE COURT OF JUSTICE

ARTICLE 19

Establishment of the Court

The Court of Justice established under Article 7 of this Treaty shall ensure the adherence to law in the interpretation and application of this Treaty.

ARTICLE 20

Composition of the Court

1. Subject to paragraph 2 of this Article, the Court shall be composed of seven Judges who shall be appointed by the Authority and one of whom shall be appointed by the Authority as the President of the Court.

2. The Judges of the Court shall be chosen from among persons of impartiality and independence who fulfill the conditions required for the holding of high judicial office in their respective countries of domicile or who are jurists of recognised competence:

Provided that no two or more Judges shall at any time be Nationals of the same Member State.

3. Not withstanding the provisions of paragraph 1 of this Article, the Authority may, upon the request of the Court, appoint additional Judges.

ARTICLE 21

Tenure of Office and Resignation

1. The President and Judges shall hold office for a period of five years and shall be eligible for re-appointment for a further period of five years.

2. The President and the Judges shall hold office throughout the term of their respective appointments unless they resign or die or are removed from office in accordance with the provisions of this Treaty.

3. Where the term of office of a Judge comes to an end by effluxion of time or on resignation before a decision or opinion of the Court with respect to a matter which has been argued before the Court of which he was a member is delivered, such Judge shall, only for the purpose of completing that particular matter, continue to sit as a Judge.

4. The President may, at any time, resign his office by giving one year's written notice to the Chairman of the Authority, but his resignation shall not take effect until his successor has been appointed by the Authority and has taken office.

5. A Judge may, at any time, resign his office by letter delivered to the President for transmission to the Chairman of the Authority, and his resignation shall take effect on the date it has been accepted by the Authority.

ARTICLE 22

Removal from Office and Temporary Membership of the Court

1. The President or a Judge shall not be removed from office except by the Authority for stated misbehaviour or for inability to perform the functions of his office due to infirmity of mind or body or due to any other specified cause.

2. If a Judge is appointed by the Authority to replace the President or another Judge before the term of office of the President or a Judge expires, the Judge so appointed shall serve in that office for the remainder of the term of the replaced President or Judge.

3. If a Judge is temporarily absent or otherwise unable to carry out his functions, the Authority shall, if such absence or inability to act appears to the Authority to be likely to be of such duration as to cause a significant delay in the work of the Court, appoint a temporary Judge to act in place of the said Judge.

4. If a Judge is directly or indirectly interested in a case before the Court, he shall immediately report the nature of his interest to the President, and, if in his opinion the President considers the Judge's interest in the case prejudicial, he shall make a report to the Authority, and the Authority shall appoint a temporary Judge to act for that case only in place of the interested Judge.

5. If the President is directly or indirectly interested in a case before the Court he shall, if he considers that the nature of his interest is such that it would be prejudicial for him to take part in that case, make a report to the Authority and the Authority shall appoint a temporary President, chosen in the same manner as the substantive President, to act as President for that case only in place of the substantive President.

ARTICLE 23

General Jurisdiction of the Court

The Court shall have jurisdiction to adjudicate upon all matters which may be referred to it pursuant to this Treaty.

ARTICLE 24

Reference by Member States

1. A Member State which considers that another Member State or the Council has failed to fulfill an obligation under this

Treaty or has infringed a provision of this Treaty, may refer the matter to the Court.

2. A Member State may refer for determination by the Court, the legality of any act, regulation, directive or decision of the Council on the grounds that such act, regulation, directive or decision is ultra vires or unlawful or an infringement of the provisions of this Treaty or any rule of law relating to its application or amounts to a misuse or abuse of power.

ARTICLE 25

Reference by the Secretary-General

1. Where the Secretary-General considers that a Member State has failed to fulfill an obligation under this Treaty or has infringed a provision of this Treaty, he shall submit his findings to the Member State concerned to enable that Member State to submit its observations on the findings.

2. If the Member State concerned does not submit its observations to the Secretary-General within two months, or if the observations submitted are unsatisfactory, the Secretary-General shall refer the matter to the Bureau of the Council which shall decide whether the matter shall be referred by the Secretary-General to the Court immediately or be referred to the Council.

3. Where a matter has been referred to the Council under the provisions of paragraph 2 of this Article and the Council fails to resolve the matter, the Council shall direct the Secretary-General to refer the matter to the Court.

ARTICLE 26

Reference by Legal and Natural Persons

Any person who is resident in a Member State may refer for determination by the Court the legality of any act, regulation, directive, or decision of the Council or of a Member State on the grounds that such act, directive, decision or regulation is unlawful or an infringement of the provisions of this Treaty:

Provided that where the matter for determination relates to any act, regulation, directive or decision by a Member State, such person shall not refer the matter for determination under this

Article unless he has first exhausted local remedies in the national courts or tribunals of the Member State.

CHAPTER 6

CO-OPERATION IN TRADE LIBERALISATION AND DEVELOPMENT

ARTICLE 45

Scope of Co-operation in Trade Liberalisation and Development

There shall be progressively established in the course of a transitional period of ten years from the entry into force of this Treaty, a Customs Union among the Member States. Within the Customs Union, customs duties and other charges of equivalent effect imposed on imports shall be eliminated. Non-tariff barriers including quantitative or like restrictions or prohibitions and administrative obstacles to trade among the Member States shall also be removed. Furthermore, a common external tariff in respect of all goods imported into the Member States from third countries shall be established and maintained.

ARTICLE 46

Customs Duties

1. The Member States shall reduce and ultimately eliminate by the year 2000, in accordance with the programme adopted by the PTA Authority, customs duties and other charges of equivalent effect imposed on or in connection with the importation of goods which are eligible for Common Market tariff treatment.

2. Notwithstanding the provisions of paragraph 1 of this Article, where, by virtue of obligations under an existing contract entered into by a Member State and such a Member State is unable to comply with the provisions of this Article, the Member State shall, upon the entry into force of this Treaty, notify the Council of this fact.

The Member State shall, however, not renew or extend such contract at its expiry.

3. Within the period specified in paragraph 1 of this Article, the Member States shall not impose any new duties and taxes or increase existing ones in respect of products traded within the Common Market and shall transmit to the Secretariat all information on import duties for study by the relevant institutions of the Common Market.

4. The Authority may at any time, on the recommendation of the Council, decide that any import duties shall be reduced more rapidly or eliminated earlier than is scheduled in paragraph 1 of this Article.

ARTICLE 47

Common External Tariff

The Member States agree to the gradual establishment of a common external tariff in respect of all goods imported into the Member States from third countries within a period of ten years from the entry into force of this Treaty and in accordance with a schedule to be adopted by the Council.

ARTICLE 48

Rules of Origin

1. For the purposes of this Treaty, goods shall be accepted as eligible for Common Market tariff treatment if they originate in the Member States.

2. The definition of products originating in the Member States shall be as provided for in a Protocol on the Rules of Origin to be concluded by the Member States.

3. The Intergovernmental Committee shall, from time to time, examine the rules referred to in paragraph 2 of this Article and propose amendments thereto to the Council.

ARTICLE 49

Elimination of Non-tariff Barriers on Common Market Goods

1. Except as may be provided for or permitted by this Treaty, each of the Member States undertakes to remove immediately upon the entry into force of this Treaty, all the then existing non-tariff barriers to the import into that Member State of goods originating in the other Member States and thereafter refrain from imposing any further restrictions or prohibitions.

2. For the purposes of protecting an infant industry, a Member State may, provided that it has taken all reasonable steps to overcome the difficulties related to such infant industry, impose for the purposes only of protecting such industry for a specified period to be determined by Council, quantitative or like restrictions or prohibitions on similar goods originating from the other Member States:

Provided that the measures are applied on a non-discriminatory basis and that the Member State shall furnish to Council proof that it has taken all reasonable steps to overcome the difficulties faced by such an infant industry.

3. The Council shall adopt criteria for determining that an industry is an infant industry.

4. The Secretariat shall keep under constant review the operation of any quantitative or like restriction or prohibitions imposed under the provisions of paragraph 2 of this Article and deliver an opinion to the Member State concerned and report the matter to the Council with its recommendations.

5. Notwithstanding the provisions of paragraph 1 of this Article, if a Member State encounters balance-of-payments difficulties arising from the application of the provisions of this Chapter, that Member State may, provided that it has taken all reasonable steps to overcome the difficulties, impose for the purpose only of overcoming such difficulties for a specified period to be determined by the Council, quantitative or the like restrictions or prohibitions, on goods originating from the other Member States.

ARTICLE 50

Security and Other Restrictions to Trade

1. A Member State may, after having given notice to the Secretary-General of its intention to do so, introduce or continue or execute restrictions or prohibitions affecting:

(a) the application of security laws and regulations;

(b) the control of arms, ammunition and other war equipment and military items;

(c) the protection of human, animal or plant health or life, or the protection of public morality;

(d) the transfer of gold, silver and precious and semi-precious stones;

(e) the protection of any item deemed to be of national importance provided that the Member State concerned shall furnish proof to the Council that the item is of national importance; and

(f) the maintenance of food security in the event of war and famine.

2. A Member State shall not so exercise the right to introduce or continue to execute the restrictions or prohibitions conferred by this Article as to stultify the free movement of goods envisaged in this Chapter.

3. Security and other restrictions imposed in accordance with paragraph 1 of this Article shall not extend for more than is necessary to achieve security aims and other risks intended to be eliminated and shall be applied on the basis of non-discrimination.

ARTICLE 51

Dumping

1. The Member States recognise that dumping, by which products of a Member State are introduced into the commerce of another Member State at less than the normal value of the products, is to be prohibited if it causes or threatens material injury to an established industry in the territory of the other Member State or materially retards the establishment of a domestic industry.

2. For the purposes of this Article, a product is to be considered as being introduced into the commerce of an importing Member State at less than its normal value, if the price of the product exported from one Member State to another:

(a) is less than the comparable price in the ordinary course of trade, for the like product when destined for consumption in the exporting Member State; or

(b) in the absence of such domestic prices, is less than either:

(i) the highest comparable price for the like product for export to any third country in the ordinary course of trade; or

(ii) the cost of production of the product in the country of origin plus a reasonable addition for selling cost and profit:

Provided that due allowance shall be made in each case for differences in conditions and terms of sale, for differences in taxation and for other differences affecting price comparability.

3. A Member State may, for the purposes of offsetting or preventing dumping, and subject to the provision of paragraph 4 of this Article, levy on any dumped product an anti-dumping duty not greater in amount than the margin of dumping in respect of such product. For the purposes of this Article, the margin of dumping is the price difference determined in accordance with the provisions of paragraph 2 (b) (ii) of this Article.

4. No Member State shall levy any anti-dumping duty on the importation of any product of another Member State unless it is determined that the effect of the alleged dumping is such as to cause or threaten material injury to an established domestic industry or such as to retard materially the establishment of a domestic industry.

5. Dumping from a third country into a Member State shall be prohibited and any affected Member State may, pursuant to the provisions of paragraph 3 of this Article, levy an anti-dumping duty on any dumped products.

6. Proceedings initiated pursuant to the provisions of this Article shall be carried out in accordance with anti-dumping regulations made by the Council.

ARTICLE 52

Subsidies Granted by Member States

1. Except as otherwise provided in this Treaty, any subsidy granted by a Member State or through state resources in any form whatsoever which distorts or threatens to distort competition by favouring certain undertakings or the production of certain goods shall, in so far as it affects trade between the Member States, be incompatible with the Common Market.

2. A Member State may, for the purposes of offsetting the effects of subsidies and subject to regulations made by the Council, levy countervailing duty on any product of any Member State imported into another Member State equal to the amount of the estimated subsidy determined to have been granted directly or indirectly, on the manufacture, production or export of such product in the country of origin or exportation.

3. Except as otherwise provided in this Treaty, any subsidy granted by a third country or through state resources in any form whatsoever which distorts or threatens to distort competition by favouring certain undertakings or the production of certain goods shall, in so far as it affects trade between the Member States and the third country, be incompatible with the Common Market.

4. A Member State may, for the purposes of offsetting the effects of subsidies and subject to regulations made by the Council, levy a countervailing duty on any product of any third country imported into another Member State equal to the amount of the estimated subsidy determined to have been granted directly or indirectly, on the manufacture, production or export of such product in the country of origin or exportation.

ARTICLE 53

Exceptions to Levying of Countervailing Duty

No Member State shall levy a countervailing duty on the importation of any product of the territory of another Member State unless it determines that the effect of the subsidisation is such as to cause or threaten material injury to an established domestic industry or is such as to materially retard the establishment of a domestic industry.

ARTICLE 54

Co-operation in the Investigation of Dumping and Subsidies

1. The Member States shall co-operate in the detection and investigation of dumping and subsidy practices and in imposing agreed measures to curb such practices.

2. Where there is evidence of dumping or export of subsidised goods by a third country to the territory of a Member State that threatens or distorts competition in the Common Market, the

affected Member States may request the Member State in whose territory the goods are being dumped or exported to impose anti-dumping duties or countervailing duties on those goods from the third country.

ARTICLE 55

Competition

1. The Member States agree that any practice which negates the objective of free and liberalised trade shall be prohibited. To this end, the Member States agree to prohibit any agreement between undertakings or concerted practice which has as its objective or effect the prevention, restriction or distortion of competition within the Common Market.

2. The Council may declare the provisions of paragraph 1 of this Article inapplicable in the case of:

(a) any agreement or category thereof between undertakings;

(b) any decision by association of undertakings;

(c) any concerted practice or category thereof; which improves production or distribution of goods or promotes technical or economic progress and has the effect of enabling consumers a fair share of the benefits:

Provided that the agreement, decision or practice does not impose on the undertaking restrictions inconsistent with the attainment of the objectives of this Treaty or has the effect of eliminating competition.

3. The Council shall make regulations to regulate competition within the Member States.

ARTICLE 56

Most Favoured Nation Treatment

1. The Member States shall accord to one another the most favoured nation treatment.

2. Nothing in this Treaty shall prevent a Member State from maintaining or entering into new preferential agreements with third countries provided such agreements do not impede or frustrate the objectives of this Treaty and that any advantage, concession, privilege and favour granted to a third country under

such agreements are extended to the Member States on a reciprocal basis.

3. Nothing in this Treaty shall prevent two or more Member States from entering into new preferential agreements among themselves which aim at achieving the objectives of the Common Market, provided that any preferential treatment accorded under such agreements is extended to the other Member States on a reciprocal and non-discriminatory basis.

4. Copies of agreements concluded pursuant to paragraph 2 of this Article shall be transmitted to the Secretary-General by the Member States parties to them .

ARTICLE 57

National Treatment

The Member States shall refrain from enacting legislation or applying administrative measures which directly or indirectly discriminate against the same or like products of other Member States.

ARTICLE 58

Customs Administration

The Member States shall apply the provisions of Chapter Nine of this Treaty in order to simplify, harmonize and standardize their customs regulations, procedures and documents to ensure the effective application of the provisions of this Chapter and to reduce the costs of and facilitate the speedy movement of goods and services across their frontiers.

ARTICLE 59

Drawback

The Member States may, at the end of the ten years specified in Article 45 of this Treaty, refuse to accept as eligible for Common Market tariff treatment goods in relation to which drawback is claimed or made use of in connection with their exportation from the Member States in the territory of which the goods have undergone the last process of production.

ARTICLE 60

Remedy for Loss of Revenue

1. The Council shall, on the recommendation of the Intergovernmental Committee, determine what remedial steps shall be taken with respect to a Member State which has suffered substantial loss of revenue from import duties as a result of the application of this Chapter.

2. For the purposes of paragraph 1 of this Article, the Member States shall conclude a Protocol which shall, *inter-alia*, determine the machinery and formula to be used in carrying out the remedial steps with respect to a Member State which has suffered substantial loss of revenue from import duties as a result of the application of this Chapter.

ARTICLE 61

Safeguard Clause

1. In the event of serious disturbances occurring in the economy of a Member State following the application of the provisions of this Chapter, the Member State concerned shall, after informing the Secretary-General and the other Member States, take necessary safeguard measures.

2. Safeguard measures taken under the provisions of paragraph 1 of this Article, shall remain in force for a period of one year and may be extended by the decision of the Council provided that the Member State concerned shall furnish to the Council proof that it has taken the necessary and reasonable steps to overcome or correct imbalances for which safeguard measures are being applied and that the measures applied are on the basis of non-discrimination.

3. The Council shall examine the method and effect of the application of existing safeguard measures and take a decision thereon.

ARTICLE 62

Trade Promotion

The Member States shall adopt measures designed to promote trade within the Common Market. In this regard, Member States shall:

(a) ensure the development and dissemination of market intelligence and trade information with a view to providing the widest possible knowledge-base of intra-Common Market trade opportunities and encourage the development of exports and markets to meet the public and private procurement needs;

(b) actively encourage the undertaking of supply and demand surveys, the organisation of buyers and sellers meetings and other multi-country contact promotion events in order to further identify and exploit the potential of intra-Common Market trade;

(c) undertake the removal of measures that have been identified during the market surveys, which restrict the flow of goods and services to their identified markets, including the establishment of agency offices, trade missions, free movement of samples and advertising;

(d) identify the possibilities of product adaptation and diversification to broaden their respective export base with a view to expanding or introducing products to new markets in the Member States;

(e) review and initiate programmes for the rationalisation and improvement of import operations and techniques to ensure that savings will accrue from such rationalisation of purchase operations;

(f) seek to ensure that donor-funded import procurement programmes allow as far as possible for the purchase of goods from other Member States;

(g) organise frequent general and specialised trade fairs;

(h) improve the performance of small-and-medium scale enterprises for export development such as marketing, business management and the provision of credits;

(i) promote export-oriented joint ventures, by encouraging and facilitating enterprise-to-enterprise contacts;

(j) support privatisation endeavours through the introduction of trade services or improvement of the trade promotion infrastructure to meet the special requirements of privatised companies; and

(k) encourage the improvement of services relating to trade such as export financing, quality control and standardisation, packaging and specification aspects, warehousing and storage operations, and others that will increase the flow of goods within the Member States.

CHAPTER 7

COMMON MARKET CUSTOMS CO-OPERATION

ARTICLE 63

Scope of Customs Co-operation

1. The provisions of this Chapter shall apply to any activity being undertaken in co-operation among the Member States in the field of customs management and the organization of customs and shall include in particular:

(a) matters concerning the application of Common Market tariff treatment for their exports and imports;

(b) the simplification and harmonization of trade documents, customs regulations and procedures with particular reference to such matters as the valuation of goods, tariff classification, temporary admission, warehousing, re-exports, frontier trade and export drawback;

(c) the prevention, investigation and suppression of customs offences; (d) national and joint institutional arrangements; and

(e) training facilities and programmes for customs officials.

2. The provisions of paragraph 1 of this Article shall not affect the gradual establishment of a common external tariff in respect of goods imported into the Member States from third countries.

ARTICLE 64

Common Market Tariff Treatment

1. The Member States undertake to co-operate in the implementation of the provisions of this Treaty concerning the treatment of goods eligible for Common Market tariff treatment and more particularly those relating to:

(a) the evolution of uniform national customs legislation and procedures;

(b) the reduction and eventual elimination of import duties and non-tariff barriers on trade among themselves;

(c) the establishment of a common external tariff; and

(d) any other aspect of customs law and practice concerning Common Market tariff treatment.

2. For the purposes of paragraph 1 of this Article, the Member States undertake where they have not already done so, to:

(a) adopt uniform, comprehensive and systematic tariff classification of goods with a common and specific basis of description and interpretation in accordance with internationally accepted standards;

(b) adopt a standard system of valuation of goods based on principles of equity, uniformity and simplicity of application in accordance with internationally accepted standards and guidelines;

(c) agree on common terms and conditions governing temporary admission procedures including the list or range of goods to be covered and the nature of manufacturing or processing to be authorized;

(d) implement the customs requirements for the re-exportation of goods provided for in this Treaty;

(e) implement the customs requirements for the transit of goods as prescribed in this Treaty;

(f) harmonize and simplify customs formalities and documents in accordance with the provisions of this Treaty; and

(g) adopt common procedures for the establishment and operation of free zones, free ports, customs supervised factories and export drawbacks.

3. The Member States undertake to harmonize their customs and statistical nomenclature and standardize their foreign trade statistics to ensure comparability and reliability of the relevant information.

ARTICLE 65

Communication of Customs Information

The Member States shall exchange information on matters relating to customs and more particularly to the following:

(a) changes in customs legislation, procedures, duties and commodities subject to import or export restrictions; and

(b) information relating to the prevention, investigation and suppression of customs offences as provided for in Article 66 of this Treaty.

ARTICLE 66

Prevention, Investigation and Suppression of Customs Offences

1. The Member States undertake to co-operate in the prevention, investigation and suppression of customs offences.

2. For the purposes of paragraph 1 of this Article, the Member States undertake to:

(a) exchange lists of goods and publications the importation of which is prohibited in their respective territories;

(b) prohibit the exportation of goods and publications referred to in sub-paragraph (a) of this paragraph to each other's customs territories;

(c) exchange among themselves lists of goods known to be the subject of illicit traffic between their customs territories and maintain special surveillance over the movement of such goods;

(d) consult each other on the establishment of common border posts and take such steps as may be deemed appropriate to ensure that goods exported or imported through common frontiers pass through the competent and recognized Customs Offices and along approved routes;

(e) exchange among themselves lists of Customs Offices located along common frontiers, details of the powers of such offices, their working hours and any changes in these particulars for the effective operation of the provisions of sub-paragraph (d) of this paragraph;

(f) endeavour to correlate the powers and harmonise the working hours of their corresponding Customs Offices referred to in sub-paragraph (e) of this paragraph; and

(g) maintain special surveillance over:

(i) the entry into, sojourn in, and exit from their customs territories of particular persons reasonably suspected by a Member State of being involved in activities that are contrary to the customs law of any Member State;

(ii) the movement of particular goods suspected by any Member State to be the subject of illicit traffic towards the importing Member State;

(iii) particular places where stocks of goods have been built up giving reason for suspicion that they may be used for illicit importation into any Member States; and

(iv) particular vehicles, ships, aircraft, or other means of transport suspected of being used to commit customs offences in any Member State.

3. The Member States shall exchange:

(a) as a matter of course and without delay, any information regarding:

(i) operations which it is suspected will give rise to customs offences in any Member State;

(ii) persons, vehicles, ships, aircraft and other means of transport reasonably suspected of being engaged in activities that may be in violation of the customs laws of any Member State;

(iii) new techniques of committing customs offences; and

(iv) goods known to be the subject of illicit traffic;

(b) on the request from a Member State and as promptly as possible, any available information:

(i) contained in customs documents relating to such exchanges of goods between countries as are suspected of being in violation of the customs law of the requesting Member State;

(ii) enabling false declarations to be detected, in particular with respect to dutiable value; and

(iii) concerning certificates of origin, invoices or other documents, known to be, or suspected of being, false; and

(c) on the request and if appropriate in the form of official documents from a Member State, information concerning the following matters:

(i) the authenticity of any official document produced in support of goods declaration made to customs authorities of the requesting Member State;

(ii) whether goods which were granted preferential treatment on departure from the territory of the requesting Member State, because they were declared as intended for home use in the other Member State, have been duly cleared for home use in that State;

(iii) whether goods imported into the territory of the requesting Member State have been lawfully exported from that of the exporting Member States;

(iv) whether goods exported from the territory of the requesting Member State have been lawfully imported into that of the importing Member States, and in accordance with the importer's declaration; and

(v) special documents which may be issued by the customs authorities of the exporting Member State for surrender to the customs authorities of the importing Member State in order that they may certify that the goods were lawfully exported.

4. Each Member State undertakes, whenever expressly requested by another Member State, to:

(a) make enquiries, record statements and obtain evidence concerning a customs offence under investigation in the requesting Member State and transmit the results of the enquiry as well as any documents or other evidence, to the requesting Member State; and

(b) notify the competent authorities of the requesting Member State of actions and decisions taken by the competent authorities of the Member State where the customs offence took place in accordance with the law in force in that Member State.

Appendix 2

The Lomé Convention

The Lomé Convention sets out the principles and objectives of the Union (at the time Community) cooperation with ACP countries. It's main characteristics are: the partnership principle, the contractual nature of the relationship, and the combination of aid, trade and political aspects, together with its long-term perspective (5 years for Lomé I, II, and III, and ten for Lomé IV). Signed in 1975, coinciding with the fourth EDF (3 BECU), the first Lomé Convention is aimed at including, after the accession of Britain to the Community, some of the Commonwealth countries in the cooperation program.

Lomé I

Its main characteristics are:

- the non-reciprocal preferences for most exports form ACP countries to EEC;
- equality between partners, respect for sovereignty, mutual interests and interdependence;
- the right of each state to determine its own policies;
- security of relations based on the achievements of the cooperation system.

It also introduces the STABEX system (to compensate ACP countries for the shortfall in export earning due to fluctuation in the prices or supply of commodities).

Lomé II

Signed in 1979 and corresponding to the fifth EDF (4.542 BECU), it does not introduce major changes, except for the SYSMIN system (help to the mining industry of those ACP countries strongly dependent on it).

Lomé III

Signed in 1984 and corresponding to the sixth EDF (7.440 BECU), it shifts the main attention from the promotion of industrial development to self-reliant development on the basis of self-sufficiency and food security.

Lomé IV

This is the first Convention to cover a ten-year period, even though the attached financial protocol has a duration of five years. The first financial protocol (1990 to 1995) provides 12 BECUS, 10.8 of which from the seventh EDF, the rest form EIB. The second goes from 1995 to 2000 and supplies 14.625 BECU through the eighth EDF. A Mid-Term Review of the Convention is also scheduled for 1995. Great emphasis is put on: the promotion of human rights, democracy and good governance; strengthening of the position of women; the protection of the environment; decentralized cooperation; diversification of ACP economies; the promotion of the private sector; and increasing regional cooperation.

Revised Lomé IV

The Mid-term review takes place in 1994-1995, in the context of major economic and political changes in ACP countries (democratization process, structural adjustment), in Europe (enlargement, increasing attention to East European and Mediterranean partners), and in the international environment (Uruguay Round Agreement).

The main amendments introduced are:

- the respect for human rights, democratic principles and the rule of law become essential elements of the Convention. This means that ACP countries that do not fulfill these criteria risk the retrieval of allocated funds;
- for the first time EDF is not increased in real terms;
- phased programming is introduced, with the aim of increasing flexibility and improving performances from ACP countries.

- more attention is given to decentralized cooperation in the form of participatory partnership including a great variety of actors from civil society.

Five Generations of ACP-EC Agreements

The new partnership agreement between the 15 European Union (EU) member states and the African, Caribbean and Pacific (ACP) states marks five generations of agreements between ACP-EC sovereign states. It is the world's largest financial and political framework for North-South cooperation.

This special partnership is characterised by its non-reciprocal trade benefits for ACP states including unlimited entry to the EC market for 99 per cent of industrial goods and many other products, especially for the Least Developed Countries (LDCs) which number 39 in the ACP grouping. In addition, aid packages for each ACP country and region are regularly updated.

A unique feature of the ACP-EC accord is dialogue and joint administration of its content by the Community and the ACP. ACP states are free to table requests which are mutually negotiated with the EC.

Institutions ensure a permanent dialogue; an annual ACP/EU Council of Ministers, regular meetings of the Committee of ACP Ambassadors which receives technical support from a permanent Brussels-based ACP Secretariat. ACP Parliamentarians and Members of the European Parliament meet twice annually in a Joint Assembly, where issues on the partnership are debated.

A 'National Indicative Programme' (NIP) is mutually negotiated by the European Commission and an ACP state and sets development targets e.g. in primary education or health and contains a five yearly spending pledge for each country tailored to meeting those needs. The NIP is funded out of the European Development Fund (EDF), the financial protocol to each agreement, to which EU member states contribute.

The EDF has also traditionally provided funds for regional cooperation, for the EU's remaining Overseas Countries and Territories (OCTs), humanitarian and emergency aid and for Non

Governmental Organisations. Additional loans from the European Investment Bank (EIB), largely for infrastructure, have become a feature of cooperation too.

The Lome "acquis"

The much valued partnership is based on a corpus of shared objectives and principles, as well as the trade and financial benefits, which have expanded overtime to become the Lome 'acquis'. Yet, the partnership has kept apace with an ever changing international environment to best respond to ACP needs.

Yaounde to Lome

ACP-EC Cooperation dates back to the birth of the European Treaty of Rome establishing the European Economic Community 1957, which expressed solidarity with the colonies and overseas countries and territories and a commitment to contribute to their prosperity.

The first association of ACP and EC member states (1963-69) Yaounde I, was drawn up in the Cameroonian capital. Yaounde II (1969-75), also signed in the Cameroonian capital, pledged the lion's share of EDF financial support to French-speaking Africa to build infrastructure in the wake of decolonisation. But the Yaounde accords importantly sewed the seeds for the new generation of Lome accords.

Lome I

Membership of the United Kingdom to the then EEC in 1973 led to the signing of the wider reaching Lome I agreement between 46 ACP and the then 9 EEC member states (1975-80). At that time, the UK was keen to put its special trading preferences for bananas and sugar under the EC umbrella and extend its assistance to some former colonies beyond bilateral support.

Separate trading 'protocols' on sugar, beef and veal and bananas became a feature of successive Lome Conventions. The banana protocol has ensured duty-free entry to the EU market for specific quotas of bananas and has been a lifeline for many small island Caribbean states.

Under the sugar protocol, the Community agrees to buy a fixed quantity annually of sugar from ACP producers at attractively high guaranteed prices aligned to EU's own internal sugar price and establishes annual quotas for sugar producers, a preference which has been valuable to the economic development of certain ACP states - Mauritius, Fiji, Guyana and Barbados. The beef and veal protocol permits a 90 per cent refund of tax normally paid on beef imports from several ACPs and has especially benefited Southern African exporters.

Lome I also prioritised infrastructure; road building, bridges, hospitals and schools and sustainable agriculture (4th EDF - 3.072 billion ECU). These priorities continued under Lome II 1980-85 (5th EDF - 4.725 billion ECU).

Stabex & Sysmin

In the 1970s, new EDF instruments were introduced to cope with the commodity crisis, demonstrating Lome's flexibility to adapt to new circumstances in ACP states.

The stabilisation of export receipts on agricultural products (STABEX) gave funds to offset losses on a wide number of agricultural products; cocoa, coffee, groundnuts, tea and others, as a result of crop failures and price falls.

Sysmin was also an innovation of the'70s. A country heavily dependent on a particular mineral and suffering export losses could access Sysmin loans which were designed to lessen a country's dependency on mining.

Under Lome III (1985-1990), whilst infrastructure funding was still required, people were still dying of hunger and rural development projects became a focus of funds for the 6th EDF (7.4 billion ECUs) to promote food security and combat desertification and drought.

Lome IV

The signing of the ten year Lome IV (1990-2000) marked another turning point in Lome's history. The then European

Community (EC) embarked on dialogue with the World Bank and International Monetary Fund (IMF) on how best to support structural adjustments as a means to economic growth.

Several ACP and EC nations agreed on balance of payments support in their National Indicative Programmes (NIPs) and sectoral and general import programmes which raised money for health and education projects by the sale of goods in short supply on the local market were financed with Lome IV's initial five year financial protocol (7th EDF 10.8 billion ECUs). The EC now provides 10-30 percent of total adjustment aid to ACP economies, notably to education and health programmes.

Other key changes under Lome IV included the banning of toxic waste movements between ACPs and EC member states and more EDF monies for decentralised cooperation and diversification of the economy.

Human Rights: An Essential Element of Cooperation

Signalling the Convention's flexibility, Lome IV became the first development agreement to incorporate a human rights clause as a 'fundamental' part of cooperation (article 5).

Further changes were made at Lome's IV revision five years later (1995-2000). An updated clause confirmed human rights as an 'essential element' of cooperation, meaning that any violation could lead to partial or total suspension of development aid by then European Union after prior consultation of other ACP nations and the abusing party. It was the first development agreement to set such a standard.

Other novelties in the revised Lome IV included a 'protocol' for the protection of ACP forests allowing the 8th EDF budget 1995-2000 (12.9 b ECU) to be tapped, for example, for the preservation of tropical forests.

In the interests of debt alleviation, all uncommitted special loans under previous Lome Conventions were transformed into grants. Further, to speed up the efficiency and effectiveness of grants, a 70 per cent allocation only would be committed at the signing of the NIP, with a further 30 per cent earmarked only on assessment of how the initial tranche had been spent.

New Millennium - New Accord

The expiry of the Lome IV in the new millennium was the opportunity for deeper changes to EU-ACP cooperation whilst preserving the Lome 'acquis.' In 1997, then Commissioner for Development, Joao de Deus Pinheiro, called for root and branch reform.

The backdrop was that in spite of Lome's successes, ACP-EU cooperation could do better and needed to adapt to a different geostrategic situation after the demise of the East-West power blocs.

Statistics indicating that generous trade preferences were not enough for economic take off were detailed in a 'green paper' published by the European Commission in 1997, ahead of the 1998 talks on a new agreement:

ACP countries' share of the EU market had declined from 6.7 per cent in 1976 to 3 per cent in 1998 with 60 per cent of total exports concentrated in only 10 products, with just a handful of nations registering economic growth as a result of the trade protocols and preferences notably; Ivory Coast, Mauritius, Zimbabwe and Jamaica.

Per capita GDP in sub-Saharan Africa grew by an average of only 0.4 per cent per annum 1960-1992, compared with 2.3 per cent for developing countries as a whole.

Only 6 per cent of African trade was with other countries of the continent.

Anti-poverty measures such as access to drinking water, improved health and education services were still a priority. And improved access to productive resources especially for women; to land, capital, credit and training, were all vital for growth.

The green paper also pondered that economic developments had gone hand in hand in some countries with the social disintegration, mounting conflicts and humanitarian disasters, etc undermining development policies and which had deflected donor focus to emergency aid and crisis management.

On the aid front, the assessment was that there had been insufficient account of the institutional and policy context of the partner country, undermining the viability and effectiveness of aid.

And there was a need to speed up disbursal of EDF monies and simplify the Convention's clauses, considered as too numerous and sometimes leading to unnecessary duplication of work.

Waning international donor support for developing nations, falling over ten years from 0.33 of donors' GNP in 1988 to 0.23 per cent in 1998, was of concern too. And this worry was heightened by an increasingly negative public reaction to cooperation, some European taxpayers viewing corruption as endemic in African nations and calling for better and more efficient use of funds.

In addition, within the European Community, the 1992 Maastricht Treaty on European Union had redefined Europe's development priorities; promotion of democracy, the fight against poverty, improved commercial competitiveness and aid effectiveness.

Further, a series of United Nations (UN) thematic conferences in the 1990's on; the Environment, Population, Human Rights, Social Development, Women, and the World Food Summit had set new standards to be met by donors and developing nations alike.

Globalisation of the economy and development of the market economy and growing regionalism in ACP nations also had to be addressed. A buzzing private sector in many ACP states, seen as an engine for economic development, merited extra support.

The new millennium was a timely opportunity for the restatement of the EC's political commitment to the ACPs.

Appendix 3

The Cotonou Agreement at a Glance

The new ACP-EU Partnership Agreement, signed in Cotonou in June 2000, is a fairly unique form of North-South cooperation. Its main elements and features are summarized here in few pointers.

A Partnership for Twenty Years

The ACP-EU Partnership Agreement is a comprehensive aid and trade agreement concluded between 77 ACP (African, Caribbean and Pacific) countries and the European Union (the community and the 15 Members state of the EU). It was signed in June 2000 in Cotonou (Benin) and is therefore commonly called 'the Cotonou Agreement.'

The Agreement lasts for twenty years and contains a clause allowing it to be revised every five years. Alongside the Agreement is a financial protocol. Covering each five-year period, this indicates the total resources that are available to the ACP through the European Development Fund (EDF). For the period now to start, the EDF (called the 9th EDF) contains euro 15.2 billion for the ACP. In addition, outstanding funds from previous EDFs can be used (approximately euro 10 billion)

The Cotonou Agreement builds on twenty five years of ACP-EU cooperation under 4 successive Lome Conventions. This provided a model of development cooperation based on the principles of partnership, dialogue, contractually agreed rights and obligations and predictability of (financial) support.

Main Objectives and Principles

The central objective of the Partnership Agreement is to reduce and eventually eradicate poverty while contributing to sustainable development and to the gradual integration of ACP countries into the world economy.

ACP-EU cooperation is based on a set of fundamental principles:

Equality of partners and ownership of development strategies. In principle, it is up to ACP states, in all sovereignty, to determine how their societies and economies should develop.

Participation. Apart from central government as the main partner, partnership is open to other actors (e.g. civil society, private sector, and local government).

Dialogue and mutual obligations. The Cotonou Agreement is not simply a pot of money. The parties have assumed mutual obligations (e.g. respect for human rights). These will be monitored through dialogue.

Differentiation and regionalization. Cooperation agreement will vary according to the partner's level of development, its needs, its performance and its long-term development strategy. Special treatment will be given to countries that are least-developed or 'vulnerable' (landlocked or island states)

Central Importance of Politics

The partnership has a strong political foundation. Through political dialogue, the parties can discuss all possible issues of mutual concern. The partnership is underpinned by a set of core values or essential elements' (respect of human rights, democratic principles and rule of law), whose violation can lead to the suspension of aid. Good government is considered to be a 'fundamental element' of Cotonou Agreement. Serious cases of corruption, including acts of bribery leading to such corruption, are grounds to suspend cooperation.

Two Main Pillars: Trade and Aid

Economic and trade cooperation is the first pillar of ACP-EU cooperation. However, compared to previous Lome Conventions, the trade regime will undergo a profound transformation. The current all-ACP non-reciprocal tariff preferences will be maintained until 31st December 2007. From 2008, a set of reciprocal Economic Partnership Agreements (EPAs) or alternative trade arrangements will normally replace them, following negotiations that will begin in September 2002. These agreements should be compatible with the rules of the World Trade Organization (WTO). ACP countries are invited to sign as groups or individually, building on their own regional integration schemes. The least developed countries (LDCs) are entitled to maintained non-reciprocal references.

Aid (or financial technical cooperation) is the second pillar of ACP-EU cooperation. The largest share of the EDF resources is grants to finance development programmes in individual ACP countries (through their National Indicative Programme) or in the 7 ACP regions (through their Regional Indicative Programme). Aid allocations will be based on assessments of each country's needs and performance.

Priority Areas for Support

Three main areas of support are identified. Economic development (including, for instance, support for structural adjustment), social and human development (including, for instance, promotion of social dialogue) and regional integration and cooperation (an area where the EC has developed an expertise ad comparative advantage). Gender, environment and institutional development are 'thematic or crosscutting issues' to be promoted in all development initiatives.

There is a comprehensive programme of action to support the private sector. A new Investment Facility aims to stimulate investment and strengthen the capacity of local financial institutions. In addition, resources are provided in the form of European Investments Bank Loans. Innovative also is the commitment expressed to support an ACP-EU Private Sector Business Forum to foster regular dialogue among ACP and EU private sector actors and with governments.

Two Main Instruments

The Contonou Agreement has rationalized the wide range of instruments that existed under the Lome conventions. Available resources will be channeled through two instruments:

Grants to support long-term development (through the national and regional indicative programmes);

The Investment Facility

Joint Management

ACP-EU cooperation will continue to be overseen by a set of 'joint institutions', including the ACP/EU Council of Ministers, the Committee of Ambassadors and the Joint Parliamentary Assembly.

Appendix 4

Agreement on South Asian Free Trade Area (SAFTA)

The Governments of the SAARC (South Asian Association for Regional Cooperation) Member States comprising the People's Republic of Bangladesh, the Kingdom of Bhutan, the Republic of India, the Republic of Maldives, the Kingdom of Nepal, the Islamic Republic of Pakistan and the Democratic Socialist Republic of Sri Lanka hereinafter referred to as "Contracting States"

Motivated by the commitment to strengthen intra-SAARC economic cooperation to maximise the realization of the region's potential for trade and development for the benefit of their people, in a spirit of mutual accommodation, with full respect for the principles of sovereign equality, independence and territorial integrity of all States;

Noting that the Agreement on SAARC Preferential Trading Arrangement (SAPTA) signed in Dhaka on the 11th of April 1993 provides for the adoption of various instruments of trade liberalization on a preferential basis;

Convinced that preferential trading arrangements among SAARC Member States will act as a stimulus to the strengthening of national and SAARC economic resilience, and the development of the national economies of the Contracting States by expanding investment and production opportunities, trade, and foreign exchange earnings as well as the development of economic and technological cooperation;

Aware that a number of regions are entering into such arrangements to enhance trade through the free movement of goods;

Recognizing that Least Developed Countries in the region need to be accorded special and differential treatment commensurate with their development needs; and

Recognizing that it is necessary to progress beyond a Preferential Trading Arrangement to move towards higher levels of trade and economic cooperation in the region by removing barriers to cross-border flow of goods;

Have agreed as follows:

Article 1: Definitions

For the purposes of this Agreement:

1. Concessions mean tariff, para-tariff and non-tariff concessions agreed under the Trade Liberalisation Programme;

2. Direct Trade Measures mean measures conducive to promoting mutual trade of Contracting States such as long and medium-term contracts containing import and supply commitments in respect of specific products, buy-back arrangements, state trading operations, and government and public procurement;

3. Least Developed Contracting State refers to a Contracting State which is designated as a "Least Developed Country" by the United Nations;

4. Margin of Preference means percentage of tariff by which tariffs are reduced on products imported from one Contracting State to another as a result of preferential treatment.

5. Non-Tariff Measures include any measure, regulation, or practice, other than "tariffs" and "paratariffs".

6. Para-Tariffs mean border charges and fees, other than "tariffs", on foreign trade transactions of a tariff-like effect which are levied solely on imports, but not those indirect taxes and charges, which are levied in the same manner on like domestic products. Import charges corresponding to specific services rendered are not considered as para-tariff measures;

7. Products mean all products including manufactures and commodities in their raw, semi-processed and processed forms;

8. SAPTA means Agreement on SAARC Preferential Trading Arrangement signed in Dhaka on the 11th of April 1993;

9. Serious injury means a significant impairment of the domestic industry of like or directly competitive products due to a

surge in preferential imports causing substantial losses in terms of earnings, production or employment unsustainable in the short term;

10. Tariffs mean customs duties included in the national tariff schedules of the Contracting States;

11. Threat of serious injury means a situation in which a substantial increase of preferential imports is of a nature to cause "serious injury" to domestic producers, and that such injury, although not yet existing, is clearly imminent. A determination of threat of serious injury shall be based on facts and not on mere allegation, conjecture, or remote or hypothetical possibility.

Article 2: Establishment

The Contracting States hereby establish the South Asian Free Trade Area (SAFTA) to promote and enhance mutual trade and economic cooperation among the Contracting States, through exchanging concessions in accordance with this Agreement.

Article 3: Objectives and Principles

1. The Objectives of this Agreement are to promote and enhance mutual trade and economic cooperation among Contracting States by, inter-alia:

a) eliminating barriers to trade in, and facilitating the cross-border movement of goods between the territories of the Contracting States;

b) promoting conditions of fair competition in the free trade area, and ensuring equitable benefits to all Contracting States, taking into account their respective levels and pattern of economic development;

c) creating effective mechanism for the implementation and application of this Agreement, for its joint administration and for the resolution of disputes; and

d) establishing a framework for further regional cooperation to expand and enhance the mutual benefits of this Agreement.

2. SAFTA shall be governed in accordance with the following principles:

a) SAFTA will be governed by the provisions of this Agreement and also by the rules, regulations, decisions, understandings and protocols to be agreed upon within its framework by the Contracting States;

b) The Contracting States affirm their existing rights and obligations with respect to each other under Marrakesh Agreement Establishing the World Trade Organization and other Treaties/Agreements to which such Contracting States are signatories;

c) SAFTA shall be based and applied on the principles of overall reciprocity and mutuality of advantages in such a way as to benefit equitably all Contracting States, taking into account their respective levels of economic and industrial development, the pattern of their external trade and tariff policies and systems;

d) SAFTA shall involve the free movement of goods, between countries through, inter alia, the elimination of tariffs, para tariffs and non-tariff restrictions on the movement of goods, and any other equivalent measures;

e) SAFTA shall entail adoption of trade facilitation and other measures, and the progressive harmonization of legislations by the Contracting States in the relevant areas; and

f) The special needs of the Least Developed Contracting States shall be clearly recognized by adopting concrete preferential measures in their favour on a non-reciprocal basis.

Article 4: Instruments

The SAFTA Agreement will be implemented through the following instruments:

1. Trade Liberalisation Programme
2. Rules of Origin
3. Institutional Arrangements
4. Consultations and Dispute Settlement Procedures
5. Safeguard Measures
6. Any other instrument that may be agreed upon.

Article 5: National Treatment

Each Contracting State shall accord national treatment to the products of other Contracting States in accordance with the provisions of Article III of GATT 1994.

Article 6: Components

SAFTA may, inter-alia, consist of arrangements relating to:

a) tariffs;
b) para-tariffs;
c) non-tariff measures;
d) direct trade measures.

Article 7: Trade Liberalisation Programme

1. Contracting States agree to the following schedule of tariff reductions:

a) The tariff reduction by the Non-Least Developed Contracting States from existing tariff rates to 20% shall be done within a time frame of 2 years, from the date of coming into force of the Agreement. Contracting States are encouraged to adopt reductions in equal annual installments. If actual tariff rates after the coming into force of the Agreement are below 20%, there shall be an annual reduction on a Margin of Preference basis of 10% on actual tariff rates for each of the two years.

b) The tariff reduction by the Least Developed Contracting States from existing tariff rates will be to 30% within the time frame of 2 years from the date of coming into force of the Agreement. If actual tariff rates on the date of coming into force of the Agreement are below 30%, there will be an annual reduction on a Margin of Preference basis of 5 % on actual tariff rates for each of the two years.

c) The subsequent tariff reduction by Non-Least Developed Contracting States from 20% or below to 0-5% shall be done within a second time frame of 5 years, beginning from the third year from the date of coming into force of the Agreement. However, the period of subsequent tariff reduction by Sri Lanka shall be six years. Contracting States are encouraged to adopt reductions in equal annual installments, but not less than 15% annually.

d) The subsequent tariff reduction by the Least Developed Contracting States from 30% or below to 0-5% shall be done within a second time frame of 8 years beginning from the third year from the date of coming into force of the Agreement. The Least Developed Contracting States are encouraged to adopt reductions in equal annual installments, not less than 10% annually.

2. The above schedules of tariff reductions will not prevent Contracting States from immediately reducing their tariffs to 0-5% or from following an accelerated schedule of tariff reduction.

3. a) Contracting States may not apply the Trade Liberalisation Programme as in paragraph 1 above, to the tariff lines included in the Sensitive Lists which shall be negotiated by the Contracting States (for LDCs and Non-LDCs) and incorporated in this Agreement as an integral part. The number of products in the Sensitive Lists shall be subject to maximum ceiling to be mutually agreed among the Contracting States with flexibility to Least Developed Contracting States to seek derogation in respect of the products of their export interest; and

b) The Sensitive List shall be reviewed after every four years or earlier as may be decided by SAFTA Ministerial Council (SMC), established under Article 10, with a view to reducing the number of items in the Sensitive List.

4. The Contracting States shall notify the SAARC Secretariat all non-tariff and para-tariff measures to their trade on an annual basis. The notified measures shall be reviewed by the Committee of Experts, established under Article 10, in its regular meetings to examine their compatibility with relevant WTO provisions. The Committee of Experts shall recommend the elimination or implementation of the measure in the least trade restrictive manner in order to facilitate intraSAARC trade1.

5. Contracting Parties shall eliminate all quantitative restrictions, except otherwise permitted under GATT 1994, in

respect of products included in the Trade Liberalisation Programme.

6. Notwithstanding the provisions contained in paragraph 1 of this Article, the Non-Least Developed Contracting States shall reduce their tariff to 0-5% for the products of Least Developed Contracting States within a timeframe of three years beginning from the date of coming into force of the Agreement.

Article 8: Additional Measures

Contracting States agree to consider, in addition to the measures set out in Article 7, the adoption of trade facilitation and other measures to support and complement SAFTA for mutual benefit. These may include, among others: -

a) harmonization of standards, reciprocal recognition of tests and accreditation of testing laboratories of Contracting States and certification of products;

b) simplification and harmonization of customs clearance procedure;

c) harmonization of national customs classification based on HS coding system;

d) Customs cooperation to resolve dispute at customs entry points;

e) simplification and harmonization of import licensing and registration procedures;

f) simplification of banking procedures for import financing;

g) transit facilities for efficient intra-SAARC trade, especially for the land-locked Contracting States;

h) removal of barriers to intra-SAARC investments;

i) Macroeconomic consultations;

j) rules for fair competition and the promotion of venture capital;

k) development of communication systems and transport infrastructure;

l) making exceptions to their foreign exchange restrictions, if any, relating to payments for products under the SAFTA scheme, as well as repatriation of such payments without prejudice to their rights under Article XVIII of the General Agreement on Tariffs and Trade (GATT) and the relevant provisions of Articles of Treaty of the International Monetary Fund (IMF); and

m) Simplification of procedures for business visas.

Article 9: Extension of Negotiated Concessions

Concessions agreed to, other than those made exclusively to the Least Developed Contracting States, shall be extended unconditionally to all Contracting States.

Article 10: Institutional Arrangements

1. The Contracting States hereby establish the SAFTA Ministerial Council (hereinafter referred to as SMC).
2. The SMC shall be the highest decision-making body of SAFTA and shall be responsible for the administration and implementation of this Agreement and all decisions and arrangements made within its legal framework.
3. The SMC shall consist of the Ministers of Commerce/Trade of the Contracting States.
4. The SMC shall meet at least once every year or more often as and when considered necessary by the Contracting States. Each Contracting State shall chair the SMC for a period of one year on rotational basis in alphabetical order.
5. The SMC shall be supported by a Committee of Experts (hereinafter referred to as COE), with one nominee from each Contracting State at the level of a Senior Economic Official, with expertise in trade matters.
6. The COE shall monitor, review and facilitate implementation of the provisions of this Agreement and undertake any task assigned to it by the SMC. The COE shall submit its report to SMC every six months.
7. The COE will also act as Dispute Settlement Body under this Agreement.

8. The COE shall meet at least once every six months or more often as and when considered necessary by the Contracting States. Each Contracting State shall chair the COE for a period of one year on rotational basis in alphabetical order.

9. The SAARC Secretariat shall provide secretarial support to the SMC and COE in the discharge of their functions.

10. The SMC and COE will adopt their own rules of procedure.

Article 11: Special and Differential Treatment for the Least Developed Contracting States

In addition to other provisions of this Agreement, all Contracting States shall provide special and more favorable treatment exclusively to the Least Developed Contracting States as set out in the following sub-paragraphs:

a) The Contracting States shall give special regard to the situation of the Least Developed Contracting States when considering the application of anti-dumping and/or countervailing measures. In this regard, the Contracting States shall provide an opportunity to Least Developed Contracting States for consultations. The Contracting States shall, to the extent practical, favourably consider accepting price undertakings offered by exporters from Least Developed Contracting States. These constructive remedies shall be available until the trade liberalisation programme has been completed by all Contracting States.

b) Greater flexibility in continuation of quantitative or other restrictions provisionally and without discrimination in critical circumstances by the Least Developed Contracting States on imports from other Contracting States.

c) Contracting States shall also consider, where practical, taking direct trade measures with a view to enhancing sustainable exports from Least Developed Contracting States, such as long and medium-term contracts containing import and supply commitments in respect of specific products, buy-back arrangements, state trading operations, and government and public procurement.

d) Special consideration shall be given by Contracting States to requests from Least Developed Contracting States for technical assistance and cooperation arrangements designed to assist them in expanding their trade with other Contracting States and in taking advantage of the potential benefits of SAFTA. A list of possible areas for such technical assistance shall be negotiated by the Contracting States and incorporated in this Agreement as an integral part.

e) The Contracting States recognize that the Least Developed Contracting States may face loss of customs revenue due to the implementation of the Trade Liberalisation Programme under this Agreement. Until alternative domestic arrangements are formulated to address this situation, the Contracting States agree to establish an appropriate mechanism to compensate the Least Developed Contracting States for their loss of customs revenue. This mechanism and its rules and regulations shall be established prior to the commencement of the Trade Liberalisation Programme (TLP).

Article 12: Special Provision for Maldives

Notwithstanding the potential or actual graduation of Maldives from the status of a Least Developed Country, it shall be accorded in this Agreement and in any subsequent contractual undertakings thereof treatment no less favourable than that provided for the Least Developed Contracting States.

Article 13: Non-application

Notwithstanding the measures as set out in this Agreement its provisions shall not apply in relation to preferences already granted or to be granted by any Contracting State to other Contracting States outside the framework of this Agreement, and to third countries through bilateral, plurilateral and multilateral trade agreements and similar arrangements.

Article 14: General Exceptions

a) Nothing in this Agreement shall be construed to prevent any Contracting State from taking action and adopting measures which it considers necessary for the protection of its national security.

b) Subject to the requirement that such measures are not applied in a manner which would constitute a means of arbitrary or unjustifiable discrimination between countries where the similar conditions prevail, or a disguised restriction on intra-regional trade, nothing in this Agreement shall be construed to prevent any Contracting State from taking action and adopting measures which it considers necessary for the protection of :

(i) public morals;

(ii) human, animal or plant life and health; and

(iii) articles of artistic, historic and archaeological value.

Article 15: Balance of Payments Measures

1. Notwithstanding the provisions of this Agreement, any Contracting State facing serious balance of payments difficulties may suspend provisionally the concessions extended under this Agreement.

2. Any such measure taken pursuant to paragraph 1 of this Article shall be immediately notified to the Committee of Experts.

3. The Committee of Experts shall periodically review the measures taken pursuant to paragraph 1 of this Article.

4. Any Contracting State which takes action pursuant to paragraph I of this Article shall afford, upon request from any other Contracting State, adequate opportunities for consultations with a view to preserving the stability of concessions under SAFTA.

5. If no satisfactory adjustment is effected between the Contracting States concerned within 30 days of the beginning of such consultations, to be extended by another 30 days through mutual consent, the matter may be referred to the Committee of Experts.

6. Any such measures taken pursuant to paragraph 1 of this Article shall be phased out soon after the Committee of Experts comes to the conclusion that the balance of payments situation of the Contracting State concerned has improved.

Article 16: Safeguard Measures

1. If any product, which is the subject of a concession under this Agreement, is imported into the territory of a Contracting State in such a manner or in such quantities as to cause, or threaten to cause, serious injury to producers of like or directly competitive products in the importing Contracting State, the importing Contracting State may, pursuant to an investigation by the competent authorities of that Contracting State conducted in accordance with the provisions set out in this Article, suspend temporarily the concessions granted under the provisions of this Agreement. The examination of the impact on the domestic industry concerned shall include an evaluation of all other relevant economic factors and indices having a bearing on the state of the domestic industry of the product and a causal relationship must be clearly established between "serious injury" and imports from within the SAARC region, to the exclusion of all such other factors.

2. Such suspension shall only be for such time and to the extent as may be necessary to prevent or remedy such injury and in no case, will such suspension be for duration of more than 3 years.

3. No safeguard measure shall be applied again by a Contracting State to the import of a product which has been subject to such a measure during the period of implementation of Trade Liberalization Programme by the Contracting States, for a period of time equal to that during which such measure had been previously applied, provided that the period of non-application is at least two years.

4. All investigation procedures for resorting to safeguard measures under this Article shall be consistent with Article XIX of GATT 1994 and WTO Agreement on Safeguards

5. Safeguard action under this Article shall be non-discriminatory and applicable to the product imported from all other Contracting States subject to the provisions of paragraph 8 of this Article.

6. When safeguard provisions are used in accordance with this Article, the Contracting State invoking such measures shall immediately notify the exporting Contracting State(s) and the Committee of Experts.

7. In critical circumstances where delay would cause damage which it would be difficult to repair, a Contracting State may take a provisional safeguard measure pursuant to a preliminary determination that there is clear evidence that increased imports have caused or are threatening to cause serious injury. The duration of the provisional measure shall not exceed 200 days, during this period the pertinent requirements of this Article shall be met.

8. Notwithstanding any of the provisions of this Article, safeguard measures under this article shall not be applied against a product originating in a Least Developed Contracting State as long as its share of imports of the product concerned in the importing Contracting State does not exceed 5 per cent, provided Least Developed Contracting States with less than 5% import share collectively account for not more than 15% of total imports of the product concerned.

Article 17: Maintenance of the Value of Concessions

Any of the concessions agreed upon under this Agreement shall not be diminished or nullified, by the application of any measures restricting trade by the Contracting States, except under the provisions of other articles of this Agreement.

Article 18: Rules of Origin

Rules of Origin shall be negotiated by the Contracting States and incorporated in this Agreement as an integral part.

Article 19: Consultations

1. Each Contracting State shall accord sympathetic consideration to and will afford adequate opportunity for consultations regarding representations made by another Contracting State with respect to any matter affecting the operation of this Agreement.

2. The Committee of Experts may, at the request of a Contracting State, consult with any Contracting State in respect of any matter for which it has not been possible to find a satisfactory solution through consultations under paragraph 1.

Article 20: Dispute Settlement Mechanism

1. Any dispute that may arise among the Contracting States regarding the interpretation and application of the provisions of this Agreement or any instrument adopted within its framework concerning the rights and obligations of the Contracting States will be amicably settled among the parties concerned through a process initiated by a request for bilateral consultations.

2. Any Contracting State may request consultations in accordance with paragraph 1 of this Article with other Contracting State in writing stating the reasons for the request including identification of the measures at issue. All such requests should be notified to the Committee of Experts, through the SAARC Secretariat with an indication of the legal basis for the complaint.

3. If a request for consultations is made pursuant to this Article, the Contracting State to which the request is made shall, unless otherwise mutually agreed, reply to the request within 15 days after the date of its receipt and shall enter into consultations in good faith within a period of no more than 30 days after the date of receipt of the request, with a view to reaching a mutually satisfactory solution.

4. If the Contracting State does not respond within 15 days after the date of receipt of the request, or does not enter into consultations within a period of no more than 30 days, or a period otherwise mutually agreed, after the date of receipt of the request, then the Contracting State that requested the holding of

consultations may proceed to request the Committee of Experts to settle the dispute in accordance with working procedures to be drawn up by the Committee.

5. Consultations shall be confidential, and without prejudice to the rights of any Contracting State in any further proceedings.

6. If the consultations fail to settle a dispute within 30 days after the date of receipt of the request for consultations, to be extended by a further period of 30 days through mutual consent, the complaining Contracting State may request the Committee of Experts to settle the dispute. The complaining Contracting State may request the Committee of Experts to settle the dispute during the 60-day period if the consulting Contracting States jointly consider that consultations have failed to settle the dispute.

7. The Committee of Experts shall promptly investigate the matter referred to it and make recommendations on the matter within a period of 60 days from the date of referral.

8. The Committee of Experts may request a specialist from a Contracting State not party to the dispute selected from a panel of specialists to be established by the Committee within one year from the date of entry into force of the Agreement for peer review of the matter referred to it. Such review shall be submitted to the Committee within a period of 30 days from the date of referral of the matter to the specialist.

9. Any Contracting State, which is a party to the dispute, may appeal the recommendations of the Committee of Experts to the SMC. The SMC shall review the matter within the period of 60 days from date of submission of request for appeal. The SMC may uphold, modify or reverse the recommendations of the Committee of Experts.

10. Where the Committee of Experts or SMC concludes that the measure subject to dispute is inconsistent with any of the provisions of this Agreement, it shall recommend that the Contracting State concerned bring the measure into conformity with this Agreement. In addition to its recommendations, the Committee of Experts or SMC may suggest ways in which the

Contracting State concerned could implement the recommendations.

11. The Contracting State to which the Committee's or SMC's recommendations are addressed shall within 30 days from the date of adoption of the recommendations by the Committee or SMC, inform the Committee of Experts of its intentions regarding implementation of the recommendations. Should the said Contracting State fail to implement the recommendations within 90 days from the date of adoption of the recommendations by the Committee, the Committee of Experts may authorize other interested Contracting States to withdraw concessions having trade effects equivalent to those of the measure in dispute.

Article 21: Withdrawal

1. Any Contracting State may withdraw from this Agreement at any time after its entry into force. Such withdrawal shall be effective on expiry of six months from the date on which a written notice thereof is received by the Secretary-General of SAARC, the depositary of this Agreement. That Contracting State shall simultaneously inform the Committee of Experts of the action it has taken.

2. The rights and obligations of a Contracting State which has withdrawn from this Agreement shall cease to apply as of that effective date.

3. Following the withdrawal by any Contracting State, the Committee shall meet within 30 days to consider action subsequent to withdrawal.

Article 22: Entry into Force

1. This Agreement shall enter into force on 1st January 2006 upon completion of formalities, including ratification by all Contracting States and issuance of a notification thereof by the SAARC Secretariat. This Agreement shall supercede the Agreement on SAARC Preferential Trading Arrangement (SAPTA).

2. Notwithstanding the supersession of SAPTA by this Agreement, the concessions granted under the SAPTA Framework shall remain available to the Contracting States until the completion of the Trade Liberalisation Programme.

Article 23: Reservations

This Agreement shall not be signed with reservations, nor will reservations be admitted at the time of notification to the SAARC Secretariat of the completion of formalities.

Article 24: Amendments

This Agreement may be amended by consensus in the SAFTA Ministerial Council. Any such amendment will become effective upon the deposit of instruments of acceptance with the Secretary General of SAARC by all Contracting States.

Article 25: Depository

This Agreement will be deposited with the Secretary General of SAARC, who will promptly furnish a certified copy thereof to each Contracting State.

IN WITNESS WHEREOF the undersigned being duly authorized thereto by their respective Governments have signed this Agreement.

DONE in ISLAMABAD, PAKISTAN, On This The Sixth Day Of the Year Two Thousand Four, In Nine Originals In The English Language All Texts Being Equally Authentic.

M. Morshed Khan
Minister for Foreign Affairs
People's Republic of Bangladesh

Nado Rinchhen
Officiating Minister for
Foreign Affairs
Kingdom of Bhutan

Yashwant Sinha
Minister of External Affairs
Republic of India

Fathulla Jameel
Minister of Foreign Affairs
Republic of Maldives

Dr. Bhekh B. Thapa
Ambassador-at-large
for Foreign Affairs
His Majesty's Government of Nepal

Khurshid M. Kasuri
Minister of Foreign Affairs
Islamic Republic of Pakistan

Tyronne Fernando
Minister of Foreign Affairs
Democratic Socialist Republic of Sri Lanka

Appendix 5

European Development Fund (EDF)

The European Development Fund (EDF) is the main instrument for Community aid for development cooperation in the ACP countries and the Overseas Countries and Territories (OCT). Articles 131 and 136 of the 1957 Treaty of Rome provided for its creation with a view to granting technical and financial assistance to African countries that were still colonised at that time and with which certain countries had historical links.

Although, following a request by the European Parliament, a heading has been reserved for the Fund in the Community budget since 1993, the EDF does not come under the general Community budget. It is funded by the Member States, covered by its own financial rules and managed by a specific committee. The Member States set the EDF budget in the Council via agreements that are subsequently ratified by the national parliament of each Member State. The European Commission and other institutions established under the partnership play a key role in the day-to-day management of the Fund. Each EDF is concluded for a period of around five years. Since the conclusion of the first partnership convention in 1964, the EDF cycles have generally followed that of the partnership agreements/conventions.

- First EDF: 1959-1964
- Second EDF: 1964-1970 (Yaoundé I Convention)
- Third EDF: 1970-1975 (Yaoundé II Convention)
- Fourth EDF: 1975-1980 (Lomé I Convention)
- Fifth EDF: 1980-1985 (Lomé II Convention)
- Sixth EDF: 1985-1990 (Lomé III Convention)
- Seventh EDF: 1990-1995 (Lomé IV Convention)
- Eighth EDF: 1995-2000 (Lomé IV Convention and the revised Lomé IV)

The EDF consists of several instruments, including grants, risk capital and loans to the private sector. The Stabex and Sysmin instruments designed to help the agricultural and mining industries respectively were abolished by the new Partnership Agreement signed in Cotonou in June 2000. This agreement also streamlined the EDF and introduced a system of rolling programming making for greater flexibility and giving the ACP countries greater responsibility.

The ninth EDF, concluded at the same time as the Cotonou Agreement , has been allocated EUR 13.5 billion over a period of five years. In addition, the unexpended balances from previous EDFs total EUR 9.9 billion.

The development aid provided by the EDF forms part of a broader European framework. Within the European Union, the funds of the Community's general budget may be used for certain types of aid. Moreover, whilst managing part of the EDF's resources (loans and risk capital), the own resources contribution of the European Investment Bank comes to EUR 1.7 billion for the five-year period of the ninth EDF.

Added to this, the Member States have their own bilateral agreements and implement their own initiatives with developing countries that are not financed by the European Development Fund or other Community funds.

Bibliography

Bibliography

Primary Sources

African Development Bank, African Development Report, 2000, Abdijan, 2000.

African Development Bank, Economic Integration in Southern Africa, Abdijan: African Development Bank, 1993.

African Regional Organizations: From Unity to Union, Key Documents of Regional Organisations, Institute of Security Studies, Pretoria, South Africa.

African Unity, Relaunching Africa's Economic and Social Development, The Agenda for Action, Egypt, March, 1995.

ECA, Progress Report by the Regional Economic Communities: COMESA – A successful venture in regional integration, Addis Ababa, 1996.

ECA, Rationalization of the operations of the PTA, SADCC and the Lusaka based MULPOC: A proposal, 1984.

Mandoza Ibbo, et.al, The Joint PTA/SADC study in Harmonization, Rationalisation & Coordination of activities of the PTA and the SADC, Harare, July 1994.

PTA, Report of the 17th Meeting of the Council of Ministers, Lusaka, P.T.A., 1992.

PTA, The Monetary Harmonization Programme of the PTA for Eastern & Southern African States, Lusaka, PTA, 1990.

Treaty of COMESA.

UNCTAD, Regional & Sub-regional Economic Integration & Cooperation among Developing Countries: Adjusting to changing realities, August, 1992.

UNCTAD, Report of the First Session of the meeting of the Heads of Secretariat of Economic Cooperation and integration groupings of Developing Countries, Geneva, April, 1989.

Website of COMESA - http// :www.comesa.int

World Bank, Accelerated Development in Sub-Saharan Africa: An agenda for Action, Washington D.C., 1981.

World Bank, Proceedings of the workshop on Regional Integration & Cooperation in Sub-Saharan Africa, Washington D.C., 1988.

Secondary Source

Adebayo, Adedeji and Timothy Shaw, *Economic Crisis in Africa – African Perspective on Development: Problems and Potentials* (Boulder Col. Lynne Reimer, 1985)

Adisheshiah Malcom, *Regional Economic Arrangements* (New Delhi, India International Centre, 1989)

Africa South of Sahara, Europa Publication, 2000.

Agyemang Attah - Poku, *African Stability and Integration – Regional, Continental and Diasporic Pan African Realities* (University Press of America, New York, Oxford, 2000).

Aly, Ahmad, *Economic Cooperation in Africa – In search of direction* (Lynne Reinner, Colorado, London, 1994)

Aryeetey, E. and Odwro, A, 'Regional Integration efforts in Africa : an overview', in J. Teunissen (ed.), *Regionalism and the Global Economy, the case of Africa* (The Hague Forum of Debt and Development, 1996).

Asante S.K.B., *The Political Economy of Regional Integration in Africa : A decade of the Economic Community of West Africa* (ECOWAS), (New York, Preager, 1986)

Bach Daniel C, (ed.) *Regionalisation in Africa – Integration and Disintegration* (Indiana, Indiana University Press, 1999).

Balassa, Bela, *The Theory of Economic Integration – III* (Homewood, Richard Irwin, 1961)

Baurename, N., "Integration in the Maghreb: Assessment and Prospects" in Nyong'o (ed), *Regional Integration in Africa* (Academy Science Publishers, Nairobi, Kenya, 1990).

Brage C., *The New Regionalism and its consequence* (Washington DC, World Bank, 1994).

CACH, *"The Experience of Central African Clearing House"*, in A CMS Seminar on Experience with payments and clearing system in African Countries, (Freetown, Sierra Leone, May 1987).

Chileste, J.H, *The Challenge of Developing Intra – African Trade* (East African Literature Bureau, 1977).

De Melo Jaime and Arvind Pangaria, (eds.) *New Dimensions of Regional Integration* (Cambridge University Press, 1994).

Foroutan, F. "Regional Integration in Sub Saharan Africa: Past experience and future prospects in J.De Melo and A Panagariya (eds.) *New Dimensions in Regional Integration* (Cambridge, Cambridge University Press, 1994.)

Green, R.H. and G.K. Krishna, *Economic Cooperation in Africa: Retrospect and Prospect* (Nairobi, Oxford University Press, 1967)

Hazlewood Arthur, *African Integration and Disintegration – Case studies in Economic and Political Union* (Oxford University Press, London, 1962)

Hoskyns, C., "Pan Africanism and Integration", in Arthur Hazlewood (ed), *African Integration and Disintegration : Case studies in Economic and Political Union* (Oxford University Press, London, 1967.)

Kadima, D. and Claude Kademba (eds.), *Whither Regional Peace and Security* (Africa Institute of South Africa, Pretoria, 2000)

Kasekande, L.A. and N. Ng'eno, "Regional Integration & Economic Liberalization in Eastern & Southern Africa", in Oyejide A.I.C and P. Collier (eds.) *Regional Integration and Trade Libralisation in Sub Saharan Africa : Framework, Issues and Methodological perspective,* Vol. III (London, Macmillan, 1997)

Landau, A., "Multilateralism and Regionalism International Economic Relations" in Daniel C. Bach (ed.) *Regionalisation in Africa: Integration and Disintegration* (Indiana University Press, 1999)

Mangoor, A. and A. Inotai, "Integration efforts in Sub Saharan Africa: Failures, results and prospects – a suggested strategy for achieving efficient integration", in A. Chibber and S. Ficher (eds.) *Economic Reform in sub-saharan Africa* (Washington DC, World Bank, 1991)

Martin, G., "Preferential Trade Area for Eastern & Southern Africa: Achievements, Problems and Prospects" in Anyang' Nyong'o (ed), *Regional Integration in Africa, unfinished Agenda* (Academy Science Publishers, Nairobi Kenya, 1990).

MC Kay V., *Africa in World Politics* (Harper and Row, New York, 1963)

Mistry, P., Regional Dimensions of structural Adjustment in Southern Africa', in J. Teunissen (ed), *Regionalism and the Global Economy : The case of Africa* (The Hague : Forum on Debt and Development, 1996)

Mistry, P., *Regional Integration and Development: Panacea Pitfalls*? (New Delhi, Research and Information system for the Non Aligned and other developing countries, 1995)

Mulaisho, D., *Post Apartheid Implications for SADCC and the Drive Towards Economic Integration* (Institute of Development Management, Gaborone, 1992.)

Nabudere, Dani Wadaba, "African Unity in Historical Perspective" in Maloka Eddy (ed.) *A United States of Africa* (Africa Institute of South Africa, Pretoria, 2003.)

Ndegwa Philip, *The Common Market and Development in East Africa* (East African Publishing House, Nairobi, 1968)

Ndongko W.A. (ed.), *Economic Cooperation and Integration in Africa* (CODESRIA, 1985).

Nkrumah K., *Africa must Unite* (New York, International Publishers, 1970)

Nyongo, A. (ed.), *Regional Integration in Africa* (Academy Science Publishers, Nairobi, Kenya, 1990.)

Omuka, R.I. and A Sessay (eds.), *The Future of Regionalism in Africa* (New York, St. Martins Press, 1985).

Oyejide A.I.C. and P. Collier (eds.) *Regional Integration and Trade Libralisation in Sub Saharan Africa: Framework, Issues and Methodological perspective* (London, Macmillan, 1997)

Robson Peter, *Economic Integration in Africa* (London, Allen and Unwin, 1986)

SADC – EU relation: Looking Back and Moving Ahead, (South African Institute of International Affairs, 2002.)

Takirambudde, Peter, "The rival strategies of SADC & PTA/COMESA in Southern Africa" in Daniel Bach (ed) *Regionalisation in Africa: Integration & Disintegration* (Indiana University Press, 1999).

Teunissen, J. (ed), *Regionalism and Global Economy, The Case of Africa* (The Hague Forum on Debt and Development, 1996.)

Thompson, V. Bakpetu, *Africa and Unity: The Evolution of Pan – Africanism* (Longman, London, 1969.)

Welerestain I., *Africa: Politics of Unity* (Vantage Books, New York, 1969).

World Bank, *Intra – Regional Trade in Sub-Saharan Africa* (Washington, DC, World Bank, 1989.)

World Bank, *Sub Saharan Africa: From Crisis to Sustainable Growth* (Washington, D.C., World Bank, 1989.)

Articles

Asante S.K.B., "Structural Adjustment Programme and African Regionalism, *West Africa* (London), October 1991.

Asante S.K.B., "What really is African Union", *West Africa*, 7-13 July, 2003.

Chidzero, B.T. Cr., "The meaning of Economic cooperation in Africa", *East African Journal* (Nairobi), December, 1965.

Davis, R. "Approaches to Regional Integration in Southern African Context", *Africa Insight* (London), Vol. 24, No.1, 1994.

Harsch, E., "Making African Integration a reality", *Africa Recovery*, Vol. 16, No.2-3 : Sept. 2000. New York.

Jalloh Abdul A., "Regional Integration in Africa Lessons from past and prospects for the future; *Africa Development* (Dakar), Vol. 1, No.2, 1976.

Keet, D., "International Players and programmes for and against – Economic Integration", *Southern African Perspective* (Cape Town), No. 36, 1994.

Kenyatta, Jomo, "African Socialism and African Unity", *African Forum*, Vol. 1, No.1, (Summer, 1965).

Leistner Erich, "Designing Framework for A Southern African Development Community", *Africa Insight*, Vol. 22, No.1, 1992.

Leistner Erich, "Regional Cooperation in Sub-Saharan Africa", *Africa Insight*, Vol. 27, No.2, 1997.

Mathews K, "Birth of AU", *Africa Quarterly* (Delhi), ICCR, Vol. 41, No.1 & 2 : Jan to June, 2001.

Mathews K, "Towards a United States of Africa", *Mainstream*, New Delhi, Vol. 339, No. 28, June 30, 2001.

Mathews K., "Regional Cooperation and Development in Africa', *Africa Quarterly*, (Delhi), ICCR, Vol. 41, No.3. 2001.

Mawencha, Erastus, I.O., "COMESA Agenda for 1999 and Beyond", *COMESA Bulletin*, Vol. 1, Issue 1, 1999.

Mehta S.C., 'African Unification: Past Experience and Future Promises", *Africa Quarterly* (Delhi), ICCR, Vol. 41, No. 4, 2001.

Mistry Percy S., "Africa's Record of Regional Co-operation and integration', *African Affairs* (London), 2000.

Nyerere Julius K., "A United States of Africa", *Journal of Modern African Studies* (London), Vol.1, No.1, 1963.

Nyerere Julius., "Nature and Requirements of African Unity", *African Forum*, Vol. 1, No. 1, 1965.

Panda, K.K, "Neo-Colonialism and African Development Strategy", *Africa Quarterly* (New Delhi), Vol. 29, Nos 1 & 2, 1989.

Panda. K.K, "Globalization, Structural Adjustment and African Development Strategy" in *Indian Journal of African Studies* (Delhi), Vol. 7, Nos 1 & 2. 1996.

Pant, V.P., "Economics of Regional Cooperation", *South Asia Forum*, Winter, 1981.

Shaw T.M., "Regional Cooperation and Conflicts in Africa", *International Journal*, Vol. 30, No.4, 1975.

Sideri S., "Globalisation and Regional Integration", *European Journal of Development Research*, 9(1), 1997.

Takirambudde, Peter, "Rethinking Regional Integration Structures and Strategies in Eastern and Southern Africa", *Africa Insight*, Vol. 23, No.3, 1993.

Journals and Magazines

Africa Quarterly, ICCR, New Delhi.

Africa Recovery, UN Publication, New York.

African Affairs, The Royal African Society, Oxford University Press, U.K.

African Chronicle, New Delhi

African Research Bulletin, Oxford, U.K.

African Studies Review, African Studies Association, Atlanta, Georgia.

COMESA Bulletin/News letter, Lusaka.

India Quarterly, I.C.W.A. New Delhi

Indian Journal of African Studies, Department of African Studies, University of Delhi, Delhi.

International Relations, London

Journal of International Affairs, Columbia University, New York

Journal of International Studies, J.N.U. New Delhi

Mainstream, New Delhi

New Africana, London

Review of African Political Economy, Roape Publications Ltd, U.K.

Review of International Affairs, Belgrade.

South African Year Book of International Affairs, South Africa.

West Africa, London

World Affairs, New Delhi

World Focus, New Delhi

Index

Index

E

F

G